TRUTH

TRUTH
Developmental, Cultural, and Clinical Realms

Edited by

Salman Akhtar

KARNAC
firing the mind

The following chapters are reprinted with permission and were first published as follows:

Chapter 6: Shoshani, M., Shoshani-Breda, N., & Shoshani, B. (2021). Heidegger and Freud—explorations into truth, anxiety, and death. In: M. Shoshani & B. Shoshani, *Timeless Grandiosity and Eroticised Contempt: Technical Challenges Posed by Narcissism and Perversion* (pp. 219–256). Bicester, UK: Phoenix. Reprinted with kind permission of Phoenix Publishing House.

Chapter 8: Spence, D. P. (1982). Narrative truth and theoretical truth. *The Psychoanalytic Quarterly, 51*(1): 43–69. DOI: 10.1080/21674086.1982.11926984.

Chapter 9: Thomas H. Ogden. (2003). What's true and whose idea was it? *The International Journal of Psychoanalysis, 84*(3): 593–606. DOI: 10.1516/HHJT-H54F-DQB5-422W. Copyright © 2003 Institute of Psychoanalysis, reprinted by permission of Taylor & Francis Ltd, on behalf of the Institute of Psychoanalysis.

First published in 2024 by
Karnac Books Limited
62 Bucknell Road
Bicester
Oxfordshire OX26 2DS

British Library Cataloguing in Publication Data

A C.I.P. for this book is available from the British Library

ISBN-13: 978-1-80013-142-2

Typeset by Medlar Publishing Solutions Pvt Ltd, India

www.firingthemind.com

To

The memory of my dogs

JACKIE & MAJNUN

Never have I ever come across more truthful beings

Contents

Part II: Cultural realm

Part III: Clinical realm

Epilogue

Acknowledgments

Twelve distinguished colleagues devoted much time and effort to writing original works for inclusion in this book. They responded to my editorial suggestions with the utmost grace. The work of five others, Michael Shoshani, Batya Shoshani and Naama Shoshani-Breda, Donald Spence, and Thomas Ogden, has been reprinted with permission. Andrew Klafter, an outstanding younger colleague of mine, procured one chapter for this book and helped in other subtle and not-so-subtle ways as well. My assistant, Jan Wright, prepared the manuscript of this book with her characteristic diligence and good humor. Kelsey Leon provided some very useful last-minute typing and formatting assistance. Kate Pearce, at Karnac Books, provided excellent and patient editorial guidance. To her, and to all the individuals mentioned here, my sincere thanks indeed.

About the editor and contributors

Salman Akhtar, MD, is professor of psychiatry at Jefferson Medical College and a training and supervising analyst at the Psychoanalytic Center of Philadelphia. He has served on the editorial boards of the *International Journal of Psychoanalysis* and the *Journal of the American Psychoanalytic Association*. His more than 300 publications include twenty-two books—*Broken Structures* (1992), *Quest for Answers* (1995), *Inner Torment* (1999), *Immigration and Identity* (1999), *New Clinical Realms* (2003), *Objects of Our Desire* (2005), *Regarding Others* (2007), *Turning Points in Dynamic Psychotherapy* (2009), *The Damaged Core* (2009), *Comprehensive Dictionary of Psychoanalysis* (2009), *Immigration and Acculturation* (2011), *Matters of Life and Death* (2011), *The Book of Emotions* (2012), *Psychoanalytic Listening* (2013), *Good Stuff* (2013), *Sources of Suffering* (2014), *No Holds Barred* (2016), *A Web of Sorrow* (2017), *Mind, Culture and Global Unrest* (2018), *Silent Virtues* (2019), *Tales of Transformation* (2022), and *In Leaps and Bounds* (2022)—as well as forty-three edited or co-edited volumes in psychiatry and psychoanalysis. Dr. Akhtar has delivered many prestigious addresses and lectures including the inaugural address at the first IPA-Asia Congress in Beijing, China (2010). Dr. Akhtar is the recipient of the *Journal of the American Psychoanalytic Association*'s Best Paper of the Year Award (1995), the Margaret Mahler Literature Prize (1996), the American Society of Psychoanalytic Physicians' Sigmund Freud Award (2000), the American College of Psychoanalysts' Laughlin Award (2003), the American Psychoanalytic Association's Edith Sabshin Award (2000), Columbia University's Robert Liebert Award for Distinguished Contributions to Applied Psychoanalysis (2004), the American Psychiatric Association's Kun Po Soo Award (2004), the Irma Bland Award for being the Outstanding Teacher of Psychiatric Residents in the country (2005), and the Nancy Roeske Award (2012). Most recently, he received the Sigourney Award (2013), which is the most prestigious honor in the field of psychoanalysis.

Dr. Akhtar is an internationally sought speaker and teacher, and his books have been translated into many languages, including German, Turkish, and Romanian. His interests are wide and he has served as the film review editor for the *International Journal of Psychoanalysis*, and is currently serving as the book review editor for the *International Journal of Applied Psychoanalytic Studies*. He has published eight collections of poetry and serves as a scholar-in-residence at the Inter-Act Theatre Company in Philadelphia.

Cobi Avshalom, MA, is a clinical psychologist, training psychoanalyst, and past chairman of Tel Aviv Institute for Contemporary Psychoanalysis (TAICP). He was a teacher in psychoanalytic psychotherapy programs in Bar Ilan University and in Maggid Institute of the Hebrew University in Jerusalem. He teaches and supervises presently in the core training program and psychotherapy program of TAICP. He has been a follower of a spiritual meditative school for almost fifty years. His papers concern ways of listening and interpreting the analytic encounter ("analytic compass"), and are about psychoanalysis and spirituality. He has presented his thoughts about various aspects of the analyst's role and being in the analytic process in conferences and seminars in Israel, Eastern Europe, and the United States.

Brett H. Clarke, MSW, is an adult training and supervising analyst at the Cincinnati Psychoanalytic Institute, where he also teaches and serves as cochair of the Child and Adolescent Psychotherapy Program. He has master's degrees in social work and English and comparative literature, and credits his literary education with introducing him to the value of listening with imagination, empathy, and critical attention. Previous publications have focused on the central place of metaphor and metaphoric "tension" in both psychoanalytic theory and practice; the philosophy of psychoanalytic knowledge; the troubled epistemology of neuropsychoanalysis; and the meaning of "science" in psychoanalysis as this relates to hermeneutic ideas about meaning. He has a private clinical practice in Cincinnati.

Mali Mann, PhD, is training and supervising analyst and child analytic supervisor at San Francisco Center for Psychoanalysis. She is a cochair of the North American Committee on Child and Adolescent Psychoanalysis/IPA. She is adjunct clinical professor of psychiatry at the Stanford University School of Medicine. After completing her medical school, Dr. Mann finished her neurology internship and psychiatry residency at the University of Kansas Medical Center. She completed her fellowship in child and adolescent psychiatry at the University of Rochester, New York and then did a second fellowship in adolescent medicine at Stanford University School of Medicine. She has published several papers in the *American Journal of Psychoanalysis*, including "Immigrant Parents and Their Emigrant Adolescents: The Tension of Inner and Outer Worlds," and "Shame Veiled and Unveiled." She has written several book chapters and a book review, including "Aggression in Children: Origins, Manifestation, and Management through Play," and "The Formation and Development of Ethnic Identity." Dr. Mann has recently edited a book, *Psychoanalytic Aspects of Assisted Reproductive Technology* (2014).

She is a member of the Pegasus Physician writing group at Stanford University. She teaches at the San Francisco Center for Psychoanalysis and Child Psychotherapy Program. She is a faculty member at China Alliance Psychoanalytic Association, and teaches at the Palo Alto Psychoanalytic Psychotherapy Training Program. She supervises residents and child fellows at Stanford University and San Mateo Psychiatry Residency Program. She has a special interest in applied psychoanalysis, maternal development and motherhood, as well as ethics in working with children and parents. Dr. Mann's community service takes her to Mexico as a member of Los Medicos Voladores ("The Flying Doctors") where she visits orphans and assists the orphanage staff in a small village near Ensenada. She maintains a private practice in child, adolescent, and adult psychiatry and psychoanalysis in Palo Alto and San Francisco.

Gila Ofer, PhD, is a clinical psychologist, training psychoanalyst, and group analyst. She has a BA in English and French literature, and MA and PhD in clinical psychology. Dr. Ofer is the founder and past president of the Tel-Aviv Institute of Contemporary Psychoanalysis (TAICP) and a founding member of the Israeli Institute of Group Analysis (IIGA). She serves on the faculty of both these institutes as well as that of the Post-Graduate School for Psychoanalytic Psychotherapy, Tel-Aviv University. She was also on the faculty of the Chicago Center of Psychoanalysis. Dr. Ofer has been the chair of the group analytic section and board member of the European Federation for Psychosynthesis Psychotherapy, and later a conjoint member of the board as the coordinator of Eastern European countries of the EFPP. She is the editor of the EFPP *Psychoanalytic Psychotherapy Review* and she is the book review editor of foreign language books in the *International Journal of Group Psychotherapy*. She is leading or helping to establish training in group analysis in Istanbul and Bucharest and other Eastern European countries. Dr. Ofer writes on theoretical and clinical topics such as gender and sexuality in psychoanalysis and group analysis; dreams in psychoanalysis and group analysis; the social unconscious; and conducting large groups. She has published her work in leading journals and presented her work and taught in Israel, Europe, and the US. Her edited book, *A Bridge over Troubled Water: Conflicts and Reconciliation in Group and Society*, was published in 2017. Dr. Ofer maintains a private practice in Tel Aviv and has online patients and supervisees from around the world.

Thomas Ogden, MD, is a graduate of Amherst College, the Yale of School of Medicine, and the Psychiatric Residency at the Yale School of Medicine. He completed his analytic training at the San Francisco Psychoanalytic Institute and is currently a personal and supervising analyst of the Psychoanalytic Institute of Northern California. He has also served as an associate psychiatrist at the Tavistock Clinic, London. He has published twelve books on psychoanalytic theory and practice, including *Coming to Life in the Consulting Room*; *Reclaiming Unlived Life*; *Creative Readings: Essays on Seminal Analytic Works*; *The Analyst's Ear and the Critic's Eye: Rethinking Psychoanalysis and Literature* (coauthored with Benjamin Ogden); *Rediscovering Psychoanalysis*; and *This Art of Psychoanalysis: Dreaming Undreamt Dreams and Interrupted*

Cries. In addition, he has published three novels: *The Parts Left Out*, *The Hands of Gravity and Chance*, and *This Will Do*. His work has been published in more than twenty languages. Dr. Ogden has served on the editorial boards of a number of psychoanalytic journals including the *International Journal of Psychoanalysis*; *The Psychoanalytic Quarterly*; *Psychoanalytic Dialogues*; and *Gender and Sexuality*. He teaches, practices, and supervises psychoanalysis in San Francisco, where he also teaches creative writing. He was awarded the 2004 *International Journal of Psychoanalysis* Award for the "Most Important Paper of the Year"; the 2010 Haskell Norman Prize, an international award for "Outstanding Achievement in Psychoanalysis"; and the 2012 Sigourney Award, an international award for "Significant Contributions to the Field of Psychoanalysis."

Louis Rothschild, PhD, is a clinical psychologist in Lutherville, Maryland. He took his PhD at the New School for Social Research where he published on the relationship between essentialist beliefs and prejudice in regard to several social categories. He then completed a fellowship at Brown University School of Medicine where he focused on the relationship between personality and chronic depression. Specializing in psychoanalytic psychotherapy, Dr. Rothschild also provides supervision, writes, and occasionally reviews manuscripts. His publications have ranged from quantitative to qualitative, social-cognitive to psychoanalysis, and clinical to philosophical. He is presently writing a book to be published by Phoenix Publishing House entitled *Rapprochement between Fathers and Sons: Breakdowns, Reunions, Potentialities*, and coediting a volume entitled *Childhood Precarities: Non-Normative Narratives of Marginalization*, with Lexington Books. He is a past president of the Rhode Island local chapter of the Society for Psychoanalysis and Psychoanalytic Psychology: Division 39 of the American Psychological Association. Outside of his professional life, he has a fondness for tennis, triathlon, and chasing a rather elusive sourdough starter in the kitchen.

Batya Shoshani, PhD, a Fulbright scholar, is a training and supervising psychoanalyst and a professor of clinical social work at the Hebrew University of Jerusalem (retired), with vast experience in teaching and supervision in social work, psychotherapy, and psychoanalysis. She is a founding member and the past chair of the training committee at the Tel Aviv Institute for Contemporary Psychoanalysis. She has been a senior consultant for public services dealing with children, adolescents, battered women, and delinquent youth. She is interested in interdisciplinary studies in psychoanalysis, weaving clinical knowledge with philosophy, literature, and art. Most recently, she has coauthored (with her husband, Michael Shoshani) a book on the technical challenges posed by cases of pathologic narcissism and sexual perversion under the title, *Timeless Grandiosity and Eroticised Contempt* (2021). Batya lives and practices in Tel Aviv, Israel.

Michael Shoshani, PsyD, MBA, a Fulbright scholar, is a senior clinical psychologist and a training and supervising psychoanalyst. He is the founding chair and a faculty member of the

Tel Aviv Institute of Contemporary Psychoanalysis. He is a faculty member and supervisor of the New York University Postdoc Program for Psychoanalysis and Psychotherapy, and an active member of the American Psychoanalytic Association (APsaA) and the International Psychoanalytical Association (IPA). For three decades, he has treated patients, taught students, and supervised clinicians. He has lectured for many years at Tel Aviv University and Bar Illan University in postgraduate programs of psychoanalytic psychotherapy, and has run workshops for many groups of professionals in Israel, the USA, Turkey, and Romania. His main interest is in clinical theories relating to the therapy and analysis of narcissistic and perverse character pathology, as well as in interdisciplinary studies in psychoanalysis, weaving clinical knowledge with philosophy, literature, and art. He is the author of the book, *Dare to Be Human: A Psychoanalytic Journey* (2009) which intimately described seven years of an analysis while emphasizing the relationship between the analyst and the analysand. More recently, he has published (with his wife, Batya Shoshani) a book on the technical challenges posed by cases of pathologic narcissism and sexual perversion under the title, *Timeless Grandiosity and Eroticised Contempt* (2021). Michael lives and practices in Tel Aviv, Israel.

Naama Shoshani-Breda, MA, obtained her degree *magna cum laude* in philosophy and digital culture at Tel Aviv University. She is currently in the process of developing her PhD proposal in philosophy. Naama has a deep understanding in continental philosophy and her interdisciplinary approach allows her to weave different areas of knowledge in her innovative work.

Ann Smolen, PhD, is a supervising and training analyst in child, adolescent, and adult psychoanalysis at the Psychoanalytic Center of Philadelphia. Dr. Smolen graduated *summa cum laude* from Bryn Mawr College and received her master's degree in social work from Bryn Mawr College School of Social Work and Social Research. She received her doctorate in philosophy from the Clinical Social Work Institute in Washington, DC. Her first profession was as a member of the New York City Ballet. Dr. Smolen has won several national awards for her clinical work, and has presented her clinical work both nationally and internationally. Dr. Smolen has published several articles including "Boys Only! No Mothers Allowed," published in *The International Journal of Psychoanalysis* and translated into three languages. Dr. Smolen is the author of *Mothering Without a Home: Representations of Attachment Behaviors in Homeless Mothers and Children* (Aronson, 2013). She maintains a private practice in child, adolescent, and adult psychotherapy and psychoanalysis in Ardmore, PA.

Donald Spence, PhD, was an eminent North American psychoanalyst who earned a place of distinction in the profession's published canon with his 1982 book, *Narrative Truth and Historical Truth.* A challenge to the limitations of recall and reconstruction, the book's message carried enormous technical significance for clinical psychoanalysis. Donald Spence obtained his bachelor's degree from Harvard University in 1949 and his PhD in clinical psychology from Columbia University in 1955. He graduated from the New York Psychoanalytic Institute in 1966 and held the rank of professor of psychiatry at the Robert Wood Johnson Medical School of the University of Medicine and Dentistry of New Jersey. Besides his highly acclaimed monograph mentioned above, he authored more than one hundred articles and book reviews and two other books. He spent the years of his retirement in Princeton, NJ, and was active with Habitat for Humanity, Pro Musica, Old Guard, and Community Without Walls. Dr. Spence died in 2007.

Vamık D. Volkan, MD, is an emeritus professor of psychiatry at the University of Virginia; an emeritus training and supervising analyst at the Washington Baltimore Center for Psychoanalysis; and an emeritus Senior Erik Erikson Scholar at the Erikson Institute of the Austen Riggs Center. He is the emeritus president of the International Dialogue Initiative and a former president of the Turkish-American Neuropsychiatric Society, the International Society of Political Psychology, the Virginia Psychoanalytic Society, and the American College of Psychoanalysts. Dr. Volkan was a member of the International Negotiation Network under the directorship of former President Jimmy Carter, an inaugural Yitzhak Rabin Fellow, Rabin Center for Israeli Studies, Tel Aviv, Israel; a visiting professor of psychiatry at four universities in Turkey, a visiting professor of psychoanalysis at East-European Institute of Psychoanalysis, Saint Petersburg, Russia; a visiting professor of law, Harvard University, Boston, Massachusetts; a Fulbright/Sigmund Freud Foundation visiting scholar of psychoanalysis in Vienna, Austria; a visiting professor of political science at the University of Vienna; and a visiting professor at El Bosque University, Bogota, Colombia. He was also a board member of the Freud Foundation in Vienna and a member of the Working Group on Terror and Terrorism, International Psychoanalytical Association. Dr. Volkan is the author, coauthor, editor, or coeditor of sixty psychoanalytic and psychopolitical books. His book, *Large-Group Psychology: Racism, Societal Divisions, Narcissistic Leaders and Who We Are Now* (2020), received the Gradiva 2021 Best Book Award. He has written hundreds of published papers and book chapters. He is a recipient of the Nevitt Sanford, Elise Hayman, Bryce Boyer, Hans Strupp, Sigmund Freud (given by the city of Vienna), and Mary Sigourney awards and the Margaret Mahler Literature Prize. He was nominated for the Nobel Peace Prize five times; letters of support were sent from twenty-seven countries.

Richard Waugaman, MD, is a training and supervising analyst, emeritus, at the Washington Psychoanalytic Institute. He is clinical professor of psychiatry and faculty expert on Shakespeare for media contacts at Georgetown University. He has written more than one hundred publications; fifty of them are on Shakespeare and on the psychology of pseudonymity. Since 2004, he has done archival research at the Folger Shakespeare Library. There he discovered one of the largest previously unknown literary sources for Shakespeare's works, in Edward de Vere's copy of Sternhold and Hopkins's *Whole Book of Psalms*. De Vere's annotations showed his unusual interest in some of these psalms, which are echoed repeatedly in Shakespeare's plays and poems. This discovery has unlocked new levels of meaning in Shakespeare's works and has helped validate Freud's theory that Edward de Vere wrote the works of "Shakespeare."

Thomas Wolman, MD, was born and raised in New York City. He attended Johns Hopkins University and the Pennsylvania State University Medical College. Subsequently he trained at the Psychoanalytic Center of Philadelphia, where he now teaches in both the psychoanalytic and psychotherapy training programs. Currently he holds the title of clinical assistant professor of psychiatry at the University of Pennsylvania School of Medicine. He has written on Winnicott, Mahler, Kohut, and Lacan, as well as on contemporary film and literary themes. He has recently published a collection of his essays on film under the title of *The Erotic Screen* (2020).

Introduction

This book is not about *the* truth. It is about truth, in all its majestic and defiled forms, in a physical and psychical sense, in prose and poetry, in history and law, in politics and philosophy, and in various phases of the human life span. As would be clear from even a cursory glance at its table of contents, not to say upon reading it, the topic it seeks to address is of great interest to large numbers of disciplines in humanities and equally fascinating to mental health clinicians. In psychoanalysis, an early preoccupation was the unearthing of childhood trauma as the etiological agent of adult psychopathology. This led to a great interest in the individual's "historical truth"; concepts such as the genetic perspective of metapsychology, reconstruction, genetic interpretation, and childhood origins of transference were all products of such conceptual zeal.

Subsequent shifts in theory challenged these assumptions. The foundations of ontogenetic certainty were shaken up by the emergent notions of "genetic fallacy" (Hartmann, 1939), "personal myth" (E. Kris, 1956a), "narrative truth" (Spence, 1982b), and the advent of intersubjective and relational perspectives in psychoanalysis (Benjamin, 2004; Mitchell, 1988; Ogden, 1994). Working in unison with the postmodern exaltation of relativism vis-à-vis "facts," these concepts threw the baby of "one person psychology" out with the bathwater of inordinately certain reconstructions of the analysand's past.

The book in your hands elucidates this and other such conundrums with eloquence and nuance. Variables of ego development, sociopolitical imperatives, and clinical praxis help organize its wide-ranging contents into a harmonious gestalt which might or might not capture the truth in this realm but certainly comes quite close to it.

Prologue

CHAPTER ONE

The meaning of "truth" and the truth about "meaning" in psychoanalysis

Brett H. Clarke

Psychoanalysis is by disposition perpetually in crisis. In fact, by now "crisis" should probably be considered a definitional characteristic of psychoanalysis. And one cannot understand the nature of its central and ongoing meta-theoretical predicament without first appreciating the essential, constitutive tension at the heart of the psychoanalytic theory of the mind. Using the vocabulary of one version (Ricœur, 1970), it would be the tension between a language of force and energy, on the one hand, and a language of reasons, intentions, and meanings, on the other. This fundamental tension has brought with it epistemological corollaries and controversies. For over one hundred years many analysts have referred to psychoanalysis as a "science," though the impressive bulk of analytic ideas, both theoretical and clinical, have emerged from groups of clinicians thinking critically about their experiences with patients over time, talking together, and writing about it. In fact, the question about "science" has proven to be a rather poor way of framing the more pertinent question of rigor. People often use the word "science" when what they really mean to convey is a concern for rigor. So in approaching the question of truth in psychoanalysis, we inevitably will also be asking what constitutes an appropriate kind of rigor in the formulation of psychoanalytic "knowledge," or how it is that we come to know what we think we know.

For those who regard the term "science" as the necessary title for any form of inquiry that claims to be rigorous, this has led to 1) a broadening of the modern definition of science (a reversion to the age-old notion of science as virtually any discipline or body of knowledge) so that psychoanalysis can fit inside, or 2) a perceived need to narrow the scope of psychoanalysis to fit into an idea of science that depends on systematic testing and empirical measurement, or 3) an effort to combine (into a single entity) epistemological frameworks that are potentially wildly disparate. But there has been an often-overlooked benefit to this vagueness about the nature of the intrinsic tensions in psychoanalytic thought, reflected in the vagueness of the term "psychoanalytic science." Fuzziness has made the discord tolerable by obscuring it, freeing analytic thinkers to imagine and reimagine the mind in creative (if sometimes misguided) ways while pretending their discipline is like a branch of archeology, medicine, or ethology. For a long while, under cover of this presumption of being "scientific" (whatever this was intended to mean), psychoanalysis was relatively free to be what it was.

Self-misrecognition has its downside, of course, and in recent decades the consequences of epistemological fuzziness have become clearer, prompted in part by cultural and economic demands for scientific accountability. The practical result has been a tilt within psychoanalysis toward research-based reforms and attempts to revise both theory and practice according to more scientific models, as we see in the ascendance of the use of measurable categories (created by one or another line of research) as the vocabulary for how we think and talk.

It is natural to locate a discipline by trying to describe its relation to other disciplines, and disciplines have traditionally been slotted into broad categories intended to help with this—thus we are given "hard sciences," "human or social sciences," "arts," "humanities," "tradecraft," etc. Every discipline shares characteristics in common with other disciplines, while at the same time every discipline is unique in the sense that nothing else is quite like it. And psychoanalysis is no different in this respect. However, my view of psychoanalysis as a discipline, and of the nature of psychoanalytic "truth," resides partly in the assertion that the ways in which psychoanalysis is different make it *qualitatively* different from most other forms of inquiry and frameworks of understanding, and that this is so for at least three reasons.

First, the epistemological imperatives of any discipline are necessarily governed to some important extent by the nature of the object of study. The question of psychoanalytic "truth" is an epistemological question—that is, a question about what constitutes "knowledge" in psychoanalysis, which includes the question of how we come to "know" things psychoanalytically. This question is especially complicated in psychoanalysis because when the object of study is subjective experience and its apposite meanings, epistemology becomes especially entangled in ontology—that is, "*how* we know" becomes especially dependent on the nature or the "being" of the thing we are looking at, in this case, human being or human subjectivity.

We should consider as inexorable the subject or target of psychoanalytic interest, which is the internal, unconsciously driven, and complexly organized dynamics of the subjectively lived experience of individuals who at once share certain human features in common while also expressing highly idiosyncratic, often unpredictable individual characteristics.[1] In his study of the "private self," Modell (1993) begins with an insight from William James, writing, "The experience of the self is a fundamental reality which cannot be transposed or reduced

[1] See Caws (2003), who calls psychoanalysis "the idiosyncratic science of the individual subject."

into something else that is more 'objective'" (p. 2). I would further suggest that there is nothing in nature comparable to individual subjective experience, a difference that is not erased by the recognition that other things might be similarly "complex": nothing else is complex in quite *this* way.

The second reason is really an elaboration of the first. Psychoanalysis is concerned with meaning—what things are given to mean, what they come to mean, what they are made to mean, all the ways in which meanings conflict, exert influence, and change over time. The notion of psychic determinism, and the need in any psychoanalytic epistemology for what Eagle et al. (2001) call a humble realism, is grounded not just in energy, but more pressingly in meaning. Ideas of psychical energies or forces, like the corporeal substrates with which they are too often confused, might be a necessary but are certainly not a sufficient condition for approaching subjectivity. One manifestation of the tensional conjunction between force and meaning in our subjective experience lies simply in how we are *moved* by what things *mean*, and by how meaning is guided and colored by affect and the experiential palimpsest of a thing's memorial history. Only in an economy of subjectively constituted meanings can reasons become causes, can *meaning* enter into a foundational dialectic with causation resulting in a psychoanalytic version of psychic determinism. Moreover, of almost peremptory relevance to the nature of psychoanalytic subjectivity as an object of inquiry is the central role of *unconscious* meaning and meanings derived and elaborated from unconscious associative links, schemas, fantasies, and beliefs.

Thus, the being (ontology) of psychoanalytic subjectivity shapes certain conditions for psychoanalytic inquiry and for what counts as truth in psychoanalysis (epistemology). Heading this list of conditions is this founding epistemological tenet: What is unconscious can only be "known" or postulated from its derivative manifestations, can only be reported or enacted by an experiencing subject in the context of an analytically framed engagement with another complex, unconsciously organized subjectivity, both of whom rely on affective involvement and imagination in order to reason about and "know" (always contextually and incompletely) their own and one another's experience. This is a constitutive, defining feature of human mental life as conceived psychoanalytically.

Third, psychoanalysis is defined by the pathways through which we register, process, organize, reflect upon, connect, delink, and reconfigure our subjective experience psychoanalytically. We come to a sense of "knowing" another person by imagining from our own experience a version of *their* experience. This will be based in part on empathic identification, stimulated by what they provoke in us (whether consciously or unconsciously), and organized by who we already are when we open the waiting-room door. But the intuitionism of empathic identification, if we are going to "know" something in a psychoanalytically useful way, must exist in tension with "knowing" from an existentially incontestable position of separateness. This involves the separateness of an analytic stance that cultivates a standing-apart-from, making possible a sense of nearness-in-distance, and ultimately and in various ways the capacity to experience and tolerate something being at once real and not real—for example, to experience a transference fantasy in such a way that it can be at once felt as real *and* understood as something that exists in a space apart from the everyday world.[2]

Psychoanalytic knowledge is only arrived at when experience occurs on multiple registers simultaneously—in terms of affect and "felt" meaning, and at the same time by organizing that experience according to one's assumptions and conceptual commitments. The type of empirical *experience* most relevant to psychoanalysis (an empiricism similar to what Morag (2016) calls "liberal naturalism") is also the foundation of psychoanalytic knowledge, and should not be confused with the quantifying and measuring kind of empiricism associated with systematic research.

Any discussion of psychoanalysis as a "science" should begin with acknowledgment that psychoanalysis is empirical in this experiential way, and that only from this premise can we make use of "objective" or "distanciated" points of reference.[3] When reasoned objectivity is viewed as emerging from and always referring back to subjective experience, it makes the experience of "knowing" something psychoanalytically an *embedded* kind of knowing, contextualized by subjectively situated moments and by an individual subject's relation to their own memorial history as this appears in their psychic world. And this brings to the process of "knowing something" an intrinsic, relative ambiguity, one that includes tensions between different levels or aspects of our experience of something, as well as tensions between the meanings that inevitably coalesce around that experience. In this way, a reasoned objectivity can also be more easily understood as in partnership with the poetic character of psychoanalysis, where the term "poetic" refers to metaphor (or "metaphorical-ness") as a property of psychoanalytic understanding—because metaphor in various forms is how human beings best capture and express a meaning or experience whose essence is polyvalent and tensional. Such is our human lot with respect to meaning.[4]

A skeletal description of a psychoanalytic hermeneutic in the sense I intend might be: A form of critical reason guided by affective and imaginative engagement, one that is dialectical

---

[2] This is where psychoanalytic knowing or "truth" intersects with versions of mature transitional experience, true play, and a properly conceptualized metaphoricity. This would involve an idea of metaphor more in line with Ricœur (1977b, 1978), Enckell (2001), and Clarke (2022), one organized around the experience of sameness through difference, as opposed to the cognitive-conceptual theory of metaphor pioneered by Lakoff and Johnson (1980), which is often cited in the psychoanalytic literature and influentially promoted by writers such as Modell (2003, 2005, 2011) and Katz (2011, 2013).

[3] In similar fashion, and as part of his effort to correct the longstanding confusion in psychoanalysis over the meaning of subject/object and subjectivity/objectivity, Lear (2003) recommends "subjective objectivity" as the appropriate form of objectivity for psychoanalytic activity.

[4] The relationship between the "poetics" of metaphor and psychoanalytic understanding is complex and would require much deeper discussion. My premise here is that metaphor has a unique capacity to capture something true about our reality, in part because it has a primordial relation to the contradictions of primary process experience and to a subjectivity rooted in unconscious processes and meanings that can only be inferred based on their derivative manifestations (for a fuller discussion, see Clarke, 2022).

in a way that fits with the processual nature of subjective experience, that is responsive to the inherent tensions and polyvalences which accompany interaction between different levels of psychic organization, and that is attuned to the constitutive tensions which accompany how we formulate meaning within particular contexts or horizons of experience. I would further suggest that an overarching hermeneutic framework offers the important advantage of being able to hold in productive tension the essential elements that make psychoanalytic meaning possible: an "empirical" objectifying distance that anchors perception and understanding *in the world*, in concert with the ongoing action of imagination and feeling that ties us inextricably to unconscious convictions, schemas, fantasies, and to the bodily organizations of psychic life.[5]

A clinical snapshot

Let me offer an illustration, intended to help in considering the epistemological complexity of grasping what is meaningful in almost any clinical moment. Ms. A arrives at her morning session and immediately reports her experience driving to my office. She explains that at about the halfway point she felt a sudden rush of panic and became frightened she would have an accident. "I was suffocating," she says tearfully. "I can't imagine what it would feel like to drown. I can't imagine being water-boarded. I think my heart would burst." Her heart is still racing, she says, her hand pressed to her chest as if holding her heart in place. I can feel anxiety in my own chest, and we are suspended together in an anxious pause.

I might have found myself moving in any number of ways in this moment. In response to my own anxiety I might have started devising ways to help her manage hers—practical ways, pharmacological remedies. The framework for such interventions would be behavioral or biochemical. Or my mind might have gone to external events or elements of her history. I might have connected her current feeling of anxious helplessness with previously reported nightmares of being confined and held down, sometimes with her suspicion that these dreams might be related to early experiences of medical trauma. I might be thinking about the neurocognitive aspects of such traumatic recursion, or about the sequelae of disrupted attachment in infancy. As I'm describing it, I would be defining her subjectivity in this moment in terms of nameable traumas, and then perhaps applying a neurobiological, a neurocognitive, or an attachment model as an organizing framework within which to develop interventions.

But what does it mean that I am working with Ms. A, and understanding her, not in terms of her neurochemistry, or cognitive patterns, or the relative, behaviorally assessed security or insecurity of her early attachment, but rather psychoanalytically? Even if speculation about psychopharmacology or discrete traumas is warranted, in every case where the thought is occurring *outside the frame of psychoanalytic reflection* I will have effectively stopped listening

---

[5]See Ricœur (1977b, 1978) for discussions of the role of imagination, feeling, and distanced reflection in the tensional structure of metaphor.

and functioning in a psychoanalytically receptive way. I would not hear her language about drowning, about passivity, helplessness, hunger for air, torture, perhaps guilt and the need for punishment, and her bursting heart in the same way, and would be less open to letting these thoughts reverberate through me or stir associations. I would probably be less aware of sensations and changes in my own body. My unconscious would still be involved in how I am listening, but I would be less receptive to and less aware of its influence.

The argument is commonly made that we can listen from within multiple frameworks simultaneously, that one does not exclude another. Most prominent in recent analytic discussion has been the example of neuropsychoanalysis, whose hybrid nature is advertised in its very name, and which operates with the assumption that a common epistemological framework (sometimes referred to as dual-aspect monism) can conjoin the discourses of neurobiology and psychoanalysis without epistemological colonization inflicted by one side or the other.[6] I would suggest instead that such multiplicity is less an integration and more an *alternation* of different modes of listening and organizing. Toggling between radically different frameworks underestimates the difficulty of occupying a single position well and immersively, and creates an *illusion* of integration based on proximity in time and on a shared attention to the same person or problem.

In this instance, that person is Ms. A, and the "problem" is her panic anxiety as she lies uncomfortably on my couch. Doing psychoanalysis, she and I are engaged in a serious kind of game, and the game has certain rules that create the possibility for certain kinds of meaning. When I am listening psychoanalytically, Ms. A is framed by my assumptions about her subjectivity. By way of example, I assume: She is complexly anchored in unconscious beliefs and fantasies; that one important version of her experience would focus on the story of her desire in relation to objects or mental figurations of objects, of desires in conflict with one another and with reality, organized adaptively or not around an array of defenses; that her desire, like all desire, is created out of the experience of absence, and lives in the play of absence, presence, and substitution. More than this, I assume that I know her by way of my particular experience of her. I imagine her based on myself and on how I am affected by her, using the material (the feelings and meanings) that are stirred up between us, and then by our interpretations and understandings of all that. I know her, in other words, by observing, engaging with, and imagining her based on my own version of the idiosyncratic, felt, but also reasoned attention characteristic of analytic listening.

[6] Advocates often focus on the need for analytic *theory* to conform to neurocognitive science, but this in itself does not avoid questions about the relationship between neurobiology and subjective mental life, or the problems that come with merging vastly different epistemological frameworks. Notable contributions to the neuropsychoanalytic enterprise include Solms (1998, 2000), Kaplan-Solms and Solms (2000), Solms and Turnbull (2002), Fotopoulou (2012a, 2012b), Kandel (2005), Modell (2003), and Opatow (1999). Critiques include those by Blass and Carmeli (2007, 2015), Brothers (2002), and Clarke (2018).

There is a psychoanalytic structure that helps to organize all of this, so that feelings of disorientation or thoughts of pharmacology can be folded into a larger process of psychoanalytic engagement. There is nothing intrinsically un-psychoanalytic about any thought until one stops listening to it psychoanalytically.

After a moment, as her breathing begins to settle, I say to her, rather obviously, "You worry that your heart will burst." Not because it is the only or the best thing to say, but because it is what occurs to me as right, perhaps because I am moved to create a new (metaphoric) tension where the words can be both literally and figuratively true, a space where meaning becomes possible. But how do we decide what is right, or more right, in any clinical moment? If not quite the way a poet chooses the "right" word, or the way a researcher counts and calculates the median value of an observable behavioral marker—then how?

Further thoughts on epistemology

It is probably safe to say that a lot of psychoanalytic writing, with its penchant for pseudoscientific jargon and disapproval of primary-process evocativeness, will never be mistaken for poetry. And indeed, as the psychoanalyst Lawrence Friedman (2000) warns, even psychoanalysts who *try* to strike postmodernist literary poses are probably (at best) foredoomed to the rank of "third-rate poets." Psychoanalysis is first and foremost a very particular, and in some ways peculiar, clinical discipline. While it is true that psychoanalysis is not poetry, it *is* in an important sense *poetic*. That is to say, there is much that comes up in the course of analytic work that has a plurivocal quality—that is allusive, sometimes metaphoric, sometimes narrative but plotted in very particular ways, full of tropes, often repetitive but then surprising, ripe with unexpected deviations of meaning. And it's not as if one can always or readily sort out the meaning of even a fairly simple dream.

Nonetheless, poems *can* be understood in illuminating and helpful ways, and so can dreams, and so can analytic sessions, and so can analytic patients. But how we reason about any of these things, and whatever objectivity we bring to bear in our study of them, must be rooted in our full experience. And with this there will always be remainders of meaning, an inherent excess. What Paul Ricœur (1973) calls the "ontological density" of subjective experience (p. 75) is compatible with an idea of "irreducibility" in the sense that I intend it. It's in the very nature of subjective experience, in its experiential density, that there is always more than can be known or articulated. This is also relevant in understanding what I mean by the word "poetic." As practitioners, psychoanalysts are less like poets and more like trained listeners and readers of the poetic; they do their best to hear what is there, but also what is in between the words in the density of subjective experience, what is suggested but never apparent, the unlanguaged in-between spaces, the poetry of the unconscious or the unconscious of the poetic.

Perhaps "irreducible" is the wrong term, but here is what I am trying to get at. I have a memory from when I am ten sitting alone in my grandmother's dining room. I say to my analyst, "I am remembering sitting in my grandmother's dining room. I am around ten. The sun is coming through the curtains. I feel sad, or something, but the sad feels like a color, a really dark red for some reason, the way the sunlight clings to the side of an apple in the bowl on the table, like it's painted on. I remember thinking that, the words, 'Like it's painted on.' The windows are open and the air around me is heavy and isn't moving. Then I can hear my relatives talking at the other end of the apartment, someone laughing, and it makes me feel good, relieved." Let's assume that in saying this, I have captured one hundredth of what I experienced in having that memory. Let's further assume that if I keep talking about that memory for the next fifty minutes, I still would capture only a fraction of what I am feeling and thinking internally, in part because my current thoughts are always changing, the memory is blending with others or with new sensations and ideas, and in theory this could go on indefinitely.[7] Already my numerations ("one hundredth" and "a fraction of") have become allusive references to a process that refuses enumeration. I could never catch up because every moment is creating new experience; here numbers become like poetic intimations of something fundamentally unmeasurable. One asks, one hundredth of what, exactly?[8]

One could further say that by its very nature, its "ontological density," subjective mental experience constitutes a *unique* kind of inaccessibility or excess. This has special importance for psychoanalysis, which is especially interested in subjective "inner" experience and the meanings we ascribe to it. Research efforts to measure and quantify aspects of this process and the minds of those involved should consider not just the complexity of the process and its content, but also its ontological density, which suggests mass, a *quality* of being or of the experience of being that is latent in the word "subjectivity."

If subjective experience includes an irreducible quality in the sense that I'm intending, surely this has epistemological implications for psychoanalysis. I don't think psychoanalysis is *above* scientifically objective inquiry, but I do think it is critical that psychoanalysis claim its right to an equal footing in negotiating that relationship. That is, it should be permitted to engage with other disciplines on its own terms and be guided by its own epistemological commitments, and to do so without apology.

This brings us back, as it must, to the vexed issue of "objectivity." The importance of objectivity in psychoanalytic thinking has traditionally been due to its role in either validating or

---

[7] Freud's concept of *Nachträglichkeit* or "afterwardness," and later elaborations of *après-coup* by Laplanche (2006) and others, capture a dimension of the dialectical and dynamic nature of memory and experienced time. Gadamer (1960) alludes to something similar in his borrowing of the notion of a *verbum interius* (the inner word) from St. Augustine. Gadamer explained, "This universality [of hermeneutics] consists in inner speech, in that one cannot say everything. One cannot express everything that one has in mind ..." (Grondin, 1994, p. xiv).

[8] In his study of Merleau-Ponty, Hass (2008) suggests something like this, writing: "There is ... a *distance* between the experiencing self and behaviour which is not a transcendental chasm or dualism, but precisely a separation (*écart*) ... This separation, this dehiscence, is why I am never *quite* at one with myself. It is why, despite all our corporeal and conversational reciprocity, there is irremediable distance between oneself and others" (p. 111).

verifying what we think we know, in giving us grounds for holding a belief to be "warranted" or justified—that is, to be "true"—or not. In order to sort out why this is a misleading place to start, however, we first have to contend with two quite different versions of objectivity, both actively employed in psychoanalytic theorizing.

The first is the familiar scientific form of objectivity rooted in the rule-governed collection and organization of observational data, and the design of experimental testing of these hypotheses using operationalized and measurable terms and categories. Traditionally this would include the ways in which such physical-science methodology has been adapted and employed to varying degrees within the social and human sciences. The second is more existentially (and epistemologically) fundamental, and is evident for example in Ricœur's term "distanciation," or in Merleau-Ponty's notion of *écart* or "separation" (see Hass, 2008, p. 211), or in Lear's (2003) more accessible and clarifying notion of "subjective objectivity." Here we have a very basic notion of "standing apart from" related to an intrinsic separateness from oneself, or to the basic otherness or separation between subjectivities, or to the positioning of one's perspective, in a relative or contextually constrained way, outside of or apart from that which one is contemplating or observing. These are fundamental, practical realities that bring us to the relative objectivity advocated by philosophical hermeneutics, not as an epistemological preference, but as an acknowledgment of a basic condition of human being.

Even advocates for a subscription of psychoanalytic theory to scientific research often acknowledge that first-order knowledge in psychoanalysis is subjective or experiential; and it is not uncommon for them to describe psychoanalytic objectivity in ways that sound to me like versions of everyday critical thinking or hermeneutics—the application of critical thought within particular contexts of activity and interpretation, one that tacks dialectically between part and whole in a process of refinement and revision. This is the procedural shape of most distanced reflection or reasoned inquiry in psychoanalysis, both in the clinical setting and in the development of theory based on clinical experience.

It is true that the warnings against relativism and arguments in favor of an enumerating "objectivity" in psychoanalysis have a certain cautionary merit. Though at times extreme, the disparaging characterizations of hermeneutics sometimes encountered in the psychoanalytic literature (as mere textualism, as relativist or postmodern, or as having a Romantic or histrionic relation to truth) should give the thoughtful reader pause. Ahumada, 1997, 2001; Hanly, 1992, 1999, 2006, 2014a, 2014b; Hanly and Fitzpatrick Hanly, 2001; and Edelson, 1988, for example, offer well-reasoned philosophical cautions against the relativist dangers of certain aspects of postmodern and hermeneutic approaches to knowledge. Laplanche (1992a) likewise associates hermeneutics with philosophical relativism, and so regards psychoanalysis as an "antihermeneutic discipline."[9] Strenger (2013) is more strident,

[9] In my reading of Laplanche, his way of reasoning about psychoanalytic questions is (in general) perfectly consistent with hermeneutic analysis as I describe it here.

characterizing hermeneutics as not just anti-scientific and unhinged from reality, but as narcissistically self-indulgent as well. In their different ways they recognize that psychoanalysis is insupportable if given over to a radical kind of relativism, social constructionism, epistemological indeterminacy, or postmodern deconstruction (which includes an emptying out of individual subjectivity).

Most everyone agrees that because the mental is intrinsically subjective, it requires a distanced perspective, a standing-outside-of, in order for relativism or an unfettered subjectivism to be fended off. But from the anti-hermeneutic perspective, hermeneutics, because of its insistence on the contextual nature of knowledge, and in some cases its focus on the protean variability of meaning, is seen as incapable of providing the kind of method-based distancing required by objectivity. And to this extent, I agree: If in fact a psychoanalytic hermeneutics were to entail an unconstrained (postmodern) kind of relativism of the sort nearly everyone is against, a relativism in which "anything goes" and everything is "constructed" or deconstructed and nothing is in any sense discovered, then it would indeed deserve correction. But the hermeneutics that I along with others either espouse or practice (without necessarily naming), and that psychoanalysis needs, is not of this sort.

What kind of discipline, exactly?

Let's allow that the epistemological question is not about whether psychoanalysis is a science. If boxing is a science, or portraiture, or interpretive studies of medieval history, or politics—if these are sciences, then yes, psychoanalysis can be called a science in this broadest of senses, but then more accurately with the qualification that it is an interpretive human science, much more dissimilar than similar to medicine or biological psychiatry. Hermeneutics suggests that better questions might be: In what sense does psychoanalytic knowledge rely on or use objective or distanced forms of inquiry? And then, what form of "objectivity" is appropriate to the study of human beings in the fullness of their subjectivity? And how should psychoanalysis interface with traditionally scientific disciplines or forms of research in a way that preserves its essential ways of working and understanding?

Two currents have been crisscrossing through psychoanalytic discussion since Freud abandoned his *Project for a Scientific Psychology* in 1895, but especially in the last forty years. First, an awareness of how fundamentally the process of psychoanalysis is a *lived* experience that includes, but goes beyond, how one thinks or how an analytic pair arrive at insight. Psychoanalysis now appreciates to an unprecedented extent that how one is thinking at any given time is rooted in how one is experiencing the moment along multiple registers. Moments of "objectivity" are only elements in a larger dialectic, pieces that move the process along while inevitably opening new avenues of experience and new potential meanings. And second, simultaneously, there is this push to reform psychoanalysis in ways intended to permit it to hold discourse with more traditionally scientific disciplines and, in so doing, rescue itself from the junk heap of discarded pseudo-sciences.[10] This awkward pairing of subjective experience (including its densities and ambiguities of meaning) with empirical research has left psychoanalytic commentators with the difficult task of reconciling two sides of an inherently gnarly fit.

Arnold Cooper (1993) voices the sponsoring idea for a reformist, research-based objectivity. "Without empirical studies," he says, "we have no way ever to discard a hypothesis …" (p. 384). Empirical research, he writes, "will be applied to psychoanalytic propositions, and many of our favorite ideas will be shown to be wrong or what amounts to the same thing, not useful" (p. 391).

Viewed in this way, psychoanalytic experience, and the ideas grounded there, are just a mess of untested data awaiting the shaping hand of systematic research. In time, Cooper tells us, many or even most psychoanalytic constructs will be replaced by empirically measurable categories. Such a shift will be based on the assumption that what resists measurement is either less real or less useful or both (see Clarke, 2017).

How should we understand these two powerful and seemingly contradictory currents in contemporary psychoanalysis—for the subjective, sometimes "poetic," and intrinsically dialectical character of the process, on the one hand, and demands for testability and quantification, on the other?

André Green (2001) addresses the challenge of a research-based epistemology by cautioning that we mustn't "give way to the temptation—under the pretext of being scientific—of forgetting the singular exigencies of the psychoanalytic method." There is a need, he writes, "for an investigation into research; that is to say, for reflection on the conditions of the application of research itself, which does not lose sight of the specificity and originality of psychoanalytic thought and the need to find ways of preserving and safeguarding them" (p. 70). Green understands the risk of a kind of scientism hidden in the push for research, at least to the extent that such reform intends a research-based epistemology that disregards "the singular exigencies" of psychoanalytic understanding.

After all, as disciplines go, psychoanalysis is no house sparrow, but a much stranger bird. Ricœur's (1970) description of Freudian psychoanalysis as combining dialectically a language of force and energy (causation, explanation) with a language of meaning (motive, reasons, understanding), outlines a dichotomy often cast in terms of psyche and soma, with psychoanalysis as the discipline operating in the interstitial space they share. From its beginnings there has been an intrinsic, tensive in-between-ness about psychoanalysis, and if you want to work and think psychoanalytically you have to be willing to navigate in that space.

---

[10] This is the common message of important contributors such as Gabbard, Fonagy, and Solms. My concern is that pluralist writers would disregard the epistemological implications of the "ontologically subjective" character of the mental, or of its irreducibility in the sense I am intending.

The hybrid nature of Freudian psychoanalysis lies in an inherent but necessary tension between biology (or its mental derivative, drive) and meaning. Biology does not traffic in meanings, and it seems important that the hybrid nature Ricœur is proposing not be misunderstood as requiring or allowing for a hybrid epistemology. What this means in a practical sense is that research findings should always be subjected to critical scrutiny, should be "investigated" or interpreted as to their value or relevance, as Green suggests.

Another way of saying this would be that an uncareful interface between psychoanalysis and scientific research will tend inherently to minimize the philosophical implications of the centrality of subjective experience (e.g., of embodiment, of lived time, of continually shifting perceptions, of variable horizons and contexts of meaning). With its special interest in subjective experience, psychoanalysis ought to require that any objective mode of attention to the mental abide by an obligation to the fundamental difference between *observing* a behavior and *experiencing* oneself behaving (see Hass, 2008, p. 111).

I experience my perceptions and thoughts as my own. I *experience* them, however one wants to characterize how I *know* them. But by experiencing them, I inevitably know them uniquely. Others can know *about* them in various partial, mediated ways (which still allows that others can know me differently, and sometimes better than I know myself), but this is all secondary to my *possessing* my experiences as my own.

The "irreducible" character of subjective experience follows first from the fact that each subjectivity possesses its experience in a way that is (to some extent) singular and private. Additionally, it is in the density of lived experience that meaning coalesces around unconscious beliefs and fantasies. Psychoanalysis's special interest in what things *mean*, both privately and between people, is part of why the subjective character of the mental is *philosophically* fundamental to psychoanalytic thought. Any critique of the scientization of psychoanalysis, if it is to be optimally coherent and effective, must anchor itself firmly in the epistemological implications of the ontological density of subjective experience, where meaning and desire intersect.

Ricœur (Changeux & Ricœur 2003) comments on the semantic dualism between the mental and the neurobiological, and in so doing articulates a danger that resides especially, but not only, in neuropsychoanalytic efforts at reform: "These discourses represent heterogeneous perspectives," he writes, "which is to say that they cannot be reduced to each other or derived from each other … I shall therefore combat the sort of semantic amalgamation that one finds summarized in the oxymoronic formula, 'The brain thinks'" (p. 14). Tensions can exist within a circumscribed discourse, but altogether different discourses, whose founding assumptions are "heterogeneous," cannot be held in tension with one another in the same way. Tensions can exist *within* psychoanalysis precisely because the terms of the tension are consistent with psychoanalysis's founding assumptions.

If one engages in an interchange between discourses with conflicting fundamental assumptions, which one can certainly do, it is best to acknowledge the preeminence of an overarching structure of inquiry, a position from which differences can be interpreted in a dynamic, evolving, context-sensitive way, and ultimately judged for their relevance, thus setting reasoned arbitration of "empirical" experience above mere quantitative verification. This is the proper role of hermeneutics in psychoanalysis at the level of discourse. I am arguing that if the pre-eminence of a reasonable hermeneutics in the formulation of what constitutes psychoanalytic knowledge is abridged or appropriated by an alternative framework founded on different epistemological assumptions—if, as Ricœur (1970) warns, psychoanalysis "bends" to the axioms of empiricism or behaviorism—it condemns itself to either being written off as non-scientific, or to "begging for a partial rehabilitation through what Skinner calls 'the simple expedient of an operational definition of terms'" (pp. 365–366).

Thoughts on embodiment

Freud described the instincts as the primary propulsive forces driving the development of desire in relation to its objects. The drives were the psychical forces at the interface between mind and body, the expression of our embodied natures. But the *psychoanalytic* body, properly understood, is not a collection of physical organs; it is the body as subjectively experienced, what Loewald (1971) calls "the body in the context of human life," a body which "is not primarily the organism with its organs and physiological functions, anatomical structures, nerve pathways, and chemical processes" (p. 125). It is the body-as-experienced that is the foundation of mental and relational life as conceived psychoanalytically (Clarke, 2018, pp. 435–436), and that ultimately functions not as an objectively observable thing, but as the idiom for psychic organization, and the ground against which meaning and its figurations become visible.

One could say, along with the neuropsychoanalyst Mark Solms, that psychoanalysis and neuroscience are looking at the same thing differently.[11] But any notion of subjectivity natural to a neuronal model bears no relation to a psychoanalytically conceived living, breathing person. So, are we really looking at the same thing? Alternate perspectives change *how* we look, but also change the character of the thing we are looking at, even if we call it by the same name. From this perspective, we are *not* two blind men investigating the same event, or elephant, from different ends, one at the tail, one at the trunk. Experientially and epistemologically, these are *different* elephants, constructed (borrowing a phrase from Loewald according to markedly "different modes of experiencing and ordering reality" (1971, p. 134)).[12]

Thus, there is a difference between being "embodied" and being "corporeal." Moreover, knowing oneself and the world by way of one's embodied nature is not secondary to the

[11] As mentioned earlier, Solms adopts a "dual-aspect monist" view of the mind–body question: two perspectives, objective and subjective, on a single reality. Whatever its merits, such an approach is inclined to see both mental and physical reality through the lens of a common epistemology.

[12] Karlsson (2010) also addresses the intrinsic problem at the heart of the blind-men-and-the-elephant metaphor as it is used to illustrate the dual-aspect position. The point is that, from the perspective I am suggesting, any effort to merge these two very different elephants into a single entity can only end up "making a bloody mess of at least one of them" (Clarke, 2018, pp. 433–434).

findings of kinesiology and neuroscience. Embodiment constitutes a foundational, first-order dimension of human knowledge, and gives the sciences of the body a context within which to be even remotely understandable.[13]

In early development we experience the mind in the idiom of the body, and this register of experience is never surmounted. Schafer (1973) writes that, as subjectively experienced,

> "feelings are substances, often fecal substances which, accordingly, may be withheld or expelled and gotten rid of or destroyed; or they may fill one up and either explode or leak (or spill) out. Or perhaps they are oral substances (milk, poison, vomitus) or other psychosexual things (urine, semen, babies). Feelings for other persons are like ties that may be cut (like umbilical cords or like the sadist's chains), or the feelings *for* others and *of* others may be engulfing, suffocating, poisonous, and soul-murdering." (p. 46)

Remember Ms. A, who felt she was drowning and like her heart would burst, a terrifying anxiety whose very existence, not to mention the eventual realization of its possible meaning, was contingent on its being first experienced as *alive* in her organs and muscles.

Biology as "lived biology" (Changeux & Ricœur 2003, p. 74) is about the embeddedness of the mind in the corporeal as a principle, as a substrate. The emphasis here is on drive as a *mental* event grounded in biology. The neurobiological details can provide guardrails for a larger process of psychoanalytic exploration. In most instances, what matters are simply the various ways in which we experience ourselves as embodied desiring subjects, not the neurobiology that underlies desire or our anxiety about feeling desire (Clarke, 2018).[14]

Despite his own neuroscientific aspirations, Freud required psychoanalysis to struggle toward some solution to the paradoxical partnership housed in the phrase "lived biology," where biology and meaning come together. I want to emphasize that better solutions uphold in some way the tension of Freud's vision of a hybrid discourse. Lesser solutions ablate the paradox and retreat to reductions or evasions 1) in which the realm of meaning is reduced to or defined by biological forces, *or* at the other extreme 2) where "drive" as a mental representative of biology is dismissed as a mere relational construction or a functionless term stripped of its primal connection to embodied experience, *or* 3) where the tension is ignored by talking about biology and meaning together as if their epistemological incongruence were unimportant.

---

[13] Ricœur (Changeux & Ricœur 2003) makes a similar point when he remarks that the researcher, especially the neuroscientist, must consult with ordinary experience in order to bring significance and sense to objective study (p. 68). Blass and Carmeli (2015) have a similar thought when they highlight neuro-psychoanalysis's reliance on common psychological understandings in formulating the relevance of neurobiological or anatomical findings (pp. 1568–1569).

[14] I refer the reader to Lear's (2003) helpful discussion of this issue (especially pp. 77–84). I borrow the term "guardrails" from Westphal (2011), who uses it to describe how distanciated or objective forms of knowledge function in Ricœur's larger hermeneutic.

Of course all experience is grounded in and dependent on biochemistry and the action of proteins, on gene expression, on the physics governing the movement of bodies in space—yet each of these disciplines adequately explains only a narrow range of phenomena, and none describes the textures, rhythms, and meanings of our subjective experience of the world.

Dialectics, not circularity

There *are* facts, of course, some of which are simply available features of an accepted reality, often organized around the foundational assumptions of a given discourse or perspective, and some of which are available for empirical measurement. There also can be more or less reasoned calculation based on uncontradicted facts in moments of clinical decision-making. But in general, the determination of what is important about any given fact, or what an accepted fact ought to mean in relation to this or that context, intention, or provisional narrative, is a judgment based on how one listens, imagines, and reasons over time. Psychoanalytic understanding is not an event, a single point in time. It has a circular but not a solipsistic character, which is to say it is dialectical and progressive, neither narrowly reductive nor radically relativist. As Ricœur (1971) the hermeneuticist says, "The construal or recognition of the parts presupposes a certain kind of whole; and reciprocally, it is in construing the details that we construe the whole. There is no *necessity* concerning what is important and what is unimportant, what is essential and what is unessential .... The judgment of importance," he says, "is a guess" (p. 158).

I think this is right: the judgment of importance in psychoanalytic work is often an educated guess, a creative projection of our sense of things, of a provisional whole. Reasoned guessing grounded in affective engagement is intrinsic to our experience of understanding something. Regarding the ongoing process of reconsideration of our guesses and provisional conclusions, Ricœur writes, "Validation is a logic of uncertainty and of qualitative probability, more like juridical argumentation, the joining of a conflict of interpretations, than like a direct arbitration by empirical facts" (p. 159). It should also be kept in mind that knowledge derived from empirical measurement must itself be interpreted in order to mean anything, both in the construction of its particular terms and system of observation, *and* in assessing its meaning in relation to the "whole" of what we are trying to understand. This is in the nature of things and not to be remedied.

This description of hermeneutic circularity as *dialectical* captures the essence of psychoanalytic clinical experience with respect to knowledge—the movement between specific part (the dream fragment remembered on this day following this event or affective moment) and the always-present, ever imagined whole (of the patient's world, the analytic relationship, etc.). This is the very material, the fabric, of analytic experience (Clarke, 2017, pp. 587–588). What does this dream about the silhouette of a man behind a window, and the feeling of confused excitement that accompanies it, mean with respect to the moment of hesitation the day before as the patient struggled with expressing a frustrated wish about the analyst, experienced now in the context of the patient's history of felt rejection? She tells me, "The man is dangerous. He wants to look in and see me undressing, like a stalker." And then she says, "In the waiting room yesterday you didn't look at me the way you usually do. I didn't realize until now, but I felt it for just a second yesterday, this … *stabbing* feeling of shame, that you weren't paying attention, maybe. It was weird." There is a pause, and then she says, "I sometimes got so angry at my father I would put cat poop in his jacket pockets, and then wait for him to find it." I say, "How did you feel, waiting for him to find it?" And she says, "Terrified. And excited. I expected him to beat the shit out of me. I waited for days. He never said a thing." I wait, and then say, "I'm thinking perhaps you felt ashamed. There was fear and excitement and it wasn't seen, like it didn't matter," and she responds, "It felt to me like you were thinking about something else, like I wasn't there. Maybe I wanted you to see something … or maybe I didn't …" And I'm left wondering what she might mean, imagining that in this moment she is unsure herself. What choice do we have but to wait and see? What is emerging illuminates or casts its shadow over what came before, even as it leans into its relation to what comes next.

I don't regard this as endlessly indeterminate in a recursive, postmodernist way. Things, stories, meanings coalesce. In order for psychoanalytic work to continue to make sense, a "humble" sort of philosophical realism is indeed required.[15] I am interested in what is real for Ms. A. I am imagining that she *really is worrying* that her heart would burst, and that there are reasons for and purpose to this feeling. The hybridity of psychoanalysis points to the poetic, to the realities that elude measurement, but without settling for a purely poetic solution. It requires tension, uncertainty, in the generation of the partial resolutions that constitute much of what we call the relative certainties of psychoanalytic meaning, but always in relation to a reasoned, subjectively objective view of psychic reality and to the world of our situated experience.

The problem of the private self

The philosopher Marcia Cavell (1993), not hermeneutic by orientation, takes issue with the idea of what she calls "an ineffable private quality" to subjective experience, of the mental having an "ontologically subjective" character. I agree that we can know about other people in various ways; we can map our own experiences onto theirs; we can imagine and to some extent feel a version of what they are feeling; we can understand their logic, their purpose, their wishes; we can study aspects of their functioning and come to more objective understandings of how they are in the world. But we *mustn't*, Cavell warns, give subjective experience a unique private quality; we mustn't make it a special "internalist" category and take it outside the purview of how we come to know *other* things that are outside of ourselves.

---

[15] While I agree in general with Eagle, Wolitsky, and Wakefield (2001) on this point, the "humble" character of the realism they espouse should also appreciate the extent to which such objectivity is *grounded in subjectivity* in the sense that Lear (2003) proposes.

Making matters worse, and further complicating my current argument, is the fact that there is in philosophical hermeneutics since Heidegger a similarly adamant objection to notions of a private interior self and to the vagaries of "psychologism" and the phenomenological foregrounding of unarticulated subjective experience. Even Gadamer's appropriation of the idea of the "inner word," upon which spoken discourse presumably is based, carries with it a stern warning, because here even the interior life is understood as "speech." Grondin (1994) explains:

> By the inner word, however—and this should be made emphatically clear—is meant *no private or psychological inner world existing prior to its verbal expression*. Rather, it is that which strives to be externalized in spoken language.... There is no "preverbal" world, only world oriented to language, the world which is always to be put into words, though never entirely successfully. This is the uniquely hermeneutic dimension of language. (pp. xiv–xv, italics added)

One would seem to find in all this more than ample justification for Laplanche's opposition to hermeneutics with respect to psychoanalysis, here in the form of two philosophical objections, arriving from opposite directions, to the idea of a private interior life. First, Cavell's objection that one's subjective inner world is not in fact private or uniquely inaccessible to others; and second, the hermeneutic insistence on the primacy of language, that everything human either is language or moving toward expression in language. This would include Gadamer's opposition to the idea of preverbal experience, and with this his hostility to the idea of an underlying private, psychologically constituted interior world. Neither, it seems to me, is consistent with a psychoanalytic understanding of the person.

From a psychoanalytic perspective, it is an absurd philosophical conceit to deny what every living human being knows experientially: I feel things without words; I know things without words, including in the sense that Heidegger intends when he talks of "knowing" as a form of "knowing one's way around" an activity, "knowing" how to do something. But also knowing in a more privately felt way, knowing oneself by knowing the affective experience of one's being in that moment. Consider a baby, in a crib, playing with his own toes. While his eyes and mind and fingers and toes exist within a matrix of organized, languaged ideas, his experience in *that* moment of *those* toes within *that* matrix is exclusively and irreducibly his own, neither described nor describable in language. Versions of this assumption permeate psychoanalytic thinking—for example, in the basic idea that affective experience precedes language and symbolization, and precedes not just differentiation between self and Other, but even differentiation between psychic and somatic space.[16]

[16] For one example among hundreds, see McDougall's (1978) discussion of early presymbolic mental organization and its expression in adult psychopathology, elaborating on ideas in Winnicott, Bion, Modell, and others. This is basic to psychoanalytic models of development.

This hermeneutic preoccupation with language, which sometimes includes hostility toward the positing of any extra-linguistic metaphysical world, seems at odds not just with common sense but also with basic psychoanalytic presuppositions. Private subjective experience does not simply come into existence when formulated in language; it equally comes *to* language and is shaped by the process of its coming to language. Reading Gadamer, the most renowned of hermeneutic philosophers, one at times feels he regards human beings as merely emergent properties of language.

Radically decentered subjects cannot be psychoanalyzed, and attempting to do so would have no purpose. Fortunately, hermeneutic philosophy does not generally advocate anything so radical. But I want to highlight two potential excesses (or misuses, depending on how you look at it) of hermeneutic ideas, both damaging to psychoanalysis.

First, Gadamer's emphasis on the game, whereby the subjects playing the game are first and foremost actors who make the game (the occasion for meaning) possible, puts the emphasis squarely on language and "languaged" meaning. To the extent that philosophical hermeneutics overemphasizes this, and denigrates the idea of a private realm of primary-process, affect-laden, unconsciously organized, pre-symbolic subjective experience, it removes itself from psychoanalytic understandings of the self.

Second, the principle of an ongoing, open-ended dialectical process *applied to the self* can lead in psychoanalysis to an overemphasis on fluidity and change in consideration of identity. One might find this, for example, in some approaches that too exclusively focus on the interpersonal psychoanalytic occasion in all its contingency, what happens between these singular actors at this time, rather than on who these actors, and in particular this analysand, are according to regularities, coherences, patterns of meaning and experience, identifiable strictures, defenses, organizing fantasies, and their evolution or sameness over time. These needn't be at odds, of course. At best it is a problem of emphasis, at worst some analysts confuse things by embracing fluidity (or a subject without a center) while at the same time (contradictorily) treating themselves and their analysands as identifiably coherent selves.[17] But the drift away from a focus on relatively coherent individual subjects can obscure the necessary tensions required of psychoanalysis with respect to workable notions of both psychoanalytic subjectivity and psychoanalytic knowledge. Once the basic assumptions about discernable, unconsciously organized continuities of self are underemphasized or even vitiated, the drift goes quite naturally toward the surface phenomenology of the interpersonal moment. This drift has surely been encouraged by the excesses of Gadamerian hermeneutics and the excitements offered by the postmodern fluidities (rather than fixities) of the self and of identity more generally.

---

[17] At times, for some writers, this seems more like an intellectual affectation than a theoretical conviction, which isn't to say it is trivial. Flirting excessively with the excitements of fluidity, even as we continue (in unacknowledged ways) to depend on the continuities of the self in order to make sense, risks confusing the issue by disregarding the needed tension.

Or so it seems to me. I feel confident about this at least: Psychoanalysis can tolerate an idea of subjectivity organized around the tension between separateness and interdependence, between the individual subject's irreducible separateness and irreducible embeddedness in an intersubjectively constituted world of language and culture. It cannot tolerate an idea of subjectivity that too radically displaces the individual subject from its existential condition of ontological discreteness, a contextually described, relative separateness that allows for individual experience and causally constructed individual historical narratives. The more radical hermeneutic rejection of a preverbal interior psychologically organized self, and the inclination of some hermeneutic philosophers to see such an inner world as "outmoded" and "metaphysical," is in my view anti-psychoanalytic. The good news is that psychoanalysis can reject it and adopt a more moderate hermeneutic, foregoing the expedient of "begging for a partial rehabilitation" through an epistemologically ill-suited empiricism (Ricouer, 1970, p. 366). Preferable is a hermeneutic that holds in tension separateness and sameness, distance and fusion, and especially highlights metaphor as a tensive relationship between asynchronous meanings as well as between reality and fantasy, between the is and the is-not.[18] Moreover, protecting the private self matters in part because it points up the difference between knowing in a broad sense and experiencing or living subjectively as a unique *form* of knowing. This is the *epistemological* obligation that follows from a recognition of the *ontological* condition of separateness, of otherness.

It is certainly true that our individual subjectivities emerge from, are constituted out of, a shared world; that "inner" and "outer" are relative designations plotted within a shared intersubjective matrix. "We are stardust," as the old song says, and so, being made from the same stuff, are able to recognize and understand one another. But as I have remarked elsewhere (Clarke, 2017), the special "private quality" of subjective experience is not a simplistic (or solipsistic) assertion of epistemic privilege; it is just the acknowledgment of a fact: my experienced subjectivity is separate from yours; the experiential dimension of subjective experience makes us ontologically distinct. This does not mean that I cannot know you in mediated ways, it only means I cannot *be* you, I cannot possess your subjective experience, and this difference is the basis for our necessary separateness. It is not first and foremost about *knowing*, it is about *being*. Every psychoanalytic theory of development depends on this distinction ("*I* am not *you*" being an essential pole in the dialectical tension required of intersubjectivity), and I suspect so does a proper formulation of psychoanalytic knowledge (pp. 591–593).

If we refuse ontological uniqueness based on this "private quality," we risk making subjectivity too much about *inter*subjectivity, the self too much an emergent property of the field

[18] My indebtedness to Ricœur stems in part from this important difference in emphasis. Taylor (2011) comments: "Gadamer's focus in metaphor remains persistently on similarity and commonality. Different horizons are *fused* … The priority is granted to nondifferentiation rather than to the abiding tension in metaphor between sameness and difference." In contrast, Ricœur's understanding of metaphor, and of understanding in general, is tensional (p. 114). See Ricœur (1977b, 1978).

(or even the field as a kind of subjectivity unto itself), or the individual subject as more function than agent in the phenomenology of an interpersonal process. And if this is so, then psychoanalysis's grounding in subjectivity *as a unique category of experience* is too easily lost in the flattening effect that inevitably comes when intersubjectivity carries too much weight.

The crucial point is that individual subjectivity is both objectively approachable and to some extent knowable, on the one hand, and epistemically inexhaustible, on the other. Moreover, there is a quality to this inexhaustibility, an experiential density that is unique to subjectivity. The quality, the very nature, the very being, of the mental is subjectivity[19]—and from a psychoanalytic perspective, this means unconsciously organized, embodied subjectivity.

Concluding thoughts

What is so poignant in psychoanalytic experience, as sometimes in everyday human intercourse, is the effort of someone trying to do the impossible and partially succeeding—of trying to convey to another person something of that irreducibly, subjectively experienced life, and engaging in a shared effort to make sense of it. One aspect of psychoanalytic work that I especially appreciate is this insistence that deeply felt, meaningful clinical experience can *only* take place in the ongoing context of an often tedious attention to one moment following another following another, day by day. And to my mind what this requires among other things is the grounding of psychoanalytic process in the quiddities of life where that irreducibly subjective dimension of experience gets played out, and upon which efforts at distanciation follow, and to which they return. For me psychoanalysis quickly loses its rootedness in felt experience, its affective gravity, when this private, experiential aspect of the dialectic is slighted and what matters becomes too much about the externalism, the public dimension, of meaning.

In this respect, psychoanalysis is an experientially based process of invention that at once rediscovers past experience in the present and creates new coherences and meanings for these experiences. In this respect, for psychoanalysis, understanding does indeed have a hermeneutic character, in the sense that understanding is always an activity of invention. Ricœur's (1977a) remarks on "invention" and metaphor apply more broadly to psychoanalytic understanding: "It would seem that the enigma of metaphorical discourse is that it 'invents' in both senses of the word: what it creates, it discovers; and what it finds, it invents" (p. 239). But more than this, what is sacrosanct in our endeavor to understand one another psychoanalytically is the prior interiority of idiosyncratic individual subjective experience, situated but irreducibly separate—our aloneness-in-relation.

In psychoanalysis we have the chance of creating with another person a version of one's singularly held subjective life in a way that is arduously shared or co-imagined. Relegation of this in both hermeneutic and Anglo-American analytic philosophy—whether by treating the

[19] See the philosophers Searle (1992) and Nagel (1995, p. 101) on the "ontologically" and "indispensably" subjective character of consciousness.

private subjective dimension of human beings as too much about language or too much about rationality—ought to chafe against any psychoanalytic notion of a psychologically comprehensible subjectivity. With many psychoanalytic versions of these philosophical approaches, and their quest to vanquish the errors of Cartesianism, Husserlian phenomenology, scientism, subjectivism, postmodern relativism, and psychologism, the separateness or alterity of the individual subject is sometimes seriously neglected. Decentering the subject does not eliminate subjects, it just allows us to appreciate them differently. You are still not me, and I am still not you. Those were *my* toes, not your toes, in *that* moment, not some other moment, seen with *my* eyes, felt with *my* fingers, in *my* moment of wonder. It is useful to keep in mind, perhaps, that philosophers are not unlike the rest of us in the sense that we are all just once-upon-a-time infants playing with our toes and figuring it out from there.

And remember as well that while we *play* with our fluidities and entangled horizons of self, however constructively and creatively, an idealized or totalizing notion of fluidity (of identity or self) is likely the expression of a wish, an everything-ism, with of course the risk that accompanies every reifying absolutism of this sort, which is the slackening or loss of essential psychic tensions, the collapse of symbolization, and the two-dimensional flattening characteristic of psychosis. Instead, from a psychoanalytic perspective, individual subjectivity can only productively possess fluidities of identity and identification as these operate in an environment of relative fixity.

Freud tells us that the infant, in the absence of what he hungers for but armed with a memory trace of previous satisfaction, hallucinates the breast. From this originating moment psychoanalysis unfolds. Both psychoanalytic desire and psychoanalytic knowledge are in their essence versions of asymptotic striving, of reaching but never arriving, because the aspirational nature of desire is encoded in the basic structure of our separateness, just as the tragic dimension of human desire resides in the irremediable nature of that separateness. Ricœur (Changeux & Ricœur, 2003) writes quite beautifully, "The price of individuation, then, is the growing otherness of the world and the growing solitude of the self. Henceforth the possibility of non-being accompanies the integration of 'being-for-life,' as though it were its shadow, and makes of life an improbable and revocable adventure" (pp. 203–204).

What I would like to propose is something like this. The psychoanalytically conceived meanings that follow from subjective experience, or accompany it, cannot escape their relation to it. Not altogether, whatever form of objectification is employed. This marks a crucial difference of emphasis which allows for what is knowable while insisting that subjective experience *belongs* to the experiencing subject in a way that gives it a permanent, "ontological" quality of hiddenness or occultation or obliqueness by virtue of its being the singular possession of one person.

At least as I conceive of it, psychoanalysis is the discourse and discipline par excellence that anatomizes and clarifies the moving parts, the motivations and mechanisms, of human desire; but it also exposes and even embraces the intrinsic ambiguities, the polysemous open-endedness of how human beings are, and appreciates this as necessary to understanding, not an unfortunate obstacle to positive psychoanalytic knowledge.

It is self-evident that certain kinds of objectivity, of critical reason, are necessary to psychoanalysis, and philosophy can be helpful, even necessary, in our understanding the nature of that. But psychoanalysts needn't feel like children lost in the dark forests of philosophy. We have much to learn, but also much to teach. Ricœur, the Continental hermeneuticist and phenomenologist, does not talk about sex or aggression in an experiential way. In my exposure to Anglo-American analytic philosophical writing on psychoanalysis, the human beings tend to be thinkers, or vehicles for beliefs, reasons, intentions, actions. There isn't a lot of blood and shit. Not that these rudiments are more real or true than obsessional anxieties or rational arguments, only that they are two things we cannot live without.

The Rat Man's cannibalistic fantasies of incorporation are not just ideas or mental representations of beliefs. These are passions that boil up from our bones and blood, terrifying and exciting. When my five-year-old patient wants to poop and pee all over the kidnapped princess, flush her down the toilet, and steal all the treasures in her castle, he isn't messing around, any more than he was messing around when he told his parents that he thought his little brother should be put at the curb with the rest of the week's garbage. Malignant envy is not a wishful regret, a stab of jealousy that motivates us to this or that course of action; sometimes it is rage that would destroy everything and everyone, including the self, rather than endure the agony of losing what is prized as an essential possession, an ontological necessity (mother's body, omnipotent power, reverence, the magic to never feel shame and the privilege to endlessly inflict it).

Consider: The compulsion to cut oneself. The compulsion to kill oneself. The abject loneliness some adolescents feel even in the embrace of a caring family. All of our quintessentially human delusions, perversions, distortions, denials, arid intellectual retreats, manic euphorias, and impregnable anti-intellectual refusals of reality. Joy, excitement, arousal, pleasure in all its varieties, passion, love. Even dissociative blankness as a response to feeling too vulnerably alive. Before these are categories for objective reflection they are states of being, idiosyncratically experienced and possessed by singular individual subjects. The uniqueness of psychoanalysis rests in part with this insistence on the driven, subjective quality of lived experience, whatever objectifications we apply to it. So I will conclude with this fundamentally Freudian idea, one that I think extends beyond him and beyond his particular metapsychology: that it is here, in the driven-ness of lived, embodied experience, that meaning and culture, thought and understanding, reasoned reflection, and even philosophy, are rooted. Forgetting this, psychoanalysis forgets itself.

Part I

Developmental realm

CHAPTER TWO

Children and truth

Mali Mann

The biographer of the first president of the United States, George Washington (1732–1799), who was an itinerant minister and bookseller named Mason Locke Weems, wrote an ironic story about the value of honesty. In the story, when Washington was six years old, he received a hatchet as a gift and damaged his father's cherry tree. When his father discovered what he had done, he became angry and confronted him. Young George bravely said, "I cannot tell a lie … I did cut it with my hatchet." Washington's father was overjoyed and embraced him and rejoiced that his son's virtuous honesty was worth more than a thousand trees. He was forgiven.

There are many fables and fairy tale stories in children's literature such as "Pinocchio," "Mercury and the Tradesmen," "Ancient Greek Fables" by Aesop, "The Crocodile's Treason" by James A. Honey, "The Emperor's New Clothes" by Hans Christian Andersen, "The Juniper Tree" by The Brothers Grimm. These stories portray the wide range of facing reality and the unreal for children and show the contrast between truth-telling, honesty, lying, make believe, and pretense.

I will give another example of such a fable that comes from a Persian fairy tale about a cat and a mouse. It is a beautiful example of Persian storytelling legacy and is attributed to Aesop (*c.*620–564 BCE), a storyteller credited with a number of fables now collectively known as *Aesop's Fables.*

> A cat tries to fool a mouse by playing dead, but the mouse doesn't fall for it. "Where is the cat?" shouted he, "that I may off with his head? I would cut off his head as if on the battlefield. A cat in front of me would fare worse than any dog who might happen to cross my path."

> After the cat catches and devours the mouse, it feels regret and continues with the next lie. It weeps and prays to Allah to ask for forgiveness: "I have repented and will not again tear the body of a mouse with my teeth. I will give bread to the deserving poor. Forgive my sin, O great Forgiver, for have I not come to Thee bowed down with sorrow?"

This story of lies evolves into the account of a war between the King of the Mice versus the King of the Cats with their armies clashing each other. The moral of the story is that the wise are not tricked by the innocence of those previously found to be dangerous. The story tells us a similar understanding of concepts such as "truth" and "lies."

The concept of truth and truth-telling is a complex one. It is not possible to touch all of the vicissitudes of this intriguing subject. Children's understanding of truth-telling requires emotional and cognitive development. The question is: At what point in their development do children develop intrapsychic capacities for differentiation between truth-telling and telling lies? In fact, the same question can be asked about children who lie and their capability to lie.

The capacity to be truthful and the capacity or prerequisites to lie are mirror opposites to each other. One can argue that a similar developmental attainment exists and operates in both scenarios. Here, I want to go over what researchers have discovered about the underlying factors that shape children's personality when it comes to truthtelling and their perception of truth.

Miller et al. (2000), in their article, "Children's Understanding of Necessity of Logically Necessary Truths" had done a study in which they examined the development of an appreciation of logical necessity. The participants were one hundred children from three age groups (seven-, nine-, and eleven-year-olds), each of whom responded to tasks drawn from four categories: logically necessary truths, physical laws, social conventions, and arbitrary facts. Questions following each task were intended to tap criteria traditionally ascribed to necessary truths, including universality, unchangeability, and the unimaginability of any alternative. Even the seven-year-olds showed some appreciation of the necessity of necessary truths, generally claiming that such outcomes hold true everywhere and will never change. Developmental changes were of two main sorts. Older children were more successful than younger children at differentiating the various forms of knowledge. Older children also showed greater appreciation of the literal unimaginability of the violation of a logical truth.

Stogner et al. (2013) examined children who had the ability to deceive. They wanted to determine whether these children were able to hide their emotional expressions intentionally. Three-year-olds were instructed to not peek at a toy while the experimenter left the room. When asked, the great majority either denied that they peeked or would not answer the question. Facial and bodily activity did not differentiate the deceivers from the truth-tellers. Boys were more likely than girls to admit their transgression. These results indicate that very young children have begun to learn how to mask their emotional expressions and support the role of socialization in this process.

The emergence and development of children's lie-telling is closely associated with their developing cognitive abilities. Telling a lie involves complicated cognitive functions including theory-of-mind understanding and executive functioning abilities. Recent research has found that telling lies emerges in the preschool years and children's abilities to maintain their lies improve with age. There has been extensive research on children's moral knowledge about lying and truth-telling and their actual lying or truth-telling behaviors. However, research to examine the relationship between the two is extremely rare. One study examined 120 seven-, nine-, and eleven-year-olds' moral understanding of lies and their actual lying behaviors in a politeness situation. Results revealed that as age increased, children increasingly evaluated others' lying in politeness situations less negatively and were more inclined to tell lies in such situations themselves. Contrary to previous findings, children's socio-moral knowledge about lying was significantly related to their actual behaviors particularly when children's rationales underlying their moral judgments were consistent with their motives for actual lying or truth-telling in the politeness situation.

Over fifty years ago, Piaget (1948) questioned approximately one hundred children aged six to twelve about eleven different aspects of moral reasoning, including truth-telling and lying. Analysis of their replies across all domains led him to postulate two distinct styles of moral reasoning, with a transition from the first to the second at around age eight. He called the first one "moral objectivity."

According to Piaget, the second subjective style had contrasting focus on such inner processes as the liar's intention to deceive results in quite different definitions, evaluations, and general ideas of lying. Another of Piaget's moral domains was that of "intentionality." Investigators such as Chandler et al. (1973) had done their own studies on intentionality and found out that by converting Piaget's verbal stimuli to motion pictures, the child's comprehension of intentionality could be improved.

Erikson's (1950) stages of development and their dangers offer one frame of reference for viewing pathological outcomes of development. Much like Sigmund Freud, Erikson believed that personality developed in a series of stages. Unlike Freud's theory of psychosexual stages, however, Erikson's theory described the impact of social experience across the whole life span. Erikson was interested in how social interaction and relationships played a role in the development and growth of human beings. Each stage in Erikson's theory builds on the preceding stages and paves the way for following periods of development. In each stage, Erikson believed people experience a conflict that serves as a turning point in development. If people successfully deal with the conflict, they emerge from the stage with psychological strengths that will serve them well for the rest of their lives. If they fail to deal effectively with these conflicts, they may not develop the essential skills needed for a strong sense of self.

He also believed that a sense of competence motivates behaviors and actions. Each stage in Erikson's theory is concerned with becoming competent in an area of life. If the stage is handled well, the person will feel a sense of mastery, which is sometimes referred to as ego strength or ego quality. If the stage is managed poorly, the person will emerge with a sense of inadequacy in that aspect of development.

Psychosocial stages: A summary chart

Age	Conflict	Important Events	Important Outcome
Infancy (birth to 18 months)	Trust vs. Mistrust	Feeding	Hope
Early Childhood (2 to 3 years)	Autonomy vs. Shame and Doubt	Toilet Training	Will
Preschool (3 to 5 years)	Initiative vs. Guilt	Exploration	Purpose
School Age (6 to 11 years)	Industry vs. Inferiority	School	Confidence
Adolescence (12 to 18 years)	Identity vs. Role Confusion	Social Relationships	Fidelity
Young Adulthood (19 to 40 years)	Intimacy vs. Isolation	Relationships	Love
Middle Adulthood (40 to 65 years)	Generativity vs. Stagnation	Work and Parenthood	Care
Maturity (65 to death)	Ego Integrity vs. Despair	Reflection on Life	Wisdom

Stage 1: Trust vs. Mistrust

The first stage of Erikson's theory of psychosocial development occurs between birth and one year of age and is the most fundamental stage in life. Because an infant is utterly dependent, developing trust is based on the dependability and quality of the child's caregivers. The infant needs to survive by being fed, loved, kept safe, and nurtured. If the caregiver fails in giving the essentials, the mistrust will happen. Conversely, if a child successfully develops trust, the child will feel safe and secure in the world. Caregivers who are inconsistent, emotionally unavailable, or rejecting contribute to feelings of mistrust in the children under their care. Failure to develop trust will result in fear and a belief that the world is inconsistent and unpredictable. During the first stage of psychosocial development, children develop a sense of trust when caregivers provide reliability, care, and affection. A lack of this will lead to mistrust.

Erikson believed that successful development was all about striking a balance between the two opposing sides. When this happens, children acquire hope, which Erikson described as an openness to experience tempered by some wariness that danger may be present. Subsequent work by researchers including Bowlby and Ainsworth demonstrated the importance of trust in forming healthy attachments during childhood and adulthood.

Stage 2: Autonomy vs. Shame and Doubt

The second stage of Erikson's theory of psychosocial development takes place during early childhood and is focused on children developing a greater sense of personal control. At this point in development, children are just starting to gain a little independence. They are starting to perform basic actions on their own and making simple decisions about what they prefer. By allowing children to make choices and gain control, parents and caregivers can help children develop a sense of autonomy. The essential theme of this stage is that children need to develop a sense of personal control over physical skills and a sense of independence. Potty training plays an important role in helping children develop this sense of autonomy.

Like Freud, Erikson believed that toilet training was a vital part of this process. However, Erikson's reasoning was quite different than that of Freud's. Erikson believed that learning to control one's bodily functions leads to a feeling of control and a sense of independence. Other important events include gaining more control over food choices, toy preferences, and clothing selection. Children who struggle and who are shamed for their accidents may be left without a sense of personal control. Success during this stage of psychosocial development leads to feelings of autonomy; failure results in feelings of shame and doubt. Succeed and they feel secure and confident, while those who do not are left with a sense of inadequacy and self-doubt.

Stage 3: Initiative vs. Guilt

The third stage of psychosocial development takes place during the preschool years. At this point in psychosocial development, children begin to assert their power and control over the world through directing play and other social interactions. Children who are successful at this stage feel capable and able to lead others. Those who fail to acquire these skills are left with a sense of guilt, self-doubt, and lack of initiative. The major theme of the third stage of psychosocial development is that children need to begin asserting control and power over the environment. Success in this stage leads to a sense of purpose. Children who try to exert too much power experience disapproval, resulting in a sense of guilt. When an ideal balance of individual initiative and a willingness to work with others is achieved, the ego quality known as purpose emerges.

Stage 4: Industry vs. Inferiority

The fourth psychosocial stage takes place during the early school years from approximately ages five to eleven. Through social interactions, children begin to develop a sense of pride in their accomplishments and abilities. Children need to cope with new social and academic demands. Success leads to a sense of competence, while failure results in feelings of inferiority. Children who are encouraged and commended by parents and teachers develop a feeling of competence and belief in their skills. Those who receive little or no encouragement from parents, teachers, or peers will doubt their abilities to be successful. Finding a good balance at this stage of psychosocial development leads to the strength known as competence, in which children develop a belief in their abilities to handle the tasks set before them.

Stage 5: Identity vs. Confusion

The fifth psychosocial stage takes place during the often turbulent teenage years. This stage plays an essential role in developing a sense of personal identity which will continue to influence behavior and development for the rest of a person's life. Teens need to develop a sense of self and personal identity. Success leads to an ability to stay true to themselves, while failure leads to role confusion and a weak sense of self. During adolescence, children explore their independence and develop a sense of self. Those who receive proper encouragement and reinforcement through personal exploration will emerge from this stage with a strong sense of self and feelings of independence and control. Those who remain unsure of their beliefs and desires will feel insecure and confused about themselves and the future.

What is identity? Identity is referred to in all of the beliefs, ideals, and values that help shape and guide a person's behavior. Completing this stage successfully leads to fidelity, which Erikson described as an ability to live by society's standards and expectations. While Erikson believed that each stage of psychosocial development was important, he placed a particular emphasis on the development of ego identity. Ego identity is the conscious sense of self that we develop through social interaction and becomes a central focus during the identity versus confusion stage of psychosocial development.

According to Erikson, our ego identity constantly changes due to new experiences and information that we acquire in our daily interactions with others. As we have new experiences, we also take on challenges that can help or hinder the development of identity. Our personal identity gives each of us an integrated and cohesive sense of self that endures through our lives. Our sense of personal identity is shaped by our experience and interactions with others, and it is this identity that helps guide our actions, beliefs, and behaviors as we age.

Stage 6: Intimacy vs. Isolation

Young adults need to form intimate, loving relationships with other people. Success leads to strong relationships, while failure results in loneliness and isolation. This stage covers the period of early adulthood when people are exploring personal relationships. Erikson believed it was vital that people develop close, committed relationships with other people. Those who are successful at this step will form relationships that are enduring and secure.

Building on earlier stages. Each step builds on skills learned in previous steps. Erikson believed that a strong sense of personal identity was important for developing intimate relationships. Studies have demonstrated that those with a poor sense of self tend to have less-committed relationships and are more likely to struggle with emotional isolation, loneliness, and depression. Successful resolution of this stage results in the virtue known as love. It is marked by the ability to form lasting, meaningful relationships with other people.

Stage 7: Generativity vs. Stagnation

Adults need to create or nurture things that will outlast them, often by having children or creating a positive change that benefits other people. Success leads to feelings of usefulness and accomplishment, while failure results in shallow involvement in the world. During adulthood, we continue to build our lives, focusing on our career and family. Those who are successful during this phase will feel that they are contributing to the world by being active in their home and community. Those who fail to attain this skill will feel unproductive and uninvolved in the world. Care is the virtue achieved when this stage is handled successfully. Being proud of your accomplishments, watching your children grow into adults, and developing a sense of unity with your life partner are important accomplishments of this stage.

Stage 8: Integrity vs. Despair

The final psychosocial stage occurs during old age and is focused on reflecting back on life. At this point in development, people look back on the events of their lives and determine if they are happy with the life that they lived or if they regret the things they did or didn't do. Erikson's theory differed from many others because it addressed development throughout the entire life span, including old age. Older adults need to look back on life and feel a sense of fulfillment. Success at this stage leads to feelings of wisdom, while failure results in regret, bitterness, and despair.

At this stage, people reflect back on the events of their lives and take stock. Those who look back on a life they feel was well lived will feel satisfied and ready to face the end of their lives with a sense of peace. Those who look back and only feel regret will instead feel fearful that their lives will end without accomplishing the things they feel they should have. Those who are unsuccessful during this stage will feel that their life has been wasted and may experience many regrets and be left with feelings of bitterness and despair. Those who feel proud of their accomplishments will feel a sense of integrity. Successfully completing this phase means looking back with few regrets and a general feeling of satisfaction. These individuals will attain wisdom, even when confronting death.

One major weakness of psychosocial theory is that the exact mechanisms for resolving conflicts and moving from one stage to the next are not well described or developed. The theory fails to detail exactly what type of experiences are necessary at each stage in order to successfully resolve the conflicts and move to the next stage.

One of the strengths of psychosocial theory is that it provides a broad framework from which to view development throughout the entire life span. It also allows us to emphasize the social nature of human beings and the important influence that social relationships have on development.

Researchers have found evidence supporting Erikson's ideas about identity and have further identified different substages of identity formation. Some research also suggests that people who form strong personal identities during adolescence are better capable of forming intimate relationships during early adulthood. Other research suggests, however, that identity formation and development continue well into adulthood.

Fischer (2009) in her paper, "What It Takes to Tell a Lie," suggests seven intrapsychic capacities as prerequisites for telling a lie. She elaborates that establishment of an attachment bond allows for both a sense of oneness and separateness, the ability to separate out self from other. Her other prerequisites are the rapprochement subphase, achievement of object constancy (Tyson, 1996), reflective functioning (Fonagy, 2001), development of the capacity to differentiate between reality and fantasy, and the integration of the psychic equivalence and pretend modes of functioning, the attainment of a certain level of cognitive development, affective containment, and the ability to play. Fischer then added an eighth criterion that involved the child's arrival at the stage of oedipal organization.

Many renowned psychoanalysts incorporated attachment theories, infant observation, and neurobiology in their work. Neurobiology, cognitive science, and attachment research highlight the importance of establishing, in the earliest stages of life, a secure attachment bond with primary caregivers so that developmental progress proceeds normally. Mother's presence as a regulator of the child's anxiety and neurophysiological system by being a solid container of the child's stress response helps affect regulation and impulse control. When we look at demarcation of self and other, Mahler et al. (1975) introduced the separation-individuation process. Although their ideas about the autistic and symbiotic phases have been questioned, still it draws our attention to the early mother and infant dyadic interaction. The maternal attunement in the interaction with her infant determines the child's developmental trajectory. Mahler understood the internal world of the infant as well as the importance of the interaction of the infant and mother from outside, which enhance the maturational process and the formation of a solid bond, giving rise to the promotion of the separation and individuation process. The object constancy is the end result of the process which starts with differentiation, practicing phase, and rapprochement subphase.

Winnicott's (1960) concept of the environment's key role in the maturation process of the infant held that "there is no such thing as a baby" (1940) and the importance of the "ordinary devoted mother" (1960). We are familiar with his idea of the "good enough mother" and his concept of true self. When mother recognizes the infant as real and separate, she contributes to her infant's establishment of sense of realness and a sense of true self. Mother's role to allow the infant to come to know and represent his own experience will help his later capacity to symbolize his inner life. Denial or absence of validation leads to the development of false self.

Tyson (1996) postulated three stages of object constancy. The first stage is attained when the infant is able to maintain a constant investment in the object irrespective of drive gratification, which correlates with social referencing; the infant copes by referencing the mother's face for affective signals and using this as a means of self-regulation. The attachment to the human face is utilized for its signaling function. Her second stage is representational object constancy which correlates with the infant being eighteen months of age. The development of speech, symbolic functioning, as well as sensory-motor thinking which tend to be be concrete yet influenced by intense emotional events are characteristic of this subphase. Wishes and external demands are being organized and categorized as coming from inner or outer bring the opportunity for creating a sense of mastery. The third stage of object constancy is Mahler's libidinal object constancy in which the representation of the object has become an inner source of sustenance, comfort, and love (Mahler & Furer, 1968). This represents a very advanced stage of development.

Reflective functioning is also the capacity to reflect on mental states and attribute intention to thoughts, feelings, and acts both within oneself and in others. It allows for a move out of the psychic equivalence mode of functioning in which psychic reality and physical reality are equivalent (Target & Fonagy, 1996). By reflecting on the child's mind and offering another mind for the child to explore, the parent supplies a road to reflective functioning. The child is able to have sense of self as a separate individual with a mind of his own as well as a consideration of mental states within oneself and others. The child is also able to distinguish thoughts and wishes from external reality and goes into a phase of pretend mode, in which ideas are represented but their correspondence with reality is not questioned. Whereas in psychic reality the child's thoughts and feelings are experienced as truth, in the pretend mode the child is able to play out all manner of feelings and scenarios as long as they are kept separated out from reality. A good enough mother can help the child to maintain a distinction between play/pretend and reality. On the other hand, the pretend mode, which is separated out from reality, allows the child to play out different roles and schemas and offers the child the opportunity to experience different feelings. Cognitive and emotional growth together with reflective functioning enable the child to see people's actions as meaningful and predictable which diminishes the child's dependence on others. It also promotes individuation. It enables the child to make a distinction between inner and outer truths and facilitates communication. The child develops a capacity to test the ideas against reality and the impact of the ideas and feelings are thus moderated. An oedipal-age child is able to engage in pretend play with a child analyst. The child is able to suspend disbelief and stay in a pretend state. Play is a means of coming to terms with reality, the reality of separateness and dependence on a caring adult. The child plays with reality and develops a transitional object. In this intermediate area of illusion, the me–not me object supplies the illusion of omnipotent control; the developmental trajectory starts from play on the body to play in the transitional space, to the use of the transitional object, to the utilization of fantasy. The capacity to fantasize is another developmental achievement. Fantasy shows the child to imagine other roles, other minds, and other solutions, all of which promotes development. The so-called "reality principle" does act in accordance with predictable consequences rather than just immediate pleasure or discharge which requires the ability to fantasize. Making the transition from the pleasure principle to the reality principle requires developmental maturation.

The child with a developed communication skill, sense of mastery, and understanding of the world, the mind, the sense of self and other external objects is ready to develop a narrative.

The child experiences mastery as play which allows him to monitor the fantasy and reality, reconstruct wishes, and face better the limitation of reality and self-capacity. The child is capable of modifying the conflict and comes up with solutions of different kinds. This capability is a sign of a developed sense of mastery. With that, the child will be better equipped with the capacity to symbolize. As adults we use play throughout our life cycle. It is an important component of our work as psychoanalysts.

In cases involving adolescents, we have to take into consideration that it is difficult to differentiate normality and pathology during adolescence; as Anna Freud (1958) said, the typical upheavals can simulate a wide variety of pathological manifestations. Adolescents avoid confrontation and do not want to talk openly with their parents and be truthful. They refuse to disclose confidences and avoid disagreements with parents. Studies show that in families, when parents use less deception, they found adolescents argued and fought more.

Here, I am not going to write about my adolescent patients who entered into analysis with me and were able to achieve their developmental tasks with successful progression. Instead, I would like to expand on the developmental capacities of younger children by presenting two case vignettes.

> **Clinical vignette: 1**
>
> Melissa, age six, refused to take ballet class even though she had taken classes multiple times in the past. After her first class, she had said she did not want to take ballet class and was not interested to continue dancing. When her mother asked her how her first class went, she said that her teacher said terrible things about her dance movements. She said her teacher asked other girls to dance and ignored her for the rest of the class period. After her mother insisted she tell her what had actually happened, she admitted that she made up the entire story and was not being honest about her account. When her mother asked her why she had to lie, she broke into tears and said she was scared of the teacher because her teacher would tell her when she made mistakes and she could not stand it.
>
> Melissa was scared of being criticized and therefore she avoided attending her class for fear of being criticized. Her mother discussed the importance of being honest and the consequences of lying, hoping she would develop the right habit of being honest. We see in Melissa's case how her mother showed empathic caring and curiosity about her daughter's omission of the real truth caused by her sensitivity to criticism. She had a younger brother when she was eighteen months old. There was intense sibling rivalry with her brother, and she competed for mother's attention. It is hard to imagine that her teacher would only pay attention to the rest of the class and not her at all. This shows her fantasy of being excluded and a repetition of her practicing phase when her brother was born.

A second case is about a young boy who had difficulty coming to terms with his early object loss, both as external reality and in his internal life. It also points out the role of his mother who had trouble believing the truth.

Clinical vignette: 2

Sam, a five-year-old boy, was referred to me by his pediatrician for analytical treatment, because of his regressive symptoms after he lost his father to leukemia. He showed regressive behavior like singing in a singsong voice, chewing his blanket, and sucking his thumb, after he was separated from his mother.

Sam's sister was two and a half years older than him. His father was diagnosed with leukemia. Father went through several rounds of chemotherapy. His mother suffered from postpartum depression after Sam was born. The attachment between mother and son was a mixture of insecure, anxious, and avoidant, which was described poignantly by his mother as "I did not care taking care of him. I was so burdened with my own depression that I wished he would turn into a three-year-old who could tell me what he wanted, not an infant! I was depressed when he was born. There was no energy to deal with him, when I had no energy left."

Father's illness lasted two years before he died in the hospital. Sam was four years old when he lost his father. During the two year period of his father's illness, father went back and forth to the hospital. Sam lived with his grandmother for the second year of his father's illness. He had not seen him for the entire year. One day, when he asked his mother to see his father, she told him that he could not see him because his father was gone to be in heaven. In my parent sessions, his mother told me that she could not remember if she had ever told Sam in words that his father died in the hospital.

In one of the earlier analytic hours, Sam asked me if I knew where his father was. Then he said his mother told him that his father was in heaven. She also told him if he was a good boy, he could see his father in heaven and if he was bad, he would end up in hell. He asked me if I could help him to go to visit him in the heaven and if I knew what kind of place it was.

Here, we see a mother who caused a whirlpool of a confessional state of mind for her son. She could not resort to the reality principle and explain in simple and understandable words the death and dying concept for her four-year-old son. Moreover, she injected fear by the way in which she gave a concrete response by introducing the idea of what would happen if he was bad or if he was good. Sam was left with two choices, either heaven or hell. It was not a big surprise that he wanted to go to heaven to be with his father and at the same time wanted to avoid hell. His grandmother told him hell was a place with burning flames and fire. How could Sam have understood that his mother might have a false belief, or an understanding of the world that was different from reality? Perhaps he was not quite convinced about the reality and existence of heaven and hell, and that was why he asked me, needing to hear my explanation. His attachment bond with his mother was an insecure, anxious, avoidant type. It is also doubtful that he achieved a sense of self from other, or if he ever reached a state of object constancy.

Sam was in a complicated situation, as I found when I tried to assess his level of cognitive development, his ability to play, or his reflective function in order to help him to experience the reality of his trauma, loss, grief, and how to differentiate the true from the false. I want to restate that this is only a case vignette, and I am not going to include my interpretations, his play content, and his analytic process in this chapter.

We know that truthfulness is a trait that many people value; truth and honesty are part of most people's sense of morality, regardless of religious affiliation. At times, the value of honesty comes into question in certain political environments. This will add a burden for parents and teachers. Parents and teachers are important figures who could reinforce honesty and help children to be truthful. Also having a good role model for honesty does matter.

Adults are able to imagine, to reason about other people's mental states. They are able to understand that other people have minds and thoughts that are different from theirs. They can make an assessment of an individual human's capacity for empathy and understanding of others, a capacity which is called theory of mind. It means that an individual is able to attribute to another or oneself mental states such as beliefs, intents, desires, emotions, and knowledge. Children are unable to use the adult's theory of mind until they are about five years of age. Children have trouble understanding that others have a false belief or a belief that is inconsistent with reality. Sam is a good example of a child who could not have understood his mother's false belief that was inconsistent with reality. This is also the case with children and their problem with lying. Lying requires an understanding that someone else can have a false belief.

Children are also more likely to tell the truth when they expect positive outcomes for truth-telling from their parents. In a study where children heard a story about a character who stole a cookie and later lied about it, those children who were most likely to endorse a confession also expected more positive parental responses from truth-telling. In other words, children who said that the character in the story should tell the truth most often had parents who praise (and do not punish) their children when they tell the truth about breaking a rule.

It is my belief, and in my clinical work I have seen, that boys and girls are not different in their relationship to truth. I qualify that view in that I have not seen a difference in the younger age group (three through seven). It is not proven that early adolescent or late adolescent boys and girls are different in their relationship to truth. Children show evidence of lying around the same time they start to pass theory of mind tasks, around the age of four or five. In a typical lab-based lying test, children are told not to peek at a toy while an experimenter looks away. This is hard for kids, so it might not surprise you that eighty percent of children peek at the toy. What is surprising is that when asked to confess later on, almost all of the two-year-olds tested admit to breaking the rules, but the older the child, the more likely he or she is to lie about peeking. The current research demonstrates a link between children's emotion expectancies and actual confession behavior. Children are also more likely to tell the truth when they expect positive outcomes for truth-telling from their parents, that is, parents who praise truthful behavior, even after a child has broken the rules; in other words, children are more likely to tell the truth after doing something wrong if they think they will be praised for their honesty instead of getting punished for their transgression.

Concluding remarks

Although it is not within the scope of this chapter to discuss all of the vicissitudes of this very important subject, I decided to touch upon a few important concepts in my case examples to approach this topic, which requires further research studies.

The concept of truth and truth-telling is very complex because children's understanding of truth-telling depends on the strength of their emotional and cognitive development and their intrapsychic capacity for truth-telling. Children develop intrapsychic capacities for differentiation between truth-telling and telling lies. The capacity to be truthful and the capacity or prerequisites to lie are mirror opposites of each other. One can even argue that a similar developmental attainment exists and operates in both scenarios.

CHAPTER THREE

The search for truth in adolescent rebellion

Ann Smolen

I begin with Anna Freud's (1958) discerning depiction of adolescence:

> His anxieties, the height of elation or depth of despair, the quickly rising enthusiasms, the utter hopelessness, the burning- or at times sterile-intellectual and philosophical preoccupations, the yearning for freedom, the sense of loneliness, the feeling of oppression by the parents, the impotent rages or active hates directed against the adult world, the erotic crushes—whether homosexually or heterosexually directed—the suicidal fantasies, etc. (p. 260)

Following Anna Freud, Erikson (1956, 1963, 1968) was a major contributor to psychoanalytic developmental theory. He describes how the adolescent finds himself grappling with his relationship to himself as well as his peers, siblings, and parents. The adolescent seeks independence while simultaneously yearning for security and dependency. The adolescent must ascertain his sexual identity, establish interests, and figure out his abilities and value. The adolescent is in search of identity … a quest for personal truth. The failure to find one's truth may lead to an "identity crisis" (1963).

More about adolescence

Blos (1962 spoke of adolescent rebellion/acting-out as an "escape from loneliness, isolation, and the depressed moods which accompany the cathectic shifts" (p. 76). Blos defined adolescent rebellious behaviors in terms of drive theory. For him the adolescent is in often-unbearable conflict as he moves away from parents and into the outside world. Blos states that the adolescent discharges these conflictual tensions in his relationships instead of "experiencing it as an internal ego-dystonic crisis" (p. 107). Both Blos and A. Freud describe the pull the adolescent experiences to be the young child once again. One way to avoid this powerful regressive pull is to rebel against the very person you are being pulled toward; hence the adolescent becomes disagreeable, argumentative, and negative. After much travail, the older adolescent is able to master this regressive pull "either by defensive or adaptive measures but primarily by a forward movement of the libido toward … non-ambivalent object relations" (Blos, 1962, p. 107).

In order to fully comprehend this turbulent yet high-spirited phase of development, we need to revisit Mahler's separation-individuation theory, specifically the "rapprochement conflict" (Mahler et al., 1975). The toddler (sixteen months to thirty-six months) becomes aware that he is no longer a baby. This is a time of conflict when he is being pulled backward to desire to once again be that infant in arms, while simultaneously yearning to be a more grown-up child. This phase of development is punctuated by a conflict of independence versus dependency. There is a push-me-pull-you quality to many interactions. For example, the toddler often demands: *I do it!* And instantly dissolves into tears demanding: *You do it!* He insists on being picked-up. The second the parent obliges, he wants to be put down once again. As the toddler strives for independence and autonomy he is often overcome with emotions as power struggles ensue with parents. His favorite word is *NO!* And his second favorite word is *MINE!* This is a time when temper tantrums may be difficult for parents to navigate. There seems to be a natural resistance to exterior authority that is coupled with striving toward autonomy. The toddler's wish to have his own way inescapably meets with resistance from the parents, often resulting in power struggles. As noted, this phase of development is experienced by parents as a disagreeable time of negativity. The toddler's stubbornness, as demonstrated in his doggedness on "no" or "yes," is essentially interrelated with a crystallization of himself as an autonomous being (Spitz, 1957). This most important power struggle with parents is a "major leap toward the formation of an independent sense of self" (Person, 2001, p. 1135).

When I work with parents, I attempt to help them understand that a temper tantrum is not malicious behavior, but rather the toddler becomes overcome with difficult emotions and literally "falls apart." The goal is to stay calm, not punish feelings, and help the overwhelmed toddler regulate and regain a sense of calm. Power struggles are challenging; however, the toddler needs his parents to set limits and boundaries. When the parent is able to do so while remaining composed and loving, the young child feels safe. When the toddler wins the power struggle he becomes frightened of his own power. It is worrisome to think you are in charge of the adults who are supposed to be keeping you safe. When this occurs on a regular basis the child may become terrified of his own aggression, which may result in fears and anxiety.

Finally, and very importantly, the toddler must mourn that he is no longer a baby. Mahler et al. (1975) observed "low-keyedness" in the toddler as he copes with his new reality. During this phase, ambivalence is experienced for the first time. The toddler feels hate for the very person he loves and depends on. By the end of this phase, we hope that the child is able to feel negative emotions toward his love object, knowing that the love does not disappear. In other words, he can experience anger toward his parent, while simultaneously knowing the love remains. When the toddler (and his parents) are able to navigate through rapprochement in a good enough manner, the now three-year-old is on the road toward object constancy, which further allows the young child to separate and individuate as he enters into the oedipal phase of development.

Now back to the adolescent. Blos (1962) coined the term *second individuation*. The adolescent revisits the rapprochement crisis and all it entails. He strives for autonomy and independence; however, instead of saying *I do it!* He now says: *You can't make me!* He experiences a regressive pull to be the dependent child. Almost simultaneously he pushes away from parents, usually by negativity and rebellious behaviors. He experiences overwhelming affects, which result in adolescent-size temper tantrums. The low-keyedness of toddlerhood is replaced by vacillating mood shifts, often cycling from exuberance to despair and back to exuberance within hours. The difference is, he no longer is a small child, but inhabits an adult body with adult instincts, and possesses a much bigger vocabulary. The goal is similar. If navigated well enough, the adolescent must mourn his childhood and move into young adulthood with all of its responsibilities. If infancy and toddlerhood went well or was good enough, object constancy is achieved. With object constancy, the adolescent has an easier time as he experiences a recurrence of separation anxieties. In addition, if object constancy is ascertained and sustained in early childhood, it "safeguards object relationships in jeopardy during adolescence" (Aarons, 1970, p. 322).

Just as parents need to set limits and circumnavigate power struggles during toddlerhood, the same remains crucial during adolescence. When I counsel parents of my adolescent patients I help them to understand their child's need for autonomy and independence. However, adolescents also need to feel safe. I explain to parents that adolescents are extremely creative as they push the boundaries and take risks. The parents' job is to understand their child's need to push back on limits and take risks as well as put obstacles in their way. For example: it is not helpful to allow a teenage girl to invite her boyfriend into her bedroom with the door closed. Or allow the consumption of alcohol in your home just to name two common "pushing the limits" behaviors. The following clinical vignette will demonstrate the early adolescent's need to rebel as she searches for her identity, and her initial pursuit for her own personal truth.

Clinical vignette: 1

Fourteen-year-old Juniper lived with her mother and two younger sisters. Her parents divorced when she was five years old. Her father quickly remarried and moved to another state, rarely visiting his daughters. Juniper began her analysis when she was twelve years old. Juniper had written an email to a classmate stating that she wanted to kill herself. This was reported to her school, which suggested that Juniper enter therapy. Upon meeting her I was struck by Juniper's pseudo maturity as well as her ability to be self-reflective and her desire to better understand the motives behind her behaviors. Adolescents often communicate through acting-out behaviors that speak indirectly to what they know and what they want to know. I understand rebellious risky behaviors such as cutting, shoplifting, binging, and restricting, as well as suicidal ideation as the adolescents' mode of communicating what cannot be said in words. Parents often claim that the adolescent is manipulative or acting-out to get attention, which may result in inaction. However, dangerous and self-directed violence such as cutting most often get adults to take notice and to begin to listen. In Juniper's case, her suicidal plea was a complex expression of hope, and a wish for a better, more fulfilling relationship with her mother.

Now at fourteen, Juniper hardly ever communicated with her father, and visits were even more rare. When her father moved far away, the three girls spent a month with him in the summer and every other Christmas. Juniper now refused to spend her summer vacation with him, preferring to spend time with peers. She reluctantly visited on Christmas. Juniper had been a compliant school-aged child. She was an excellent student, but she was painfully shy, longed to be popular, but had few close friends. When she entered adolescence her close relationship with her depressed mother suffered. Power struggles ensued as she asserted her independence and strived to be treated differently by her mother. Angry arguments erupted where hurtful words from both mother and daughter sharply penetrated leaving gaping wounds. Juniper felt mistreated, rejected, and misunderstood. Mother made her preference for Juniper's younger sisters well known, which only made Juniper feel more justified in her rage and aggression. Juniper tearfully bemoaned the fact that her mother never said: "I love you."

Juniper's rebellious act was to seduce the worst boy she could find. It was as if she was screaming at her mother: *So you won't love me but somebody will and you will hate him, and you will finally be sorry!* Juniper's rebellious conquest of the worst boy continued until her senior year of high school. During these adolescent years, Juniper experienced a resurgence of separation anxiety. She could not tolerate it when her mother went away, even for a day. Juniper's defiance of her mother served several uses; however, a main purpose was it helped her to resist the regressive pull back to childhood. Juniper's acting-out years were certainly an emotional testing period in which the "drives place ego and superego under the greatest stress" (Aarons, 1970, p. 309).

As Juniper matured, the "worst boy" no longer held her attention or her desire. She worked hard in her analysis as she came to understand her motives for her rebellious behaviors. Juniper was able to make that crucial transition from rebellion to healthy age-appropriate risk-taking. Juniper was able to navigate college and graduate school successfully as well as reestablish a close relationship with her mother.

Clinical vignette: 2

Judy began her analysis when she was nine years old. Her presenting problem was severe separation anxiety and a host of many other fears and phobias. I will focus on her newfound strength and her ability to search for her own truth and identity as she rebelled against family norms.

Judy's family was religious and followed strict orthodox Jewish rituals and laws. As stated above, Judy was afraid of just about everything from spiders, cats, and dogs, to school phobia where she needed to be homeschooled for a year. She was terrified of growing up because that meant the people you love will die. She refused to allow cut flowers in the home because she could not bear to see them wilt and die. When her pet rabbit died, she mourned for months, refusing play dates and other fun outings. When her body began to develop she became angry. When she menstruated for the first time she refused to acknowledge its occurrence. Needless to say, Judy had a long and sometimes painful analysis as we worked through many of her fears and conflicts.

By the time Judy entered high school, many of her presenting problems had resolved and she began a type of metamorphosis. Her once plain appearance slowly began to change. Judy was enamored by the Gothic style. She ordered interesting items online, such as corsets. She began to wear heavy dark eyeliner, black lipstick, and black nail polish. She spoke about how she never felt she fit in anywhere and this was her way of finding a comfortable place for herself. As her appearance altered, she began to really like herself. She would state: "I like that I am different. I am a rebel and I'm proud." In this way Judy demonstrated a willingness to take risks in her relationships and demanded to be heard. Judy's rebellion took the form of nonconformity. She was against fitting in with the popular group or the jocks and was not the academic nerdy type. Judy established her own look that attracted a few other adolescents who were like-minded. In this way Judy rejected her old child identity and refused to be treated like a child. Judy's parents were not exactly thrilled, in fact her nonconformity offended them, but to their credit they did not stop Judy from experimenting with her appearance, as long as she promised to marry within their faith.

However, Judy needed to further rebel against her parents. She claimed that she no longer wanted to be Jewish, but instead wished to convert to become a Buddhist. In addition, she began a relationship with a boy who was not Jewish. At this point in her search for identity and personal truth, Judy thought she knew who and what she did not want to be; however, she had no idea yet what she wanted to be. These developments pushed her parents a bit too far and many fights and disagreements took place. After many parent sessions, I managed to persuade Judy's parents to back down and stay calm. Judy's flight into Buddhism (or fight against her parents' beliefs) was short-lived. Judy remained within her faith, although not religious. She continued to date non-Jewish boys through college and eventually married within her religion.

The impact of the pandemic on adolescent development

As I write this chapter, we have been in quarantine for nearly two years. As analysts, we are among the lucky few who could continue seeing all of our patients remotely. The transition to remote therapy with my adolescent patients went smoothly. I attribute this to their expertise with computers and their ease with socializing online. That said, that is about the only thing that has been easy for adolescents during the pandemic. This age group was faced with isolation from peers as well as coping with multiple losses. My patients who were in their senior year of high school lost out on those important last few months when they find out which college they will be going to, with whom to go to prom, and of course, graduation itself. In addition, they could not visit the colleges where they were accepted to aid in their final decisions. As summer waned, a couple of my college-bound patients opted to defer their freshman year. The few who went to college faced isolation in a new place as they were assigned single rooms with strict no-visitor rules as well as classes online once again.

As the months rolled on, many adolescents were faced with rituals gone, peer interactions gone, and being stuck at home with their parents whom they were trying very hard to leave. As we know, as adolescents head toward leaving home, their peer group becomes most important. This, perhaps, was and continues to be the most difficult loss for this age group to contend with. The following short vignettes demonstrate some consequences of the pandemic on adolescent development.

Clinical vignette: 3

Wes was devastated that he missed out on his last few months of high school. He came into treatment at the beginning of his junior year with suicidal ideation. Wes was insightful and was able to explore his fears that centered upon separation and growing up, and most difficult for him, his sexual identity. He longed to take "normal" adolescent risks such as sexual experimentation as well as wanting to try smoking marijuana and drinking alcohol; however, whenever an opportunity arose, he was able to make an excuse and avoid all of these social interactions with his peers. Wes grew up with parents who believed in and practiced a very strict and often harsh parenting style. They were unable to acknowledge and understand developmentally normal autonomous behaviors in their young son. Wes grew up worried that any behaviors not approved by his parents would result in anger and withdrawal of love.

For ten months Wes remained isolated, interacting with friends online as his first semester of college was deferred. Wes's rebellion took the form of a moral and ethical dilemma. He and a few of his buddies applied online for the special unemployment benefit that was being offered during the pandemic. He told me he answered all of the questions truthfully and qualified for benefits. He soon began receiving weekly payments from the government. Wes felt justified in receiving this money, but kept it a secret from his parents, acknowledging to me that these government funds were meant to go to families who needed the money to pay rent and feed their children. Yet he could not give it up and spent the money on designer clothes and expensive gifts for his family and friends. Wes was too conflicted and inhibited to act out and take risks in expectable adolescent mischief. He did not sneak out to meet friends or figure out ways to outmaneuver his parents' rules about curfew. The shutdown proved to be a convenient excuse not to take any risks at all. However, when Wes told me about obtaining unemployment benefits, I seriously worried about his moral compass.

Lampl-de Groot (1960) states that in adolescence, internalized moral standards are threatened as the young man rebels against his parents. "To disengage oneself from the love object and that for which he stands is to disengage oneself from a part of one's own personality" (Aarons, 1970, p. 325). Wes was kindhearted and a good friend. He worried about his parents and showed compassion in many ways. So what was this action about? Wes felt inadequate sexually, and worried that if a girl saw his penis she would laugh and broadcast to all who would listen that he was a failure as a lover. In addition he was homophobic and was terrified that he was homosexual. Perhaps duping the government made him feel powerful. Maybe if he possessed expensive items they would compensate for his feelings of sexual insufficiency. Wes described how he felt like a strong man when he sent extravagant gifts to his friends.

Wes complained bitterly that the pandemic robbed him of his opportunity to prove his manhood before leaving for college. He lied to his friends about his sexual prowess and was terrified they would discover that he remained a virgin. Wes's dreams and fantasies were often filled with homosexual desires. Perhaps Wes's moral lapse, in addition to trying to feel powerful, was his way of expressing his anger toward a mother he had difficulty separating from, toward an emotionally disengaged father, the pandemic in general, and most importantly, anger toward himself for struggling with his sexual identity. In this way, Wes rejected his parents' demand for compliance. His insistence that he was owed this money was a defensive posture that allowed him to rebel against his parents. In addition, it is possible that Wes's reluctance to enter into intimate relationships is connected to his history where his independent strivings were not appreciated or enjoyed by his parents. Because of his parents' approach to childrearing, Wes might assume "that others will have no genuine interest in what he thinks or feels" (Herzog, 2015, p. 309). This was Wes's attempt at a trial independence where he took the stance of "You can't make me, nobody is going to tell me what to do."

Clinical vignette: 4

Emma was in treatment for generalized anxiety for two years before the pandemic hit. She had always been the perfectly compliant little girl. She was the "good" child in the family, while siblings struggled. It is vital to realize that "the overly accommodating child has had to face a specific conflictual dilemma throughout her development" (Herzog, 2015, p. 301). As her older siblings demanded their parents' attention, Emma needed to choose between her own needs or the approval, and in her mind, the love of her parents. As a compliant child, Emma enjoyed knowing she pleased her parents and in this way won their love. Giving up this "gratification associated with incestuous wishes, contributes to uncertainty and guilt" (Aarons, 1970, p. 325). Emma needed to renounce "parental omnipotence in which [she] participated" (Aarons, 1970, p. 325). In doing so, she was now left to figure out her own strategies. Pickhardt (2009) noted that the adolescent who rebels against always being the compliant good child may be more prone to engage in dangerous risk-taking.

Emma celebrated her sixteenth birthday during the shutdown. A few months later, her parents began to allow her to visit with her best friend outside with masks. Emma and her friend rebelled in "normal" adolescent fashion such as raiding her parents' liquor closet and getting drunk, and securing pot and getting high. These are activities that many adolescents engage in regardless of pandemics. She spent many sessions worried/anxious that getting drunk or high would mean she was terribly bad and more importantly, it would be proof that she was unlovable as it would disappoint her parents. She was also able to begin to understand her fear of loss of control. What would happen if she were not always good (or sick/anxious)? Would her rage erupt like a volcano? Would her sexual desires run amuck? I was not concerned by her rebellious actions and saw them as a step forward as she was on a path to discovering her own personal truths about her identity. As in most cases, her parents discovered both her forays into their vodka and found her pipe not well hidden in her room. Emma learned that although her parents disapproved of both underage alcohol use and pot smoking, they continued to love her as much as when she was the perfectly behaved little girl.

Emma's moral dilemma occurred a few months later as social restrictions were becoming a little more lax. Emma was now permitted to gather with up to ten friends outside with masks. At one of these gatherings Emma engaged in "hooking-up" with a boy she had feelings for. As we know, in normal times, hooking-up is an exciting and often a wonderful experience. However, for Emma it caused extreme guilt. She was terrified that she could potentially kill her parents and/or grandparents if she were to contract Covid. Emma spent several anguishing hours as she awaited her negative Covid test. Only then was her guilt alleviated.

Earlier in this chapter, I reminded the reader of how the adolescent revisits and reworks earlier pre- and post-oedipal phases of development. In addition, the adolescent experiences more mature sexual impulses that need to be contained. This is a difficult feat because the adolescent must simultaneously reject external controls by parents as he becomes more independent.

Clinical vignette: 5

Fourteen-year-old Billy seemed to have grave difficulties tolerating this phase of his development. Billy had always been a shy child. He had difficulties making friends and avoided play dates, parties, and any type of team sport. His presenting symptoms were night terrors, separation anxiety, and social anxieties. Billy did very well in his analysis facing his many fears until puberty. In middle school, he became withdrawn from both academics and friendships, often refusing to attend school. He refused to go on outings with his family and spent the majority of his time playing computer games and surfing the internet. Just as Billy celebrated his fourteenth birthday, the pandemic hit. Billy abruptly began remote school as our world shut down. Billy's whole existence centered on screens. Parents who had enforced limited use of computers and phones before the pandemic now felt compelled to allow their adolescents unlimited access as it was their only connection to their friends and the outside world. Even before the pandemic, Billy's parents were ineffective in limit setting, allowing Billy unlimited time with television, computer, and phone. With my urging they were, at times, able to set some boundaries; however, they quickly slipped back to old behaviors.

As the months wore on, Billy became more and more addicted to his screens that took on a compulsive quality. Billy's compulsive computer use seemed to take on an autistic quality; as Tustin (1987) described, Billy seemed to encapsulate his self behind an autistic-like barricade. In addition, his addiction to the internet encouraged magical thinking. "Computers can reinforce magical thinking through speed, displacement, and the nullification of distance" (Tyminski, 2015, p. 220). The shutdown wore on and Billy, now fifteen years old, continued to relate on a concrete level as he remained lost, and isolated from peers, living in a magical land of video games. I wonder if Freud (1911b) would say that Billy, and so many other children like him, turned away from reality because the reality of the situation was unbearable. Billy sought comfort and pleasure. Freud's (1911b) "pleasure principle" explains Billy's desire to turn away from reality, and the "reality principle" causes us to stop and think and postpone gratification. For Billy, magical thinking overtook his ability to confront reality. He became deadened, unable to even know what he was thinking or feeling.

Billy's social anxiety resurfaced with a vengeance as he refused almost all social interactions. "If one is afraid of intimacy yet afraid of being alone, a computer offers an apparent solution. The illusion of companionship without the demand of friendship" (Turkle, 2004, p. 21). Billy turned to cyberspace in order to defend against what is felt as an intolerable emptiness and loneliness. Billy's dependence on the internet stalled his development and allowed him to remain regressed. He was unable to move through this vital developmental phase. I also question if the use of the internet for this purpose is no different than other defensive behaviors such as binge drinking or drug use.

The analyst's role

Aarons (1970) claims that every adolescent is a delinquent. The role of the analyst is not to side with or condone rebellious risk-taking, but to explore with the adolescent "what it is that is threatening in his infantile attachments" (Aarons, 1970, p. 315). From infancy, we begin to separate from our love objects. It is imperative to recognize that separating and individuating does not mean disconnecting from those we love and depend on. Attachment is not negated. We remain connected and attached as we simultaneously separate and individuate. There is a "continuous tension between contact and separation, between recognition of the other and the affirmation of the self" (Valvo, 2007, p. 30). As adolescents become independent and autonomous, they often become dependent on another such as a peer group, a best friend, or a first lover. These attachments are often reenactments of their earliest relationships with parents. Sometimes, as with Juniper and Judy, first lovers serve as the catalyst of rebellion against parental values. As the adolescent becomes aware of his separateness, he must confront his own vulnerabilities. As the relationship to parents alters, the attachment feels unstable. The adolescent often becomes deregulated and cannot calm himself. This is when rebellious acting-out may occur. Just as the rapprochement crisis in toddlerhood needs parents who can remain calm and understanding of the toddler's conflicts, the second individuation of adolescence also needs to be well managed by parents. Parents need to be able to respond to adolescent angst with love and support in order to navigate through this crucial passage successfully. As the analyst, we are not a friend, nor do we render judgments. The acting-out behaviors may cause us anxiety, and at times, it is difficult not to pass judgment or intervene. Treating adolescents can be challenging; however, it is awesome to be along for the journey as our young patient searches for his identity and his own personal truth.

Final thoughts

Our psychoanalytic knowledge of adolescence was shaped by Anna Freud (1958) and those who came after her; most prominent is Blos (1962). Both theorists based their understanding of this developmental phase through an ego psychology lens, the leading theory of their time. Over the last sixty years a lot has changed, including the nature of adolescence in this culture and our understanding of this developmental phase. Over the past decades, we have seen exacerbated grandiosity among adolescents as well as intensified feelings of "invulnerability attached to the feeling that they do not need their parents any more. Dependence is split off and projected into the parents, who have their own conflicts about letting their children go" (Altman, 2007, p. 8). Adolescent grandiosity is manifest in the teen's preoccupation with his own self-interests. He inflates and devalues and is overcome by oscillating moods and reckless impulses. "Two propulsive emotional forces are ever present and interdependent viz., the struggle to be free of attachment to parental figures, and the quest for independence and self-identity" (Aarons, 1970, p. 315).

Many times, in my practice, I have observed overly anxious parents which results in a counterphobic attitude of invulnerability in the adolescent. It is not uncommon for adolescents to feel as if nothing bad could happen to them. Adolescents often make the adults around them apprehensive and uneasy. Altman (2007) reminds us of our own teen years as we took risks, experienced invulnerability, and rebelled against our parents' rules and limits. Most of us could not understand our parents' anxious behaviors and worries; however, most of us survived, developed our adult identities and discovered our personal truths. Remember, the ultimate goal and resolution of adolescence is to integrate our need for pleasure with an acceptance of accountability, dependability, and responsibility.

The adolescent often appears to feel contempt for the parents' values, expectations, and even their morality. As we saw with Wes, he could no longer passively adhere to his parents' expectations. Instead he threw his family values aside in search of his own personal goals and mobilized his energy toward conspiring with his buddy (a new object) to fool the government. Wes was plagued by his unresolved conflicts resulting in building defenses that in turn further prevented resolution of his most difficult conflicts. I believe this threatened his ability to mature as he remained juvenile in many respects.

Lastly, it is vitally important to comment on how adolescence is a painful period because it is during this phase of development that the adolescent discovers that his parents are not all-powerful, and do *not* know everything there is to know. Parental flaws become known as they fall from the lofty heights of omnipotence. It is this uncomfortable reality

> that supports the adolescent's irrational opposition to the offer of parental guidance and intervention. Mood swings are the adolescent's manifestation not only of discontent with himself, but of a despondency born of a new conviction that his parents cannot solve problems as they could in the days of their omnipotence. (Aarons, 1970, p. 325)

As parents fall from their pedestal, the adolescent incurs a deep narcissistic wound, which in turn propels him to search for new objects and develop his own intellectual goals. Aarons (1970) claims that this narcissistic injury is the cause of the mood swings and the deep feeling that he is misunderstood.

In conclusion, I am grateful and privileged to have been allowed to journey with my adolescent patients through both their ecstatic and desolate moments. It is often a rollercoaster ride, exciting, and at times terrifying. I am in awe of them as they share their deepest worries and struggle with their interpsychic conflicts. In many cases I am extremely fortunate to treat these children from pre-adolescence through young adulthood. I am honored to have known Wes, Billy, Emma, Juniper, and Judy.

CHAPTER FOUR

Truth in later life

Thomas Wolman

I begin this chapter on truth and later life with a generalization: The existential dilemmas of later life coalesce within the area of "human finitude." According to Dictionary.com, "finitude" and its correlate, "finite" means 1. Having bounds or limits, 2. Subject to limitations or conditions, as of time, space, circumstances, or the laws of nature. Of course, one of these laws of nature insists that, in Freud's (1913c) words, "We owe nature a death." Yet finitude in time entails more than just our endpoint: it implies that identity—our "I"—disappears and reappears as another "I" (or an Other "I") at every inflexion point in our history, a "truth" at variance with the "fiction" that sustains us all: the illusion that the "I" of today is the same "I" as the "I" of yesterday and tomorrow, that therefore identity is permanent, that the self exists outside of time and its predations, and that continuity is the order of the day.

If we list the main challenges to individuals in middle and later life, we have the following: aging, illness, loss of parents, spouses, and peers, marginalization (occupational, social), and what I call the shrinking of the ego's domain (Colarusso, 1998). We can think of the latter, alternatively, as the downsizing that takes place regarding one's living space, personal possessions, attachments and—with the exception of King Lear—one's egoistic pretensions.

In this piece, I propose that "truth" in the psychoanalytic sense always bears a relationship with human finitude and therefore has a particular affinity with the issues of later life. And because, as I will try to show, psychoanalytic truth affects the individual's sense of identity, it will always pose some version of Hamlet's question: To be or not to be—the fundamental question of human existence.

Telling the truth in Moverman's *The Messenger* (2009)

At the outset, I posit that truth must be spoken. Now, we can all agree that the starkest reality in human life is death. But for death to enter the realm of truth, it must be delivered in words to the person most affected by it—the next of kin. In this regard, I offer the following example from the film, *The Messenger* (directed by Oren Moverman, 2009), set within the US army.

The messenger in the title refers to the "casualty notification team" charged with notifying the next of kin that their loved one has died in the line of duty. In a two-person team, the senior officer, Tony—played by Woody Harrelson—lays down strict conditions—a kind of "ten commandments," if you will, for the proper conduct of their painful duty. And as we review these conditions, I invite the reader to consider these seemingly arbitrary rules in relation to truth, and to compare them to those governing the psychoanalytic situation.

Rule number one states that: we do not speak from a script. Reading from a script detracts the speaker from full and direct engagement with the person who must hear and digest this news. In the same vein, the speaker must not vacillate, waver, hesitate, or stammer. Vacillating makes it seem as if the speaker is of two minds about what she is saying. For the same reason, one must ensure that the name and address of one's interlocutor is correct. In this case, the truth can only be told to one unique individual. A bit later, Tony clarifies that "We don't speak to anybody other than the next of kin"—that is, "no friend, neighbor, coworker or mistress."

These constraints together comprise aspects of the messenger's "character." We may infer that such character entails a kind of solidity and stolidity, thus a single-mindedness and unity of purpose. I propose that such attributes can only come about through an almost complete *identification with the role of messenger.* In Tony's words, "You represent the Secretary of the army," ergo, you are not speaking for yourself or on your own behalf. Indeed, you do not even identify yourself by name because that would draw undue attention to yourself and "it's not about you." You must put to one side, therefore, your own inclinations and impulses, particularly the temptation to offer succor and consolation. You are even prohibited from touching the bereaved except in a medical emergency.

It is not that such help is inappropriate, but that it extends outside the messenger's brief. The messenger delegates such assistance to others who will be meeting with the next of kin in future. We would say that any attempt to comfort the bereaved in this moment would interfere with the format of the message as a "categorical imperative," meaning without conditions or exceptions: absolute. "Imperative" as a modality of speech implies the unavoidable and direct engagement of the listener, as in a command, for example.

Nevertheless, one feature of the mode of address works to mitigate the harshness of the message: the fact that "each casualty" is spoken of by name. He or she is never referred to as a "body" or as "the deceased." Thus, calling him or her by name is more than a matter of correctness. It is meant to honor the fallen soldier and thus to afford him a "place" or a "place-holder" in the annals of history. For similar reasons, you never use euphemisms, such as "lost," "expired," or "passed away." Instead, you say "killed" or "died." This frankness of speech recalls Freud's practice of calling a spade a spade (or in his words, "*appeler un chat un chat*") (Freud, 1905d) when discussing sexual matters.

Several constraints apply to the matter of time. You do not, for example, visit the family in the "dead of night." Optimally, you arrive in the morning. Your timing is not meant just to spare the family pain, but to ensure they are alert and able to hear what you have to say. Indeed, once a positive ID is made, time is of the essence. You have a twenty-four-hour window (or less) to deliver your message before the news media broadcast it to the world. The truth cannot wait, and it cannot be postponed. The "moment of truth" comes only once; and, once expired, it devolves into mere "knowledge." Truth in the telling differs from knowledge accessible to all.

En route to your destination, you do not ask for directions, nor consult GPS or MapQuest. Instead, you navigate. No explanation is offered for this apparently unnecessary restraint. But we must assume something more here than male pride. On one level, it fits with the previous injunction against following a script. That is, the act of telling the truth must be a spontaneous act and not a performance based on advance knowledge. The injunction also implies that truth-telling cannot be put in writing. In this regard, let us note, the army's use of "casualty notification teams represents a break from its time-honored policy of informing next of kin by telegram. But it's not just writing per se; any mediating device such as cell phone or email would blunt the directness of the message.

An interesting choice confronts the messenger at the front door: to knock or ring the doorbell. In Tony's words, "knocking is ominous, but ringing is jarring." You want to avoid the possible diversion of a silly jingle or musical motif emanating from the bell. In contrast, a knock on the door imparts just the right amount of gravitas to the encounter, as implied in the phrase "Death knocks at the door." For the same reason, you avoid meaningless small talk and greetings such as "Good morning." At this point, the team stand on the threshold of their first encounter with the next of kin and their rule book is put to the test. After some minor distractions, Tony informs the mother of her son's death. The effect of his "truth-telling" is explosive: "A scream comes out of Mrs. Burrell—a sound so raw, so loud, coming from so deep inside her that it literally shakes Tony and Will in their shoes" (scripts.com). In addition to this "punch in the gut" reaction, Mrs. Burrell slaps Tony once across the face, and when Tony continues his remarks, she tells him: "Stop saying that; you don't know what you're saying" (ibid.).

Thus, the effect of truth-telling can be unpredictable, devastating, and destabilizing. Nothing ensures that truth-telling is therapeutic. And we must distinguish "the effects of truth-telling" from "truth effects." The team's action must be distinguished from an intervention that produces a "truth effect" in the listener, that *allows her to reach her own truth.* The slap in the face reflects the mother's visceral reaction to being "left out of the conversation." Indeed, if Tony's declaration produces any "truth effect," then he and Will are its target. The mother's outburst reveals the "truth" repressed in both men. In Will's case, it is his reaction to horrific battlefield trauma; in Tony's case, by contrast, it is the shameful knowledge that he has never been tested on the battlefield. Furthermore, the scene of the two men stoically standing amid a swirling sea of chaotic emotion is powerfully moving for the viewer. It evokes those feelings of "pity, fear and catharsis" (Aristotle, 335 BCE) that are the truth effects of tragic drama.

I will now amend my first definition of truth as "telling" to the related idea of truth as a possible outcome of verbal intercourse. In papers such as "Constructions in Analysis," Freud (1937d) draws a distinction between truth as correctness and accuracy versus truth as an *effect of the analyst's intervention.* Indeed, it is possible to reel in a "carp of truth" from a "bait of falsehood" (Freud, 1937d). In this light, I offer three illustrative vignettes.

Clinical vignette: 1

I saw a woman in her mid-thirties for brief psychotherapy. She had been suffering from depression most of her adult life and her ostensible reason for consulting me was to renew an antidepressant she had been taking since her teens. When I saw her, her depressed mood wasn't crippling, but it hung over her like a dark cloud. Taking her history, I learned that her parents had shamelessly neglected her and left her to her own devices. At the age of seventeen, she consulted a lawyer and got herself declared an "emancipated minor." A family friend stepped in and paid her tuition so she could attend college. At the time of our meeting, she was living with her boyfriend, a writer, and working as a visual artist.

At one point, I asked her if painting gave her a reason to go on living and she said, yes, it did. She then told me that a course she had taken in New York on the techniques of the Old Masters had had a profound effect on her. I then asked her—off the top of my head, so to speak—did she consider herself to be a photographic realist? She paused to reflect. Then: "I'd say I'm more of a classical realist."

When I heard these words, I knew in my bones that "the truth had been said" but I wasn't sure if the effect took place in the patient or within myself. In any case, I did not attempt to interpret her words; I didn't ask her what she meant; I didn't ask her for further associations. I just let the matter stand. In retrospect, I must have sensed that any further interventions on my part would have diluted the truth effect.

However, I was free to think about the implications of what she said. Her "realism" conveyed the idea that no matter how her life improved, she could never erase the damage done to her ego ideal. Thus, she could look at the world and herself "realistically" but without much youthful idealism. Yet she was able to avoid the deadening of her internal world characteristic of melancholia. Thus, in identifying herself with classical realism—which I later discovered refers to a modern art movement that seeks to return to the roots of Western art (Wikipedia.com)—she links herself with the "old masters" and thus maintains in her work a link to the original parental ideal.

I later wondered why she didn't become an expert art forger, a vocation for which she had the skills and through which she could have made a good living. I believe the answer lies in her rejection of photographic realism. To merely reproduce the work of

> others or make an exact copy of nature would return her to the static inertia of the "depressive real."
>
> **Clinical vignette: 2**
>
> This vignette is actually an excerpt from an interview given in 2011 by the groundbreaking neurologist, Oliver Sacks (1933–2015). In that interview, Sacks revealed that he had been in analysis with the New York–based psychoanalyst Leonard Shengold for forty-six years and that he had sought analytic help at a critical inflexion point in his life, when he was floundering. Sacks said that in one of his early sessions, he asked Shengold if—in the latter's opinion—he was psychotic. The analyst answered without hesitation: "No." Then Sacks asked: "Do you think I'm an ordinary neurotic?" This time, after a brief pause, the answer again was: "No." At this point, Sacks and, we infer, the analyst, let the matter drop.

Can a simple clarification of diagnostic impression count as a moment of truth? I think it can, although the full extent of the truth effect may not have emerged until years later. In my view, the truth of this brief exchange lies in its subtext. On the literal level, Shengold implies that Sacks falls somewhere between neurosis and psychosis. Perhaps, given some of his patient's extreme behaviors such as daily methamphetamine use and thirty-six-hour motorcycle rides undertaken without sleep, he felt that Sacks met the criteria of that all-purpose category: borderline state. However, I heard another message whose truth only blossomed with the passage of time: Sack's truth was that he was and is unclassifiable—unclassifiable as a person and as an intrepid explorer of the human mind. Today, after his death, we still marvel at the different lives he lived and at his unique vocation at the frontier (borderline?) of neurology, psychiatry, and his own genre of medical literature.

Near the end of my time at the Philadelphia Veterans Affairs Medical Center, a colleague referred a patient to me because I was known to take on psychotic patients in psychotherapy. Here is a brief recollection from my encounter with that patient.

> **Clinical vignette: 3**
>
> In the opening sessions, I had serious qualms about whether I could continue. The patient was a floridly psychotic man in his mid-fifties. This fact in itself did not deter me. However, the patient was overtly menacing toward me and I did not feel safe in his presence. Moreover, he recounted a series of the most perverse fantasies imaginable: scenes of rape, torture, murder, pillage, cannibalism—you name it. These fantasies were narrated with a savage glee, and the possibility of acting out was ever present. In addition, the patient harbored three kinds of delusions: the demonic (the Irish demon), the grandiose, and the persecutory. The latter two all involved the belief that he was being followed by multiple government agencies including the CIA and the Department of

Homeland Security. The one grandiose delusion—and the one that dominated his psychical life—asserted that he was a five-star general of the army.

Nevertheless, I noted a few positive signs. The patient—whom I will now call the general—always appeared on time for his appointments. He lived with his sister, and the arrangement seemed peaceable. He had no history of violence or legal troubles. And for better or worse, he used his sessions to verbalize every crazy and bizarre thought that entered his mind.

After a few sessions, his menacing attitude lessened. He developed a relatively benign delusional transference toward me. He believed that I could intervene with the director of Homeland Security to get them to stop following him. In each session, he implored me to write a letter to the director, yet he was not overly insulted when I explained why this was not possible.

It was at the end of each session that his attachment to me became apparent. Over several meetings he found it increasingly difficult to let go of my hand. The issue came to a head during one session when he brought my hand up to his mouth with the intention of biting me. His cannibalistic fantasies had become so compelling that he wanted to devour me and "swallow me whole" so that I would not disappear.

At this point, I knew I had to do something, and for once, my intuition did not fail me: I wrenched my hand away and immediately drew my hand to my head in a military salute. The general saluted me in return, and we continued saluting each other several times, at which point the patient felt able to leave the office. I should add that by this time, I was calling the patient "general"—his preferred term of address. In succeeding partings, I would salute the general and he would return the gesture, sometimes multiple times.

This intervention proved to be a turning point in the therapy because, although his multiple delusions continued unabated, his level of anxiety decreased. But a few months later, I had to tell him that I was retiring from the VA and would not be able to see him anymore. I introduced him to a colleague who would see him in follow-up. In our last session the patient announced to me: "I know I am not a five-star general." I was flabbergasted. Not in a hundred years did I think he would willingly give up a delusion of this "magnitude." And of course, I realized that his admission was in part a response to the fact of my leaving; and the delusion might therefore reappear at any time.

Yet these factors do not undo the "truth effect" at work in his declaration. He was not merely "stating a fact," he was articulating his "truth" and addressing it specifically to me—for my ears only. I would posit that the salute enabled the patient to set a boundary between himself and me while still recognizing his dignity as a human being. It was as if he were saying: "Because you recognized me as a person worthy of respect, I do not need—at least in this moment—to pretend I am more than what I am."

Interestingly, I only found out later that the category of five-star general has been left unfilled and unoccupied since the era of Marshall and Eisenhower (Wikipedia.com).

The delusional metaphor therefore may have provided the patient with a stable "place" in a chaotic world with "nobody in command."

Truth versus knowledge in Bergman's *Wild Strawberries* (1957)[20]

This film recounts a journey undertaken by its protagonist, Professor Isak Borg, a seventy-eight-year-old widower, from Stockholm to Lund where he will be granted the honorary degree of doctor jubilaris in recognition of his half century of contributions to bacteriology. But in the first scene a somber note is struck in what ought to be a jubilant mood. A bell peals and the wall clock ticks loudly reminding us of the passage of time. A dream filled with death symbols casts a pall over Isak's planned journey. He offers a hint to the problem in his admission that he has "withdrawn from most human relationships," and as a consequence feels "somewhat lonely." On a subterranean level, he senses that a key element is missing from his life. In the film, Bergman reimagines the journey as a search for this missing element. We will argue that the missing element is "truth." At each of the journey's turning points, a critical encounter allows Borg an opportunity to revisit the decision points when truth was evaded.

The first encounter features Marianne, Borg's daughter-in-law, wonderfully played by Ingrid Thulin. She is pregnant and on the verge of leaving her husband, Evald (Borg's son). She complains that Isak's insistence on their paying back a loan is causing them hardship. Isak remarks that he and his son are alike in holding to firm principles and that "a promise is a promise." But here Marianne counters with: "But he hates you!" Isak's stricken look shows that her words have gotten under his skin. Yet he does not reject what she says out of hand, but instead asks what she has against him. "Do you want me to be frank?" she asks. "Yes," he answers, and she lets him have it: "You're selfish, ruthless, and you never listen to anybody but yourself."[21] As evidence, she cites his refusal to allow her to stay with him when she needed help. When he seems surprised, she repeats back to him his own words: "I have no respect for mental suffering." He had added: "If you need therapy, you had better see a shrink." This slightly ironic comment expresses a truth, namely that Isak has repressed his own "mental suffering." Yet once again he does not repudiate Marianne's words.

Instead, Isak draws Marianne to a secluded spot in the country, the site of his childhood home. Wistfully, he tells her that, here, wild strawberries used to grow. The "wild strawberries" represent the "pleasures (and pain) of the flesh" that Isak has forsaken. Suddenly—and against a background of storm clouds—Isak relives a memory of Sara, his first love. He sees her in the flower of her youth picking strawberries. Then, Siegfried, Isak's brother enters. He proceeds

---

[20] See *Ikiru* (1952) for a strikingly similar Japanese film directed by Kurosawa. Here too, the diagnosis of stomach cancer prompts an older man to reevaluate his life. He too, finds his moment of truth in a series of conversations with a vivacious female coworker.

[21] All quotes from *Wild Strawberries* are from this source: https://scripts-onscreen.com/movie/wild-strawberries-script-links/.

to flirt with Sara and despite her half-hearted resistance boldly kisses her. He is everything that Isak is not: slick, flirtatious, comfortable with women and a bit "nasty." During the kiss the strawberries spill to the ground—this time suggesting Sara's loss of virginity as well as the annulment of her secret engagement to Isak. Later Sara complains to her mother that Isak's sensitivity and hyper-moralism makes her feel "worthless." Witnessing this humiliating scene, Isak feels overwhelmed with sadness and emptiness, the very "mental suffering" he has long suppressed. Indeed, this "primal scene" puts him squarely in the role of "impotent" observer.

But just then, the scene jumps back to the present and he sees before him another Sara, played by Bibi Anderson—a young vivacious hitchhiker accompanied by two male friends. The ongoing subplot involving the threesome enacts another version of the "primal scene" between Isak, the original Sara, and Siegfried. In this case, the two men are both in love with Sara and are constantly feuding with each other and vying for Sara's exclusive love. During a leisurely lunch, the two men argue the relative merits of science and religion. The one advocating religion declares that rationalism is "dry as dust" and that "modern man believes only in himself." He adds that man still has a horror in the face of death and that the non-belief of modern man is simply a failure of the imagination. Thus, the intellectual back and forth replicates the dichotomy between nasty, sensual Siegfried versus "dry as dust" moralist Isak. However, it is also Isak the rational scientist who sees all human affairs through the lens of a microscope who is contrasted with a more creative and therefore quasi-religious engagement with others.

A second brief encounter at a gas station presents a second and more benign version of the scene. The married couple running the gas station—the Akermans—remember Isak from when he worked in this rural area as a busy general practitioner. They treat him with warmth and respect. When Isak offers to pay for the gasoline they refuse to take his money. Mr. Ackerman—played by a young Max Von Sydow—says: "Some things simply cannot be paid back" (Akhtar, 2012). His words express the couple's gratitude for Isak's past contribution to their community. Note that their view contrasts with Isak's more draconian viewpoint that debts must be paid back to the penny. The couple's kindness recalls Isak to that decision point in his history when he opted for the ideal of pure science over that of helping others. He now questions that decision.

A third iteration of the scene ensues when Borg's car almost collides with another vehicle that veers off the road. Isak and company offer a ride to the stranded motorists, a married couple named Allman. The minute they enter the car they resume what must be a long-standing feud between them. It is immediately apparent that their fighting is both vicious and vitriolic. The husband adopts a lofty and distant approach to his wife's allegedly "imaginary complaints" and her so-called "hysteria." The wife—for her part—keeps trying to get under the husband's skin and break through his veneer of imperturbability. At one point and out of desperation, Mrs. Allman starts slapping her husband but to no avail. The feuding reminds Marianne of her own troubled marriage, and, having it up to here with the couple, she demands that they leave. Isak too, sees in the couple a mirror image of his own contentious marriage. He too must have adopted the infinitely understanding but patronizing role while his wife did her utmost to provoke him. In a later scene, Isak sees her being seduced by her lover, a nasty sensualist in the mold of Siegfried. Thus the images of *Scenes from a Marriage* (Bergman, 1973) replicate Isak's original trauma.

After a visit with his hard-bitten mother, Isak nods off while Marianne drives. Once again finding himself at the site of the "wild strawberries," he engages with the original Sara and his personal truth finally emerges. She gives him a hand mirror and asks him to look at himself. She tells him that her image as a woman on the threshold of a vibrant life has stayed in his mind. She guesses that her conduct must have hurt Isak's feelings. He immediately denies that this is the case. But she counters with: "It did hurt your feelings because you can't bear the truth." Thus, we are witness to Isak's "moment of truth" because on this occasion he *can* bear the truth of what she tells him.

Moreover, she does not spare herself. She admits that, in reaction to her own conflicts she was unintentionally cruel to Isak. Isak reflexively answers that he understands. But Sara asserts that in fact he doesn't "understand" (Fink, 2010). She is getting at the fact that—in saying "I understand"—Isak is once again evading the truth he has just attained. In his pain, he truly cannot understand why she is rejecting him. "Understanding" forms the defensive pose he will later use to protect himself from his utter bafflement during the original scene (part of which might be attributed to perplexity when faced with the parents' overt sexuality, he being one of ten children). Sara compares Isak's incomprehension to "speaking different languages." And in exhorting him to reexperience the pain of that moment he must recognize that "he knows nothing" and that all his accumulated knowledge counts for little when confronting the truth of his being.

A final version of the scenario occurs when Marianne and Evald confront the truth about their marriage. In this encounter, Evald embodies a more extreme version of Isak (whose similarity to his father has been noted). When Marianne informs Evald that she is going to have a child and that she intends to bring this child into the world, her husband is dismayed. He admits that he "doesn't want to bring children into this world," a point of view he attributes to being an "unwanted child in a hellish marriage." In a tone that will send chills up and down your spine, he avers that his only passion—such as it is—is to be "stone cold dead." Can this contrast between Eros and Thanatos be any more stark? The death drive embodied by Evald represents the dark path on which Isak was headed, the one heralded by his opening nightmare. The "end" it represents is not just "end of life" but the "dead end" that his life had become.

But even before this late-stage cautionary tale, Isak had been processing the stations on his journey and coming to a new "decision point" at which he will start to reconnect with others. He acknowledges that his weird dreams seemed to be telling him something that he refused to accept in the waking state. In his words, "It is as if I'm alive but dead, or dead while alive." That is, he was enacting the part of a dead man who has repudiated the "living germ" within, or a living man who carries within himself the "dead child" he imagined himself to be. In taking leave from him, the new Sara in all her "abundant vitality" as the personification of Eros, tells him with only a trace of her usual irony, that she loves him most of all, and that she loves him in the past, present, and future all at once. In what seems like a hyperbole, she imparts Isak's truth that—like a magic portal in space-time—he has regained *access* to love.

Truth and identity in Glatzer and Westmoreland's *Still Alice* (2014)

The first scene of Richard Glatzer and Wash Westmoreland's *Still Alice* (2014) depicts Alice Howland at—what will turn out to be—the pinnacle of her life. She is surrounded by her loving husband and two of her three children, one a lawyer, the other a doctor. Her husband, John, runs a successful biochemistry research program. She is in robust health. Moreover, she is a distinguished professor of linguistics at Columbia University and a world-renowned expert on language acquisition. Perhaps the only missing piece in this otherwise idyllic picture is Alice's daughter, Lydia. Alice worries about Lydia because, unlike her other two children, both professionals, Lydia is a struggling actor working in Los Angeles. Not having attended college, Lydia has failed to measure up to Alice's (and the family's) ideal of higher education.

Early in the movie, Alice has a frightening experience while jogging on the Columbia campus. As she enters the main quad, the background of the scene goes out of focus to suggest Alice's spatial disorientation. Momentarily dismayed, she is relieved when things quickly fall back into place, and she sees the famous Butler Library in clear definition. Visually, this shot accents the monumental library as a vast treasure trove of linguistic resources. For Alice, the library becomes her temporary anchor, the buttress of her own linguistic mastery. In a certain sense then, it represents her self-image as a linguist and her specialty in "language acquisition" as a massive "repository."

This experience, along with minor word-finding difficulties, prompts Alice to consult a neurologist. In short order, Dr. Benjamin informs her that she has early onset Alzheimer's disease, a particularly virulent type, and that medications will not halt disease progression.[22] And as the *coup de grâce*, her children have a 50/50 chance of inheriting the condition. The doctor is compassionate but utterly frank in his assessment. He doesn't mince words. Truth in this instance means complete conformity with the facts. But this "reality" is not Alice's truth. Indeed, the enormity of it leaves her momentarily at a loss for words.

It is only somewhat later when, awakening in the middle of the night, Alice tells her husband what she has learned. His response is one of complete denial: "This makes no sense, it's insane," he says. He opines that "We all make mistakes." But upon hearing these words, Alice flies into a rage. She accuses John of not taking her seriously and ignoring her rising feeling of panic. Then she laments that everything she's ever worked for is going up in smoke.

[22] A more recent and truly remarkable portrayal of dementia is by Anthony Hopkins in the 2020 movie, *The Father*. His tenaciously held paranoid stance insulates him from any access to truth. Only in the last ten minutes of the film, in the company of an experienced nurse, does his rigid façade begin to crumble.

Thus, she begins to speak a truth that is personal and specific to her. It is perhaps ironic that her husband's attempts at denial—denial that she herself is grappling with—brings about a "truth effect."

And once she has acknowledged the impact of the diagnosis on her life, a plan begins to form in her mind—a stratagem to outwit the "enemy" so to speak. She begins by inserting a series of basic questions into her smart phone[23] such as: "What is the name of your oldest daughter?" and "What is the street where you live?" In her mind, these questions establish a baseline of mental functioning. She also asks her doctor for a prescription for Rohypnol, ostensibly to help her sleep. In the following scene, she is addressing herself on FaceTime as if she were another person named Alice. She tells her counterpart that "I am you" and that she needs *that other* "Alice" to listen carefully. When she can no longer answer any of the questions on her phone, she will be prompted to open a file on her laptop labeled "Butterfly." Opening the file, she will be given instructions on locating a hidden bottle of pills. She is enjoined to swallow them all, to go to sleep, and to not tell anybody what she has done.

In undertaking this plan, Alice places herself in a position of "master of her domain" modeled upon her husband's single-minded approach to life. She views the plan as a "logical" course of action that will spare her the pain and suffering of losing her wits, and in engineering her future death by suicide, offers her a measure of control over her own fate. But the plan assumes that she and her future self are exact counterparts just as—up until now—she and John had shared mastery over their respective domains (linguistics, biological research). Moreover, her instructions to her future self are delivered as commands that must be obeyed with no questions asked. Hence, her "rule by fiat" cannot possibly speak her truth because her counterpart in the mirror is given no opportunity to speak for herself.

Yet in the same time frame, a realignment of the family is taking place which sets in motion changes that will render moot the plan's outcome. As noted, the family had been united in their shared ideals of professionalism, with Lydia the sole exception. Alice had been aligned with her husband and two older children. Now, however, Lydia, with whom she has the most contentious relationship, steps into the breach. The two begin to renegotiate their relationship during a walk on the beach. During that walk Alice shares memories with her daughter and specific hopes for the immediate future. However, when she asserts her long-held wish that Lydia attend college, her daughter hears it as yet another assault on her autonomy. But when Alice implicitly adds the words: "before I die" Lydia is moved. From this moment forward, their ongoing conversation becomes the crucible in which Alice's truth emerges.

Responding to John's suggestion that she read one of Lydia's plays, Alice sorts through a half-dozen of the latter's scripts, including *The Three Sisters* by Anton Chekov (1901) and *Angels in America* by Tony Kushner (2014). It so happens that during Alice's fiftieth birthday celebration with her family, Lydia had been appearing in Sartre's *No Exit* (2015), in Los Angeles.

---

[23] The smart phone has become a heavily invested object for Alice. It serves as an "auxiliary" ego that incarnates the "mastery" she is in the process of losing.

It is perhaps no accident on the part of the screenwriters that *No Exit* encapsulates Alice's horrific situation to a tee. Indeed, the director of *Still Alice* wants to showcase the importance of tragic drama (a genre that fits this film) because of its direct address to the audience in real time and its relentless pursuit of human truth. In this light, a scene depicts the twosome discussing *Angels in America*. Lydia wants to hear Alice's personal "take" on the play. Alice remarks on how "big, wide is the scape." By "scape" she means to say "scope" but the slip of the tongue reveals a certain truth about herself: Even in her more limited capacity, her listening partner can hear the truth in what she says. Thus, Lydia hears "scape" as "scope," but perhaps also as "landscape," "soundscape," or the "cloudscape" inhabited by angels.

In perusing the scripts, Alice comes across Lydia's diary (Lydia's name is written boldly on the cover). Alice begins to read it. We could infer that, in this stage of her illness, she conflates the diary with the other plays, and blurs the boundary between public and private. Yet could we not say that in the pursuit of truth, the diary should be read aloud to a listener, like a patient revealing a "secret" from the psychoanalytic couch, for example? This question becomes acute when Alice inadvertently reveals that she has read the diary. At first, Lydia takes umbrage as if Alice intended to trespass on her domain, and as if they were two "autonomous egos" vying over disputed territory. After all, this issue had been the basis of their ongoing struggle over the years. But now, Lydia finds herself at a crossroads that bears on the issue of her own personal truth: Is she willing to read her diary out loud (or allow it to be read) just as if it were a play like *Angels in America*?

In their next private moment, Lydia has made her choice. In response to Alice's apology for an argument whose content Alice no longer remembers, Lydia apologizes to *her* and asserts that her diary is no longer "off limits." She attaches a Post-it note to its cover that reads "no secrets." She can now ask Alice what it is like *to be you* during this ordeal. Through this act, Lydia recognizes that what she saw as the boundary of her "self" was also an obstacle to the full disclosure that truth requires. Alice tells her that she has always been so defined by her intellect, by the fluency of her articulation, that, on her bad days, she loses the sense of who she is. Indeed, on those days, she can "see the words hanging in front of me and I can't reach them, and I don't know who I am." Yet by speaking her truth, *she becomes who she is in the moment of articulation*, despite having to jettison the sense of mastery that formerly bolstered her ego. A few days later, Alice attends a production of *The Three Sisters* (Chekov, 1901) in which Lydia plays the middle sister. Alice listens attentively and engages with the play; for the first time, she grants Lydia's vocation the respect it deserves.

Meanwhile Alice is slated to give a speech about her condition to the local medical society. She rehearses the speech on FaceTime with Lydia. Her first drafts focus almost exclusively on the scientific aspects of Alzheimer's disease such as "myeloid plaques." Lydia tactfully suggests that she make her speech more personal by telling her audience what it feels like to experience the effects of the disease. Alice at first balks at the idea. She feels the group pressure to make her speech about *knowledge* rather than personal truth. She also agonizes over the difficulty of writing even one paragraph in scientific terminology.

But when she gets up before her audience, we hear immediately that she has taken Lydia's suggestion to heart: Her speech focuses solely on the subjective dimension. She begins by quoting a phrase from Elizabeth Bishop's poem (Bishop, 1979, "One Art"), "losing isn't hard to master." Listing her various losses, the pages of her speech suddenly fall to the floor. But she "comes back" with an actual witticism: "I think I'll try to forget that that just happened." It strikes a chord with her audience because it wistfully looks back on her former self who thought she had "control" over her own memories. At the same time, it acknowledges that she will inevitably lose the memory of "what just happened." And yet the witticism shows the connection between the two Alice(s)—it affirms that she is "still Alice" in the moment of its being said. Indeed, she is "still Alice" because she wants her listeners to know that she is not "suffering"; she is "struggling ... struggling to be a part of things, to remain connected ... to what I once was." And finally, she notes that delivering this speech reestablishes her identity as a "linguist" contributing to the fund of scientific knowledge while presenting her personal truth as the "art of losing."

With the passage of time, Lydia and John change places, and Alice reaffirms her commitment to life. Lydia takes over the role of caretaker for Alice, a move that allows John to move to Minnesota and a project at the Mayo Clinic. However, he and Alice do share one final moment of truth. John asks her if she still wants to be here. The question is relevant due to the recent aborted suicide attempt. But Alice answers: "I'm not done yet."

In one of the last scenes, Lydia is reading or reciting from memory a scene from *Angels in America* in which the souls of the departed join hands and form a great web in the sky. She asks Alice what she thinks the play is about. At this point, Alice has few words left to draw upon. After a struggle she answers with one word: love. This affirmation of love serves as a holophrase for all the words Alice has spoken in her quest to be herself while struggling with loss. Lydia responds: "Yes, mom, it was about love."

Concluding remarks

In this contribution, I have explored the intrinsic connections between the "truth" and the acknowledgment of human finitude. In the psychoanalytic arena, the appreciation of human finitude is equivalent to acknowledging that "the ego is not master in his own house." In simple terms, the ego comprises the area of knowledge and the domain of self-mastery. Thus Dr. Borg's valorization of science and moral principle served as bastions of permanence, unaffected by the vicissitudes of personal history. In the same vein, Alice's view of "language as acquisition" offered a seemingly immutable foundation, immune to the vagaries of time and fate. In both cases, truth contradicted the stability of self-knowledge and impugned self-mastery. Its articulation at auspicious moments altered the identity of its "bearers" and shifted their historical trajectories.

These distinctions point to unresolved problems, three of which I will mention in closing. The first involves the analyst's tendency to offer "knowledge" to the patient in the form of "insight." In these instances, the analyst presents an interpretation such as "You are like this or that" or "You must be feeling this or that" or "You have a pattern of doing this or that." A good rule of thumb, however, is to leave such insights to the patient to figure out (Fink, 2010). The analyst, for her part, should avoid adding to the patient's store of self-knowledge (which in many cases derives from the analyst's knowledge of her own alter ego). Yet there are times when doing precisely this unlocks a previously unmentioned "truth" that contradicts the presumed "knowledge." Thus, the relationship between "truth" and "knowledge" is complex and, during a lengthy analysis, "truth" and "knowledge" may overlap as they did during Alice Howland's speech before the medical society.

A second problem concerns the status of self-analysis. A recent rereading of a book chapter I wrote nearly three decades ago entitled "The Death of the Analyst in the Post-termination Phase of Analysis" (Wolman, 1990) concluded that something was missing at the heart of the endeavor, the nature of which was left obscure. In the same volume containing that chapter, a brilliant essay by Jacob Arlow (1990) on his near-death experience after a heart attack concluded that its underlying truth lay in the "awareness of a sudden, drastic confrontation with mortality, warded off by the idea: 'If this is death, it's not bad at all. I'm not afraid of it. In fact, I could really enjoy it.'" In my 1990 chapter, there was likewise a kind of "denial in fantasy" of the analyst's death but also the analyst's necessary presence in some form or other as an auditor. According to what I have argued here, any attempt at self-analysis must address a listener who is not a mere "double" of the "self-analysand" for it to stand any chance at success. In Freud's "self-analysis" the position was filled by Wilhelm Fliess (Masson, 1985), for Dr. Borg, the two Annas and Marianne; for Alice, Lydia.

But these examples also show that persons in late life are receptive to the truth under the right conditions. If we view the "prime of life" as the period of maximum expansion of the self-image, then its "shrinking," or as I prefer to think—its jettisoning of inessential elements—promotes a greater investment in one's history, legacy, and symbolic representations. Hence, older individuals may be more motivated to find words for who they were, who they are, and who they still might be. And in this regard, we may note that old age is no longer deemed a detriment to psychoanalysis. The limited time available is, if anything, an incentive to make the most of one's time on the couch—or for that matter, behind the couch and beyond the couch. A study (Jeffery, 2001) found that on average, psychoanalysts live longer than other medical professionals. And if we can cite many analysts who have practiced into their nineties, why should we not expect the same for their analysands?

Part II

Cultural realm

CHAPTER FIVE

"Nothing is truer than truth" and Shakespeare

Richard M. Waugaman[24]

When we want objective truths about the world, we turn to science. But when we want truths about human experience, in all its complexity, we often turn to great literature. In this essay, I will explore some of Shakespeare's insights into the vexed topic of truth. After four years of President Trump trampling the truth, the topic could not be more timely. This essay will examine Shakespeare's play, *All's Well that Ends Well*, after putting it in the context of the real Shakespeare's approach to human truths.

"Tell all the Truth but tell it slant," advised Emily Dickinson (1830–1886) in *Poem 1129* (1872). In her succinct admonition, she captured a core aspect of Shakespeare's sophisticated approach to the truth. In her day, there was a vogue for collections of Shakespeare quotations, under the premise that they offered straightforward moral advice. Editors of those anthologies mistook Shakespeare as someone who wrote transparently, mistaking superficial appearances for the disguise necessary for an Elizabethan nobleman to speak truth to power. A lover of Shakespeare's works (Paraic Finnerty, 2006),[25] Dickinson knew more about poetry than did those editors. She knew that truth can be so unsettling that our conscious mind wards off such unwelcome news. It is tempting to think that her famous advice, "tell it slant," was indebted to her more accurate understanding of Shakespeare.

Dickinson's contemporary Nathaniel Hawthorne wrote, "Whatever you seek [in Shakespeare] you will surely discover, provided you seek truths." Yet Hawthorne recognized that Shakespeare's words need to be interpreted, since they have "surface beneath surface, to

[24] My ninety-five publications on Shakespeare are available at https://gufaculty360.georgetown.edu/s/contact/00336000014RkZiAAK/richard-waugaman

[25] "Shakespeare was the first author she chose to read, and … she regarded him as the only necessary author" (p. 3).

an immeasurable depth, adapted to the plummet-line of every reader; his works present many faces of truth, each with scope enough to fill a contemplative mind" (cited in Finnerty, p. 63). Delia Bacon believed Elizabethan authors used "esoteric" writing—that is, writing between the lines—to escape the pervasive censorship of their day, so their publications would speak to future generations, provided we peer deeply beneath the surface of Elizabethan literature. None of this will come as a surprise to psychoanalytic readers, who spend their work day constantly shifting back and forth between the surface and the unconscious depths of their patients' associations.

Hawthorne helped Delia Bacon publish her heretical 1857 work, *The Philosophy of the Plays of Shakespere Unfolded*, the first book to challenge the traditional Shakespeare authorship theory, replacing it with her theory that a group of authors wrote the works. Before delving into what Shakespeare has to say about truth, we first need to address the truth about who wrote Shakespeare (as I see it). This proves to be such a surprisingly controversial topic that Delia Bacon was harassed mercilessly, after she rejected the conventional wisdom that is still cherished by Shakespeare scholars and by most lovers of his works. Ironically, Bacon's theory that a group of writers wrote the Shakespeare canon has recently come into its own, with the 2016 *New Oxford Shakespeare* proposing that a dozen playwrights collaborated with Shakspere of Stratford. The fierce reaction against Delia Bacon contained misogyny and possible homophobia, as conveyed in an 1883 slur that claimed questioning Shakspere's authorship was "a literary bee in the bonnets of certain ladies *of both sexes*" (Richard Grant White, quoted in Finnerty, p. 62; emphasis added). In fact, the majority of Shakespeare authorship skeptics in nineteenth-century America were women (Finnerty, 2006, p. 66).

As Hawthorne noted, much was "done to assail the prejudices of the public, but far too little to gain its sympathy" for Bacon (cited in Finnerty, 2006, p. 10). Like Ignaz Semmelweis, an obstetrician who traced maternal deaths from puerperal sepsis to his colleagues not cleansing their hands sufficiently before delivering babies, she enraged the "experts" with her new discoveries, and she was rewarded for her pains by so much verbal abuse that she ended up in a mental hospital. Sometimes, a prophet is not only without honor, but even becomes the victim of gaslighting.

Who wrote Shakespeare?

The issue of who wrote Shakespeare should be a simple question of history, but it has become complicated by our intense idealization of these literary works and of their author. Since the late 1500s, there were numerous hints that many people knew the actual author was concealing his identity. We might think this was unusual, when nowadays most writers want credit for what they write. However, that was not true in Shakespeare's day. Most Elizabethan plays were published anonymously. With rare exceptions, the nobility did not publish literary works under their own names during their lifetimes. The courtiers' ideal was called *sprezzatura*, or cultivating the appearance of nonchalance as to one's reputation. Penn State scholar Marcy North's *The Anonymous Renaissance* is a paradigm-shifting book about the many complex motives and meanings of all forms of anonymous authorship in the Renaissance. Her broad concept of anonymity also includes the use of a pen name, or pseudonym, as well as the name of an actual person to conceal the true author (a so-called "allonym"). Writers who use one pen name tend to use others as well.

North noted that the paucity of literary works signed by Edward de Vere, Earl of Oxford, does not explain his exceptional contemporary reputation as a writer. In 1589, he was called one of the best courtier poets, and one of the best playwrights of comedies. North concluded that many of his works must have been anonymous, although his authorship of them was known to court insiders. In the early twentieth century, a simple English schoolmaster named J. Thomas Looney became skeptical of the traditional theory that the questionably educated Stratford merchant William Shakspere (that was how he usually spelled his name) wrote the canon. Remarkably, Looney created a sophisticated methodology for validating authorship attribution that has been imitated by scholars in other fields (Ostrowski, 2020), and that may be more reliable than the highly questionable computerized stylometry whose very obscurity has led to its being idealized. With his long list of characteristics of the author based on the literary works, Looney researched biographies of Elizabethan writers, and determined that there was a nearly perfect fit between the authorial "profile" he discerned in the plays and poems, and the biography of Edward de Vere, 17th Earl of Oxford (or "Oxford"). For example, it is generally assumed that Shakespeare, as a commoner himself, was primarily sympathetic with other commoners. But Looney, like many who have read Shakespeare closely and dispassionately, instead found a consistent pattern of sympathy with the aristocracy, along with contempt for commoners such as Jack Cade, leader of a rebellion of Kentish men in 1450.

The backlash against Looney, Bacon, and other authorship skeptics has been ferocious and relentless, and it suggests that the traditional theory has a deep psychological appeal, perhaps even an unconsciously religious quality. Ironically, traditional Shakespeare scholars have shown no interest in ascertaining the truth about this matter, as they instead direct their energies toward suppressing the authorship question, and slandering the motives of those who challenge their authority as the putative experts in this matter. The growth of the internet, however, has thwarted their efforts to enforce a taboo against the work of authorship dissidents.

This bizarre attack on academic freedom forces us to ponder what factors can limit our love of truth. Perhaps what we love more than objective truth is the psychic truth of a good narrative, that reflects what we *wish* were true, such as the beloved narrative of Shakspere's ascent from humble beginnings to lasting worldwide fame. And this preference echoes the original meaning of "truth" as "loyalty," going back to the word's oldest Germanic etymology. Unfortunately, being true to a false theory means betraying the facts. Unconsciously, traditional Shakespeare scholars engage in groupthink, starting with a premise they refuse to question, then reasoning circularly rather than objectively, and attacking rather than listening to anyone who offers contradictory evidence. One can sympathize with them in a way, since unless they succeed in branding authorship dissidents as cranks and crackpots, they will be forced to admit that their contention about who wrote Shakespeare is based more on tradition and authority than on solid evidence. Yes, such groupthink exists even in academia, which we often idealize, just as we idealize Shakespeare. We cannot hope to pursue the truth unless we are mindful of the workings of our unconscious resistances to it.

In a letter to Oskar Pfister, encouraging him to continue writing, Freud noted, "the truth often has to be said many times" (October 30, 1923). Freud also wrote, "Of the three powers which may dispute the basic position of science, religion alone is to be taken seriously as an enemy [art and philosophy are the other two] (1933a, p. 160). Freud was the world's first prominent intellectual to accept Looney's 1920 theory that Oxford, not Shakspere of Stratford, wrote Shakespeare's works. And Freud was attuned to the methodological challenges of investigating the truth in this matter—"Very strict scrutiny is necessary, and one must keep one's critical faculties alive; one must be ready to meet sharp criticism, and to work against one's own inclinations" (November 7, 1935 letter to Percy Allen; first published in Waugaman, 2017).

Was Freud's authority sufficient to persuade psychoanalysts that Oxford may have written Shakespeare? Hardly. This should reassure anyone who worries that analysts are sheepishly submissive in their attitude toward Freud. No, analysts have been the last to even give Freud's and Looney's theory a hearing. One respected psychoanalytic society invited me to speak on Shakespeare, until someone raised a red flag, and the invitation was then revised to indicate I could not address the authorship debate. Another time, a colleague who is expert about Shakespeare's works and I had both given presentations at an event. Afterwards, I overheard him reassure an attendee, "It doesn't make a bit of difference who wrote Shakespeare." So, the truth doesn't matter? Devotees of the traditional authorship theory can be at their most anti-intellectual when this issue arises. Contending that it's only the plays and the poems of Shakespeare that matter violates our understanding of psychic determinism as it illuminates creativity, and serves to rationalize a deep discomfort with questioning one's tenacious attachment to the traditional author.

Truth in Shakespeare

When we search Shakespeare's works for what he says about truth, we find the seeming tautology, "truth is truth" in one of his first plays, *Love's Labour's Lost* (IV.i.), where he also writes, enigmatically, "truer than truth itself" (IV.i.). He repeats "truth is truth" in *King John* (I.i.); in *Measure for Measure* (V.i.), he is still more emphatic—"Truth is truth to the end of reckoning." Ramon Jiménez writes, "Oxford was passionate about, if not obsessed with, the idea of truth, and used 'true' hundreds of times in his plays and sonnets, in at least nine different meanings. He also used it to form some twenty compound adjectives …" (2018, p. 16).

These quotations bring me back to the related words in my title, "Nothing is truer than truth." That phrase, also ostensibly redundant, is a rough English translation of Edward de Vere's Latin motto: "*Vero nihil verius.*" "Ver" referred to the French town the family originated from, before an ancestor who served under William the Conqueror relocated to

England in the eleventh century, where he was rewarded for his loyal military service. "*Vere*" and "*vero*" are also the Latin words for "truly," and Oxford's motto uses Shakespearean word play with the various meanings of his family name. The motto also implies "No one is more loyal than Vere."

As in psychoanalysis, we must distinguish between surface truths and deeper truths in Shakespeare. Arthur Melzer's book (2014), *Philosophy Between the Lines: The Lost History of Esoteric Writing*, encourages us to dig deeper in Shakespeare's texts to find his most controversial truths. Inspired by the work of Leo Strauss, Melzer "aims to re-establish a general recognition of the several reasons for the near-universal prevalence of *esoteric* writing among the major philosophical writers of the West prior to the nineteenth century" (p. 6; emphasis added). That is, some of the most profound thinkers—and Melzer joins Delia Bacon when he includes Shakespeare—were not free to write explicitly about their most controversial ideas, but had to disguise the truth under a conventional veneer. Giovanni Boccaccio, in his 1357 *Life of Dante*, said great poets write on two levels, so that their work "simultaneously challenges the intellect of the wise while it gives comfort to the minds of the simple" (cited in Melzer, location 460). Think of the contrast between court versus public performances of Oxford's plays. At court, the audience could read between the lines as Oxford spoofed powerful court figures, but these subversive attacks were concealed from the general public.

In 1605, Shakespeare's contemporary, Francis Bacon, called esoteric writing "enigmatical," in contrast with "disclosed" [or overt]. And none other than Nathaniel Hawthorne, in his introduction to the 1857 book by Delia Bacon, approvingly quoted her observation that "The great secret of the Elizabethan age [i.e., who wrote Shakespeare] ... was buried in the lowest depths of the deep Elizabethan Art ... in the inmost recesses of the *esoteric* Elizabethan learning" (Finnerty, 2006, p. 9; emphasis added).

In sharp contrast with our idealized images of a merry Elizabethan age, writers back then were jailed, tortured, and maimed for offending those in power. Curiously, in his *Richard II*, Shakespeare got away with staging the deposal of an English monarch. And Queen Elizabeth knew exactly what this meant, since she observed, "I am Richard II. Know ye not that?" Despite the prominence of concealment in Shakespeare's works, this deposal scene was undisguised. Holinshed's *Chronicle*, one of Shakespeare's top four literary sources, tells us that Richard III was an able warrior, who had one shoulder higher than the other. His skeleton, exhumed from under an English parking lot in 2012, confirms that he had some scoliotic, lateral curvature of the spine. What of the severely hunchbacked Richard III ("an envious mountain on my back," (*Henry VI*, III.ii) who treads the Shakespearean stage? Did he depict the truth about the historical Richard III's body? Of course not. Between the lines, though, it was a savage attack on the hunchbacked Robert Cecil, who succeeded his father, Lord Burghley, as Queen Elizabeth's principal adviser. Oxford was here using the disguise of an historical character to warn Queen Elizabeth that she should not trust the scheming, dishonest Robert Cecil, who happened to be the brother of Oxford's wife Anne. Yet the soliloquy that alludes to his hunchback also allows Richard to enlist our empathy for why he feels so cheated and vindictive, because of his disability, which makes him feel that "love forswore me in my mother's womb." Oxford captures our minds and hearts because he grasps and communicates complex truths.

What are the truths that lie beneath the "esoteric" surface of Shakespeare's works? Here, we must remind ourselves of the profound lesson that Hermann Rorschach taught us: An ambiguous stimulus predictably leads us to see things that are actually projections from our inner worlds. Unless we realize this, we are at risk of false certainty that what *we* see in Shakespeare's dramatic and poetic ink blots constitutes their sole underlying meaning. Shakespeare not only holds up a mirror to us in all his works, but he also holds up Rorschach cards, inviting us to say what we see in them. So we gaze at our own reflection in Shakespeare's works, confronting truths about ourselves that will often make us squirm. Yet, as Justin Frank has noted, "pursuit of truth is as necessary to the mind as food is to the body, and without it the psyche starves" (2018, p. 105).

Delia Bacon was probably correct that Shakespeare was writing a powerful critique of the corruption of the Elizabethan court, between the lines. Some of her nineteenth-century contemporaries, such as Walt Whitman, correctly perceived beneath the mask of the commoner-playwright a profound aristocratic sympathy, and therefore condemned Shakespeare as anti-democratic.

Shakespeare never spoon-feeds us. To find consoling truisms in his works is usually to misread him. Helen Vendler (1999) has observed that when a Shakespeare sonnet ends with a proverbial sounding couplet, it suggests that Shakespeare has despaired of finding a true solution to the problem described in the preceding three quatrains. Another example—tee shirts sometimes bear the popular Shakespeare quotation, "First, let's kill all the lawyers." Did Shakespeare truly advocate that? Or even joke about it? No, looking at the context shows that he was mocking the common rabble during a peasant's revolt. Conflating details from several past such revolts, he reminds us that overthrowing the established government risks anarchy. Further, like other nobles, Oxford had legal training, and peppers his works with legal terms and metaphors, always used correctly. We have created some fallacious "truths" about Shakespeare out of our compelling need to identify with him, and to claim him as one of us. Coming to terms with our fundamentally flawed idealization of Shakspere of Stratford is the first step toward discovering concealed truths about the pseudonymous works of Oxford, and about him.

Earlier, I quoted from *Measure for Measure*: "Truth is truth to the end of reckoning." As Paula Blank (2006) insightfully observes, this passage says a great deal about Shakespeare's attitude toward truth—and its measurement. Isabella is speaking. She has been horribly betrayed by the evil Angelo. It is in condemning Angelo that she says "Nay, it is ten times true, for truth is truth/To the end of reckoning" (V.i.45–46). Blank comments that Shakespeare's characters "generally maintain a belief in a truth that transcends ... the reckonings of men" (p. 39). Blank also explores Shakespeare's deep and sophisticated interest in law, noting that "The purpose of law, in fact, is to guarantee that a single truth will apply in all determinations of equality ... Shakespeare makes continual reference to the oath that Renaissance monarchs took at their coronation, to provide [equal justice], despite their personal allegiances" (p. 174). In *All's Well that Ends Well*, the buffoonish character Parolles (from the French word for "speech") lies pathologically, and shows that words can be a poor measure of truth. He is called a "linguist," meaning a persuasive speaker, who is skilled in persuading people of what is untrue.

Freud once said that Friedrich Nietzsche knew himself better than any man who ever lived (Waugaman, 1973). And it's true that Nietzsche anticipated Freud's insights into our capacity for self-deception with his famous aphorism, "I did that, says my Memory. No, I could not have done that, says my Pride. And Memory yields." However, with due respect to Nietzsche's brilliant self-awareness, Freud surely knew that it is actually Shakespeare who deserves that honor, with a seemingly superhuman capacity to face unwelcome truths about himself. Hamlet may be Oxford's most autobiographical character; he is viciously self-critical in his "O what a rogue and peasant slave am I!" soliloquy (II.ii).

Paradoxically, fiction is better suited than nonfiction to present some of life's most important truths. Perhaps because it can speak at once to both our conscious and unconscious selves. And because it is better designed to grasp and convey complexity. The truth is often multilayered, far more complex than we can easily describe explicitly. Shakespeare had a genius for communicating with our various conscious and unconscious self states, through both explicit language, and, perhaps more importantly, by activating networks of affectively charged implicit memories. He knew that language is most saliently *spoken* language. It wasn't just that most of his contemporaries were illiterate that led him to write plays. He used theater to communicate some of his most profound insights because hearing spoken language is far more effective than reading a text, so that multiple aspects of our identity and of our conflicts become activated in a way that allows for new insights and compromise formations. Because he understands us so well, we trust Shakespeare to help guide us in our search for truth, in all its stubborn complexity.

In one of his most enigmatic poems, "Let the bird of loudest lay" (Waugaman, 2014) Oxford wrote, as he was grieving the deaths of Queen Elizabeth and the Earl of Essex,

> Truth may seem but cannot be;
> Beauty brag but 'tis not she;
> Truth and beauty buried be.

Perhaps Oxford was hinting that the new political realities under King James, with Robert Cecil victorious in a power struggle, only allowed Oxford to tell the truth between the lines.

J. Earle (1881) offers profound insights into truth in Shakespeare's works in his 1881 essay "The History of the Word 'Mind'." One way he underlined Shakespeare's understanding of the complexity of the human mind was by counting the number of different words and phrases that one of Shakespeare's French translators had to use for "mind": six major ones, as well as some twenty others, less frequently. Earle concludes that the word "serves on all occasions to express anything whatever that is of the inner sphere of human nature" (p. 319). This reflected a shift away from an earlier era, when "soul" was of paramount interest. "[W]e may say that the

Soul's approach was by the way of the Good, and that there had risen up in humanity a fresh demand that the whole province of Thought should be newly explored by way of the *True*" (p. 320; emphasis added). The emphasis of Renaissance humanism on the individual as a central concern required a fresh examination of human capacities and limitations in ascertaining what is true, independently of faith.

Sky Gilbert in his 2020 book posits that Oxford was medieval in some of his worldview, which celebrated the polysemous potential of poetry to communicate complex human truths that are poorly suited to the more strictly denotative language that emerged from an incipient scientific worldview by the early seventeenth century. Similarly, Gilbert notes that Shakespeare celebrates paradox, because it helps us get at complex truths that are difficult to capture in words. Gilbert believes that the literary worldview was shifting in Shakespeare's day to one that was strongly influenced by scientific views of objective truth that are less helpful in understanding the truths of our inner experiences.

All's Well that Ends Well

Truth and deception are a theme that permeates *All's Well that Ends Well* [*AWEW*]. "Truth" is used much more often here than in any other Shakespeare play, exceeded only by how often it occurs in the Sonnets. In this play, Bertram has a striking blind spot for the dishonesty of his companion, Parolles. One of the most hilarious scenes in the play is when other characters trick Parolles into thinking he has been captured by the enemy. Under threat of torture, he badly betrays Bertram—he is anything but true in its original meaning of loyal. His exposure as a fraud is a moment of supreme shame, but Parolles's reaction is remarkable. He has an instantaneous character change, as he drops his false façade and faces the truth about himself:

> Yet am I thankful: if my heart were great,
> 'Twould burst at this ...
> ... simply the thing I am
> Shall make me live. Who knows himself a braggart,
> Let him fear this, for it will come to pass
> That every braggart shall be found an ass. (IV.iii)

Similarly, the entire plot of the play turns around the exposure of Bertram as a shallow snob, unable to recognize the value of his new wife Helena, merely because she is beneath him in social rank. After Helena miraculously cures the King of a fatal illness, he rewards her by allowing her to choose Bertram as her husband. But Bertram objects:

> A poor physician's daughter my wife! Disdain
> Rather corrupt me ever! (II.iii)
> Somewhat unconvincingly, Bertram's final words in the play are
> "I'll love her dearly, ever, ever dearly." (V.iii)

Helena herself practices deception repeatedly, in the course of exposing Bertram's dishonesty. She tricks her estranged husband, Bertram, into impregnating her, through the famous "bed trick," when he assumes he is sleeping with Diana, a Florentine who, in cahoots with Helena, arouses his lust. Helena also tricks most of the characters in the play into thinking she is dead, so that when she reveals herself to be alive at the play's end, it recalls the resurrection of Jesus. Such a parallel with Jesus (and with the Virgin Mary?) was earlier hinted at by her miraculous healing of the King. It leads the awe-struck courtier Lafeu to exclaim, "They say miracles are past" (II.iii), as he then rejects rational explanations for such events, speaking instead of "heavenly effect in an earthly actor," and "the very hand of heaven." Since Shakespeare alludes to the Bible constantly, a biblically literate audience might think of Jesus saying "Ye shall know the truth, and the truth shall make you free" (John 8:32) and "I am the way, the truth, and the life" (John 14:6; John's word for truth is αλήθεις from λήθεις, the root of *lethe*, implying that truth is freedom from forgetfulness, or oblivion). Just as "truth" appears more often in *AWEW* than in other Shakespeare plays, that word appears in the Gospel of John far more often than in the rest of the New Testament.

The theme of truth in Shakespeare is linked with his deep interest in all forms of deceit that hide the truth. Literal and figurative masks are common in his works. Shakespeare's plays often warn Queen Elizabeth to beware of courtiers who flatter her, since there is usually self-serving duplicity in flattery. The plot of *AWEW* involves multiple instances of lies and deception. It is a detailed study of the use of words to evade the truth.

AWEW offers some fascinating insights into truth. Note the implication that song lyrics are one way to reveal the truth, in the first two uses of the word in the play:

> *Countess* Wilt thou ever be a foul-mouthed and calumnious knave?
> *Fool* A prophet I, madam, and I speak the *truth* the next way:
> (*he sings*) For I the ballad will repeat
> Which men full *true* will find:
> Your marriage comes by destiny;
> Your cuckoo sings by kind. (I.iii)

In the Elizabethan era, ballads were often written and sung to share noteworthy news. The cuckoo was so named because of the repetitive mating call of the male. The *OED* credits Shakespeare with coining "cuckoo-bird," and also "cuckoo-spell" for his English version of an obscure term of rhetoric (epizeuxis, meaning the immediate repetition of a word or phrase). The fool implies that it is natural sexual instincts ("kind") that lead the cuckoo to seek a mate.

Freud famously wrote that "that no mortal can keep a secret. If his lips are silent, he chatters with his finger-tips; betrayal oozes out of him at every pore" ("Dora," 1905e, p. 78). Shakespeare was also fascinated with the way our faces, specifically, can give us away. The Countess asks Helena if she loves Bertram, but then quickly adds, "Therefore tell me *true*/But tell me then 'tis so, for, look, thy [blushing] cheeks/Confess it th' one to th' other, and thine eyes/See it so grossly shown in their behaviours/That in their kind they speak it" (I.iii.; emphasis added).

AWEW has been called "perhaps the most problematic of [Shakespeare's] so-called 'problem plays,'" principally because it "lacks unity" (Calderwood, 1963, p. 61). Critics have overlooked the role of autobiography in the play, with their false assumption about who wrote it. The Oxfordian authorship hypothesis clarifies many enigmatic aspects of the plot—especially plot elements Oxford added from the play's source in Boccaccio's *Decameron*. It is one of Oxford's confessional plays that make amends for Oxford's horrible mistreatment of his first wife, Anne Cecil (as do *Othello* and *A Winter's Tale*). They had grown up together, since Oxford was the ward of Anne's father—just as Bertram is the ward of the King of France, and Helena is the ward of Bertram's mother, the Countess of Rousillon. Helena says to the Countess, "Would … that my lord your son were not [equivalent to] my brother" (I.3.161–162). Just after marrying Helena, Bertram deserts her to go from France to the war between Florence and Siena. Soon after impregnating Anne, Oxford abandoned her for fourteen months, spending most of that time in Italy. The play's marriage is unlike other marriages in Shakespeare, in that it is not between social equals, just as Anne was Oxford's social inferior in class-conscious Elizabethan England.

Oxford's bisexuality receives some possible "slanted" allusions in the play. Bertram's dishonest servant Parolles twice calls him "sweet heart." Oxford's servant Rowland Yorke may have had a sexual relationship with Oxford, and may have, Iago-like, convinced Oxford that his wife, Anne, was pregnant by another man. Like Parolles, he was a traitor, betraying knowledge about English military positions to the Spanish (Anderson, 2005, p. 115).

This somewhat neglected play was among the eighteen plays that were not published until 1623, seven years after the death of the traditional author (and no one ever claims *he* must have written plays after he died, which is one of the standard slanders against the authorship claims of Oxford). No one has successfully explained why half the plays were withheld from publication until such a late date. Since Oxford's son-in-law was one of the dedicatees of the 1623 *First Folio*, it's likely that Oxford's daughter had the manuscripts of his unpublished plays. One theory is that the political implications of those eighteen plays were too inflammatory for their earlier publication. Or that they revealed too much about their hidden author.

When was the play written? Anne Barton believes it was written around 1602. That was two years before Oxford's death. It was also a year before the end of Queen Elizabeth's life, a time when she was deeply depressed. Belatedly confirming Delia Bacon's groundbreaking thesis, scholars now increasingly recognize that Shakespeare wrote primarily for court performance, and only secondarily for the general public (Dutton, 2016; Lake, 2016). This new perspective encourages us to look between the lines of his plays for controversial truths he intended for the ears of the Queen and her courtiers. It is always illuminating to recall that the Queen was the most salient spectator of Oxford's plays, so he always wrote them with her in mind. She was often compared by poets with the goddess Diana; the character Diana in this play may allude to her. The psychoanalyst, Marvin Krims, has written eloquently, from personal experience, of how therapeutic it can be to watch Shakespeare's plays. I believe Oxford, once one of the Queen's favorite courtiers, knew he could lift her spirits with his theatrical entertainments, performed at court for her, especially when he self-deprecatingly satirized his own many notorious flaws. He helped her escape her present cares by transporting her into the 1570s, when Oxford married Anne, then escaped her by living in Italy for a year.

Ramon Jiménez, among other scholars, has documented that Shakespeare's plays were revisions of earlier, anonymous sources that were also written by Oxford. In 1579, a now lost play was staged at court that may have been an earlier version of *AWEW*. It was called *The Rape of the Second Helen*, alluding to Helen of Troy (in *AWEW*, the names Helen and Helena are used interchangeably for the same character). Bertram resolves never to have sex with Helena, so he can later have their marriage annulled. The crucial plot element of the bed trick, where Bertram has sex with and impregnates Helena, thinking she is Diana, not only has many sources in folklore and literature, including *Decameron*, but it also has an autobiographical source. The Essex antiquarian Thomas Wright wrote in 1836 that Anne's father, Lord Burghley, arranged to have Oxford sleep with Anne, while Oxford believed he was having sex with another woman. The bed trick recurs in three other Shakespeare plays. Since Burghley was mercilessly spoofed as Polonius in *Hamlet*, it seems likely that *Hamlet* was written before Burghley's 1598 death. Oxford seemed to make penance toward those he had wronged, following their deaths, and I suspect the addition of the "good old counsellor Lafew" (Garber, 2004, p. 622) to Boccaccio's tale served as a fonder, reparative depiction of Burghley in *AWEW*.

Scholars agree that Shakespeare borrowed plot elements for *AWEW* from Boccaccio's *Decameron*. That work, set in 1348 Florence at the height of their devastating plague, has special relevance for our Covid-19 pandemic. Shakespeare's true connection with Boccaccio is even stronger, since evidence strongly suggests Oxford wrote not only Shakespeare's works, but also the first full English translation of *Decameron*, appearing anonymously in 1620 (Waugaman, in press). Isaac Jaggard published it in two lavishly illustrated large folio volumes, three years before Jaggard also published the famous *First Folio* of Shakespeare's plays. Both works were dedicated to Oxford's son-in-law, the Earl of Montgomery, whose wife Susan may have owned her father's unpublished manuscript of the Boccaccio translation, as well as of the eighteen plays first published in 1623.

Close reading of the 1620 *Decameron* translation shows many phrases that appear in the works of Shakespeare. For example, "There shall we hear the sweet birds sing." This image is unusual for its era, but Shakespeare wrote "where late the sweet birds sang" in Sonnet 73, as well as closely similar phrases in *The Winter's Tale* and *The Rape of Lucrece*. The Ghost in *Hamlet* tells Hamlet, "I could a tale unfold whose lightest word/Would harrow up thy soul … *And [make] each particular hair to stand on end/Like quills upon the fretful porcupine*" (I.v). That vivid trope for terror is apparently used nowhere else except in this phrase in the English version of *Decameron*: "*his hair stood upright like porcupine's quills.*" The *Oxford English Dictionary* cites Shakespeare as the first writer to use "over-plus" to mean excess libido, in Sonnet 135. The 1620 translation uses the phrase in just the same way.

Marjorie Garber makes the intriguing observation that *AWEW* alludes to its own title more often than do Shakespeare's other plays. She speculates that this suggests "a certain self-consciousness about its identity as a fiction" (p. 619), perhaps to disguise to the wider public its allusion to so many embarrassing events in Oxford's life. Garber sometimes hints that she has doubts about the authorship of Shakespeare's works, but she stops short of admitting that explicitly. She shows a deep interest in psychoanalysis, so Freud's authorship opinion likely influenced her. Garber cites G. K. Hunter's observation that the play "begin[s] with plans for the education of a *brash* young courtier … and address[es] the question of stepparents" (p. 619; emphasis added). We still have the daily schedule of tutorials that Oxford's "step-father" (that is, guardian) Burghley assigned for young Oxford's education, starting at twelve. And "brash" is an understatement for Oxford's notoriously impulsive behavior. He killed a servant with his rapier at seventeen. A contemporary wrote that "his perverse sense of humor was a source of grave embarrassment" to Lord Burghley (think Polonius in *Hamlet*). He repeatedly defied the hot-tempered Queen Elizabeth as her most wayward courtier until she eventually banished him from court for two years.

Garber unwittingly names another autobiographical theme when she notes that there was "a quasi-incestuous relationship" (p. 625) between Bertram and Helena, since they grew up in the same household—that of Bertram's mother, the Countess of Roussillon. When Bertram's father dies, he succeeds him as Count, and leaves his mother, going to live at the court of the King, as a royal ward. When Oxford was twelve, his father died, leaving his son as the 17th Earl of Oxford. Queen Elizabeth then ordered him to leave his mother's home and become the Queen's first royal ward, assigned to be raised in the home of William Cecil (cf. the "old and loyal lord and counsellor," Lafew in *AWEW*). In *AWEW*, Bertram initially balks at the King's order to marry Helena, after the King promised to grant anything she wished for healing his near fatal illness. Bertram arrogantly complains that Helena is far beneath him in social rank. The King replies, "'Tis only title thou disdain'st in her, the which/I can build up … If thou canst like this creature as a maid,/I can create the rest." Similarly, fifteen-year-old Anne Cecil's marriage to the twenty-one-year-old Oxford, like that of Bertram to Helena, was "quasi-incestuous" (Garber, 2004, p. 625). Anne was far beneath Oxford in social rank. So Queen Elizabeth elevated Anne's father to Lord Burghley shortly before Anne married Oxford—a match ordered by Anne's father. And this detail of the King offering to raise Helena to a higher rank is not in Boccaccio's story of Bertrand and Gillette (she is named Juliet in Oxford's 1620 translation). Further, like Helena, Anne was known to be a successful healer, a skill she learned from her mother, a highly scholarly woman (in *AWEW*, Helena learned to heal from her physician father)—"the noble Countess of Oxford most charitably … did many great and notable cures upon her poor neighbours" (from notes of Sir William Pickering, 1516–1575).

The ninth story of the third day in Boccaccio's *Decameron* is well known to be the primary literary source for *AWEW*. In the first complete English translation, Oxford emphasizes a parallel with his own life. The Italian version[26] said "*morto il conte e lui nelle mani*

[26] The version I used is Boccaccio, 1966.

del re lasciato ..." ("once the Count [his father] died, he was left in the hands of the King"]. But Oxford translates this as "Old Count Isnard dying, young Bertrand fell as a *Ward* to the King ..." (emphasis added), just as Oxford became the first royal ward in Elizabeth's new wardship system at age twelve, after the death of his father, the 16th Earl ("Conte" in Italian). Later in the story, the Italian version has the King say to Bertrand, "*Beltramo, voi siete omai grande e fornito*" ("Beltramo, you are henceforth great and provided"). Once again, Oxford's English translation introduces a key autobiographical word: "Noble Count, it is not unknown to us, that you are a Gentleman of great honour, and it is our royal pleasure, to discharge your *wardship*" (emphasis added; only instance of "discharge your wardship" in the database Early English Books Online). It is likely that Oxford thus drew attention to a pivotal parallel with his life not only because he identified with Bertrand, but because he wished that at least some readers of his translation would recognize this parallel with his life. It would lead readers to understand, further, that Oxford identified with Bertrand's unwillingness to marry the woman he was ordered to marry.

As I mentioned earlier, Oxford sometimes used his plays to expiate his guilt toward those he had wronged—following their deaths. One disguised truth in *AWEW* is the playwright's confession of his culpability in ruining his marriage to Anne with his arrogance about his social superiority to her, with his abandonment of her when she was pregnant with their first child, and with his pathological jealousy of her. Like Leontes's wife Hermione in *The Winter's Tale*, Bertram's wife Helena appears to be resurrected from the dead at the play's end. This is probably the playwright's wishful fantasy, and helps explain some of the blatant disconnects from reality in the play, as Anne Barton perceptively notes. She comments on several parallels with *Hamlet*, which is probably Oxford's most autobiographical play.

Like Hamlet, Bertram lost a father who is portrayed as an ideal, a paragon of virtue. Bertram is an obnoxious snob, while his father is described as more of an egalitarian. Oxford, after losing his father at twelve, may have idealized him. Bertram becomes the ward of the King of France, as Oxford became the ward of William Cecil (later elevated to Lord Burghley) at twelve. There's a subtle allusion to Burghley in the mention of one Corambus in *AWEW*. Like Corambis, the earlier name of Polonius in the first quarto of *Hamlet*, this name satirizes Burghley's motto "*Cor unum, via una*" (one heart, one way) in a word that implies "double-hearted," or duplicitous. Shakespeare often doubles plot elements, for emphasis and for creating complexity. Here, the theme of wardship is doubled, since Helena is herself the ward of Bertram's mother, the Countess of Roussillon.

It is always surprising when otherwise discerning people who love Shakespeare's works claim that the truth about who wrote them does not matter in the least. Unconsciously, they may be expressing their quasi-religious attitude, with the canon being like holy scriptures, whose human authorship is regarded as irrelevant. When people truly love Shakespeare, I am amazed that they do not share my excitement about expanding the range of his possible authorship to several other Elizabethan works (see Waugaman, 2007, 2008, 2010, 2013, 2015, 2016, 2018, in press). Oxford understood our conflicting feelings when searching for the truth—about ourselves and about others. His empathy was extraordinary. Occasionally, he overwhelms us with the truth, but mostly he tells it "slant" enough to make it nearly bearable.

The Emily Dickinson poem whose first line is "Tell all the Truth but tell it slant" ends,

> The Truth must dazzle gradually
> Or every man be blind.

CHAPTER SIX

Explorations into truth, anxiety, and death by Heidegger and Freud

Michael Shoshani, Batya Shoshani, and Naama Shoshani-Breda

In what follows, we have attempted to formulate certain lines of thinking which we find worthy of further development in order to broaden the lens through which we observe our patients in general and individuals with perverse organizations in particular—both in order to better understand them and in order to be more able to accept them. We are inviting our readers to join this project, as we believe many hearts and minds are required for completing this task.

Psychoanalysis and philosophy

Much has been said about the complex relationship between psychoanalysis and philosophy. The intricate affinity between these two disciplines is intuitively apparent to us and many others, especially when one realizes that the problems that frequently arise in psychoanalysis are not far removed from the core concerns of Continental philosophy. Psychoanalysis grapples with problems surrounding consciousness, freedom, anxiety, death, meaning, language, self-and-other, and self-worth. Similarly, Continental philosophy explores such matters as consciousness, thought, experience, anxiety, memory, justice, language, the "Other," etc. Philosophical investigation centers on epistemology and the individual's *conscious parts* and relies on *reason and logic*. Psychoanalysis, however, is preoccupied with *unconscious motivations*. Still, both disciplines relate to the individual's emotional experience, each through its unique prism. Thus, many prominent psychoanalytic theorists draw their representations and ideas from Continental philosophers. Freud himself was greatly aided in consolidating his ideas by the philosophies of Plato, Sophocles, Aristotle, Kant, Schopenhauer, and Nietzsche.[27]

Since their inception, both philosophy and psychoanalysis have sought to present a complete and comprehensive portrayal of the human being and his world, by defining a host of eternal and absolute truths about man. The psychoanalyst and philosopher Roger Money-Kyrle (1952, 1968) argued that the classical philosophers could not have been philosophers of "life" since, absorbed as they were with the ideal of a primary philosophy, they aspired to formulate general and all-inclusive approaches so that anything not included therein could not be regarded as "philosophy." They attempted to base their approach on consistent, coherent, and minimalistic principles so that each part would fit in with all the others: Any argument regarding epistemology had to be in harmony with statements made about ethics and so forth. According to Money-Kyrle, this limitation led to a warping of various aspects of these philosophies so that the gap between philosophical thinking and life eventually became a gaping chasm. He argued that the confrontation between philosophers and psychoanalysts in the first half of the twentieth century proceeded along the following lines: Philosophers ridiculed and criticized psychoanalysts for their *blatant carelessness in handling concepts, explanations, and contradictory definitions.* Psychoanalysts, on the other hand, *ridiculed philosophers*, particularly the classical philosophers who, they claimed, were *textbook examples of obsessive-compulsive disorder (OCD).*

A further fundamental difference between philosophy and psychoanalysis is the claim that even though both disciplines are preoccupied with similar and, at times, identical questions about the world and the individual, philosophy attempts to interpret these in theoretical and general terms, whereas psychoanalysis tackles them from a practical and individualistic perspective. This distinction was epitomised by Bion, in noting that the fundamental questions discussed by philosophers in theory confront psychoanalysts in practice in their consulting rooms (Bion, 1962a). Indeed, psychoanalysis intertwines the practical and the theoretical and its central interest is in the living individual and his or her psychic experience, in human nature and its drives, in particular unconscious ones. Theory monitors practice and is consequently altered. Thus, in our view, in contrast to most philosophical approaches, psychoanalysis' epistemic, ontological, and ethical insights into human life have an impact on people's actual lives, as do its concepts of what constitutes truth and reality.[28]

From the middle of the nineteenth century onwards, Western classical philosophy's altar of reason began to crack and novel revolutionary ideas started to permeate. Thinkers began to realize that the rational compulsion to find theoretical correspondence, consistency, and connection in relation to human existence, notwithstanding their substantive inner

---

[27] For example, in developing fundamental concepts that describe psychic dynamics, he adopted two key allegories from Plato: that of the cave and that of the chariot.

[28] Nietzsche thought that the origin of this gap between philosophy and life could be traced back to Plato and even berated him for reversing the correct hierarchy by contending that the world of ideas was more representative of reality than the physical world and life itself.

contradictions, misses the objective and even distorts it. From there, philosophy and especially Continental philosophy turned its attention to dealing directly and immediately with reality, the physical world, life, and the individual in all his complexity and irrationality. The roots of this trend during the nineteenth century lie in the thinking of Kierkegaard, Husserl, and Nietzsche, who were followed in the twentieth century by Sartre, Marx, and, of course, Heidegger (Mills, 1997). This trend facilitated a greater proximity between philosophy and psychoanalysis so that, today, one can see the seeds of a more productive dialogue than that made possible in the past.

In this chapter, despite and perhaps precisely because of the abovementioned gaps between philosophy and psychoanalysis—and their eventual and gradual rapprochement—our focus will be on exploring ways in which psychoanalysts can draw on philosophical inquiries for inspiration and for greater understanding. Within this overarching investigation of the multitude of issues that one can address in the context of the potential affinity between philosophy and psychoanalysis, we have chosen to focus on the subject of truth and authenticity, as well as to explore its relation to two additional but integrally connected themes—anxiety (*Angst*) and death. These subjects are prominent in the experiences of patients with perverse organizations and other difficult patients, and are thus highly pertinent to understanding their psychic-existential distress, as portrayed throughout this book. We will focus on the way these subjects are illuminated by Freud and Heidegger.

Freud is a natural choice for this comparison, seeing as his thinking serves as the theoretical and clinical foundations for the entire edifice of psychoanalysis, including its contemporary developments. As for Heidegger, our choice is a more intricate and a more personal one. In a previous work (Shoshani & Shoshani, 2013) we depicted resorting to the writings of Argentinian author Jorge Luis Borges in order to better understand the patient we called "the bottle man." In this exploration, we were struck by a sentence from Borges: "I have spent most of my life puzzling over time, the problem of time and, of course, my own identity. At least they go together, because I feel that time is the stuff that I'm made of" (Borges, 1960, p. 8). Our attempt to delve deeper into this fascinating idea, which resonated for us the experiences of this and other patients, has eventually led us to encounter Heidegger's monumental book, *Being and Time* (1927). Despite the almost insurmountable difficultly of tackling Heidegger's language and his enigmatic thinking, we felt that his doctrine held ideas that have the potential to illuminate and enliven various aspects and layers in the psyches of difficult and perverse patients in ways that may broaden our ability to understand and accept them—to enrich our toolbox, our emerging associations, and our ways of understanding them.

Approaching truth through falsehood

In the final lines of Tolstoy's *The Death of Ivan Ilyich* (1886), the protagonist comes to the realization that his entire life, including his relationships with his wife and children, had been a falsehood. He felt that the only sliver of truth in his whole false existence had been the devotion and integrity of the simple servant who cared for and comforted him in his final months, the only person to tell him of his imminent death. The narrator ends the story by saying that Ivan had succeeded, for the first time in his life, in seeing the truth and so regained his life and, in a sense, succeeded in living for the first time.

In such poetic language, Tolstoy touches upon one of the foundation stones and driving forces of both philosophy and psychoanalysis: the search for truth. In effect, he expresses a profound insight into what one can term "the therapeutic power of truth." There have been numerous philosophical attempts to formulate various aspects of this notion, including Plato's allegory of the cave. This allegory exemplifies the importance and centrality of truth for the individual, alongside an understanding of the difficulty in tolerating and knowing it (*The Republic*, *c.*381 BCE, 514a–520a). Similarly, in Nietzsche's view (1873), the man of truth will inevitably reach the realization that he has been lying throughout his life. Heidegger expressed it thus: "For humans a home for dwelling is the truth of being" (1947, in Pimentel, 2018, p. 6). According to Freud, bearing the truth in all its nakedness represents the peak of control.

The many theories of truth illustrate its complexity, its multiple faces, and its elusiveness. Among the prominent approaches in defining the concept of truth are the "correspondence," "coherence," and "pragmatic" approaches. According to the correspondence theory of truth, an assertion is true if there is correspondence between it and a given reality. This theory is based on the metaphysical assumption of existence and presence. The assumption that some objective reality exists independently of consciousness is also the source of certain reservations about the validity of the correspondence theory. For example, how is one to know and prove that such a reality indeed exists, if all our knowledge and experience are transmitted to us via consciousness? The coherence theory of truth originates in the analytic tradition in philosophy. This theory posits that a truth is a justified belief based on logical coherence, a methodological approach, axioms and clear definitions, and the avoidance of contradictions. Third, the pragmatic theory of truth focuses on the extent to which an individual's belief can be said to be "useful" to him. Thus, a belief is true so long as it advances the desired outcome. The latter two theories can also be challenged: the fact that a claim is based on logical coherence or that it has certain benefits offers no guarantee that it is true. There is no way of knowing the extent to which a *coherent* claim matches reality, whilst a pragmatic assertion may have led to the desired result merely by good fortune (Mills, 2014).

In psychoanalysis, the concept of "truth" has no formal definition. However, even without such a definition, the question of "truth" is the formative basis of every psychoanalytic idea. As philosopher and psychoanalyst Charles Hanley described it so well: "The concept of truth is the 'cornerstone' of every theoretical or clinical approach in psychoanalysis" (Mills, 2014, p. 271). Were we to investigate the various psychoanalytic approaches, we would discover that they rely on definitions of truth offered by various schools of philosophy. Psychoanalytic approaches that rely on the correspondence theory strive to attain the patient's remembrances (the case of Freud's patient, Dora, for example) or, in other words, to gain access to the patient's truth, which he has forgotten and repressed ("truth" here being a specific content that corresponds to events that occurred in objective reality). Approaches that rely on "emotional" pragmatism regard truth as dependent on context and as coconstructed by therapist and patient. Accordingly, the critiques leveled against these approaches are, in fact, aimed at the underlying assumptions they harbor about truth, cautioning against the relativistic postmodern worldview they explicitly or implicitly support. According to such critics, such relativism regarding truth negates and nullifies the concept and thus "throws out the baby with the bathwater."

Because we find the elusiveness and controversiality of the concept of truth in both philosophy and psychoanalysis fascinating and believe it is a potential basis for a fertile encounter between the two disciplines, we have chosen to examine the perception of truth in psychoanalysis—umbilically tied as it is to the Freudian concept of the unconscious—and pit it against Heidegger's concept of truth. Since anxiety is a central emotion in an individual's experience and existence, in what follows we will want to see how each of the thinkers analyzes and interprets anxiety as a fundamental of existence. We will then examine the link between anxiety and knowing the truth according to both thinkers.

Freud and Heidegger—from critique to common grounds

In the Europe of the 1930s and 1940s, Freudian psychoanalysis was dominant as the main intellectual influence of the period. Everyone was captivated by the novel theory that offered an interpretation of various aspects of human existence that had hitherto remained elusive and concealed. German philosopher Martin Heidegger (1889–1976) did not join the chorus of praise and even frequently criticized Freudian psychoanalysis. The peak of Heidegger's critique was reached in the ongoing seminars he gave in the Swiss town of Zollikon (1959–1969) before an audience of philosophers and psychoanalysts. These seminars have encouraged us to investigate the basic ideas of the two theoreticians—Freud, the father of psychoanalysis, and Heidegger, the founder of the ontological-existentialist approach in philosophy—and the possibility of a dialogue between them.

It is important to note that we approach Heidegger's writings with a considerable feeling of abhorrence given his political involvement in the Nazi regime. And yet, as we turned the pages of Heidegger's work, we came to realize that in addition to the disgust we felt for his support of Nazism, Heidegger's philosophy was of unparalleled importance,[29] as described by Jean Francois Lyotard: "The greatest thought can lend itself, as such, to the greatest horror" (1990, p. 57). Immediately after World War II, Heidegger was questioned about his political activities and his membership of the Nazi Party by the Denazification Committee.[30]

---

[29] It is important to point out that Heidegger "joined the Nazi party because of its opposition to western culture [...] He saw modernity as an historical expression of the forgetfulness of Being and so supported Nazism—which opposed modernity" (Pimentel, 2018, p. 74). Heidegger believed that only the German nation could overcome this forgetfulness of being.

[30] The Denazification Committee asked the German philosopher Karl Jaspers for his evaluation of the danger involved in permitting Heidegger to return to teaching students. Jaspers was both very clear in his appreciation of Heidegger's philosophical work and in his assertion that Heidegger should not resume his teaching career as of yet and recommended to suspend him from teaching for several years.

As a result, he suffered a mental breakdown and was hospitalized for a few months in a Swiss psychiatric hospital. There, he also underwent psychoanalysis with Emil Von Gebsattel (Askay & Farquhar, 2011) and became personally acquainted with the practice of Freudian psychoanalysis, of which he had been so critical. In the hospital, Heidegger also met the psychiatrist Medard Boss who, in time, became his close friend and the initiator of the Zollikon seminars (Heidegger, 1987). Boss had been a patient of Freud's in 1925 and even treated some of his patients through psychoanalysis. Boss is thus a kind of link between Freudian psychoanalysis and Heidegger's existential ontology, both through his personal biography and through his theory of *Daseinsanalysis*.[31]

Freud's approach to truth

> *My whole make-up is intuitive, and that in setting out to establish the purely empirical science of PA, I subjected myself to an extraordinary discipline.*
>
> —From a letter written by Freud to Jung, December 17, 1911 (McGuire, 1974, p. 650)

As a loyal supporter of the scientific method, Freud determined that the object of the psychoanalytic investigation is the individual psyche and that this scientific, objective, and empirical investigation aims at uncovering the person's truth. Contrary to his attraction to the rational, in the spirit of the Enlightenment, Freud was also influenced by contrary ideas such as ancient Greek philosophy and the German Romantics. Ancient Greek philosophy, as represented by Socrates, Plato, and Aristotle, highlighted the centrality of the person's drives, instincts, inner contradictions, and the irrational internal forces. Similarly, German Romanticism, whose representatives include Fichte, Schelling, Schiller, and Goethe, identified the limitations of reason and opposed the exclusivity of its rule. Instead, they gave center stage to the person's complex and unconscious psychic events. This opposition to the regime of reason and such focus on instincts, urges, and unconscious desires represents a central axis in the thinking of Nietzsche and Schopenhauer who, in turn, greatly influenced Freud's psychoanalytic theory and his perception of truth. Indeed, one can find many contradictions and tensions between Freud's loyalty to objective and positivist science and his focus on the subjective experience and the unconscious in their various shades of irrationality. Accordingly, Freud alternated between relating to the individual as a scientific object and as a hermeneutic creation (Ricœur, 1970). One solution to this contradiction is the proposed distinction between Freud's meta-psychological theories, which are grounded in scientific principles, and his clinical technique, which he formulated for the purpose of psychoanalytic treatment (Boss, 1963).

---

[31] According to Mitchell, Hans Loewald was influenced by Heidegger's ontological existentialism and incorporated some of the ideas of *Daseinsanalysis* in his thinking, as one can see in Loewald's writings (personal communication, 1999).

Nevertheless, from the outset, Freud placed the concept of truth at the very center of his psychoanalytic theory, as a necessary and constitutive condition in his thinking and practice. This can be seen in the first and most important fundamental rule of psychoanalytic treatment, which demands that the patient be absolutely genuine and honest with himself and the analyst. This centrality is reinforced by Freud's determination, later on, that the origin of neuroses and symptoms is *repressed truth* and that treatment, therefore, must focus on exposing this truth. Thus, Freud deals mainly with psychic truth, which is located in the unconscious.

Freud defines the unconscious as the force that initiates, activates, and leads the individual as well as the psychic faculty housing the greatest and most genuine accretion of human knowledge (of which consciousness is merely the tip of the iceberg). This psychic layer houses memories and emotional contents that have been repressed and become "nonexistent" as far as the individual is concerned, alongside innate phylogenetic preconceptions. Psychoanalytic investigation is thereby directed at probing into the unconscious in search of the patient's truth, as is evident from *Studies on Hysteria* (Freud & Breuer, 1895d). In contrast with scientific or philosophical knowledge, which is objective, universal, and absolute, the kind of knowledge psychoanalysis is concerned with is therefore experiential, subjective, individualistic, and dynamic.

While the purpose of psychoanalysis is to discover such truths about ourselves, it is not clear what "truth" is and in what way we can "know" for certain that something is true (Greenberg, 2016). There is scarce explicit reference to these questions in Freudian theory, as Freud seems to have relied on a rather vague and ambiguous concept of truth. In his final years, Freud's early emphasis on the remembrance of actual contents also began gravitating toward a notion of truth as a construction:

> Quite often we do not succeed in bringing the patient to recollect what has been repressed. Instead of that, if the analysis is carried out correctly, we produce in him an assured conviction of the truth of the construction which achieves the same therapeutic result as a recaptured memory. (Freud, 1937d, pp. 265–266)

To this very day, there is still an animated debate among thinkers from various psychoanalytic schools about the tension between emphasizing truth as a simple and direct recollection of repressed contents and focusing on the process of discovering the truth as facilitating the formulation of a past psychic event (that for some reason could not be registered at the time) as an experience. The latter approach represents a transition from dealing with repression and resistance to dealing with ways and tools that facilitate knowing, such as symbolization, mentalization, dreaming, creativity, etc. Accordingly, the aim of psychoanalytic therapy changed from discovering the patient's "lost" truth (i.e., that which they do not allow themselves to know), to developing the patient's capacity for knowing. Blass warns against the contemporary trend which she sees as liable to lead to relativism and an abandonment of the search for truth. Nevertheless, Blass (2016) agrees that the task of therapy is to establish an openness to truth: "What is ultimately sought in analysis is *openness to truth*, a capacity to know, rather than the knowledge of this or that truth. However, I see this as a stance that has always lain at the very foundation of psychoanalysis, not as a new perspective" (p. 306).[32]

Finally, Blass argues that, for Freud, the individual finds himself in a constant inner conflict in relation to truth: "The capacity to know, like the truths to be known, are given, available to the individual but in a conflicted way. The patient is driven to know but also does not want to know" (2016, p. 314). We believe that such a reading of Freud opens up a possibility of identifying similarities between Freud and Heidegger around the concept of truth. Let us then present the concept of truth in Heidegger's thinking and his basic philosophical tenets.

Heidegger—a brief introduction

> *I am not a substantial subject or thing. I have no permanent essence that constitutes my core nature [...] I am merely a way of existing [...] a "happening" in the process of realizing itself.*
>
> —Askay & Farquhar, 2011, p. 16

Heidegger's first book, *Being and Time* (*Sein und Zeit*, 1927), is generally regarded as having brought about a revolution in philosophical thinking. Heidegger's thinking places the question of the meaning of being, of what is (*Sein*), at the center of the philosophical domain, as is evident in the title of the book's introduction: "The Necessity, Structure, and Priority of the Question of Being." Heidegger based his ideas on the thinking of his teacher Husserl, the father of phenomenology. However, in contrast to Husserl, he shifted the emphasis from epistemology to ontology. Heidegger believed that philosophy should investigate and discover the ontological conditions that enable "beings" to appear in the way they are revealed to us in daily life and allow us to gather information or "ontic" knowledge about them (Pearl, 2011). Medard Boss describes Heidegger's point of departure thus: "His prime aim is to adhere to the immediately given objects and phenomena of man's world, to remain with man's undistorted perceptions, and to let the phenomena speak for themselves and show us their essence and meanings" (Boss, 1963, p. 59).

Heidegger believed that such ontologically based philosophy could shed light on man's existence, ease the individual's suffering, and perhaps even become a new platform for psychoanalytic thought. His main efforts were aimed at developing a philosophy that could also be relevant to human life and, in particular, serve as a useful instrument for medical doctors in helping their patients. He also thought that psychoanalysis had been mistaken in embracing the scientific approach which, in his view, was not an appropriate tool for seeking an understanding of human existence and human suffering.[33]

---

[32] This idea is illustrated and discussed in Shoshani and Shoshani (2021, pp. 169–187).

[33] This is the basic assumption that underlies the revolutionary hermeneutic tradition in human thought, brought about by Heidegger and later leading to such important cultural ideas as the fusion of horizons and the hermeneutic circle.

Heidegger argues that the concept of "being" is the most general concept that permeates everything and bestows fundamental meaning to everything. He is critical of the ways traditional metaphysics approaches the "question of being," claiming that all its attempts at defining being have been found wanting:

> Being is the nearest [to the human being]. Yet the near remains farthest from the human being. Human beings at first cling always and only to beings. [...] thinking thinks only of beings as such; precisely not, and never, being as such. [...] Philosophy [...] always follows the course of metaphysical representation [...] This means that the truth of being as the clearing itself remains concealed for metaphysics. (1947, pp. 254–255)

Echoes of Heidegger's criticisms of Western philosophy for failing to assimilate the *ontological difference between beings (Seiende) and being (Sein)* abound in his writings. Heidegger argues that attempts by traditional metaphysics to investigate being have amounted to fixing general and absolute definitions of beings *perceived only as "things"* while neglecting the dimension of being in and of itself as well as "the difference between being and beings" (ibid., p. 246). Heidegger rejects such "essentialist" thinking, arguing that these determinations are only partial: "Metaphysics does not ask about the truth of being itself. Nor [...] in what way the essence of the human being belongs to the truth of being" (ibid., p. 247). This failure has led us to lose the dynamism and openness of being and its way of coming into existence in an individual's life. That is to say, the way it is uncovered, becomes manifest, and reveals itself to a person at any time and in every context. Therefore, Heidegger argues that what is needed is a different analytical tool.

Heidegger observes being in a novel way, by bestowing it with an ontological dimension and examining the concept of being via the existence of the individual: by his existence (*Dasein*) the individual establishes himself and the world by means of a continuous process. The individual is reality and his relation to being is the essence of his humanness. It is important to explain that Heidegger believed that being is uncovered in the reciprocal encounter between the individual and the world, which are *one and the same.*[34]

In an attempt to undermine traditional metaphysics and resolve the basic rift in the history of philosophy between conceptual theory and life itself, Heidegger thus engages in a philosophy of life that is both conceptually serious and systematic and seems to emerge from the dynamism of life itself (Boss, 1963). In order to discuss being, Heidegger first introduces the concept of *Dasein* (which literally means "being there") as defining the individual's state

---

[34]This stance stands in contrast to other theories, in particular Kant's, that differentiate between consciousness and things themselves. Whereas, for Kant, man projects his consciousness (the categories of his consciousness) onto the world and the individual can therefore be seen as "imprisoned" in his consciousness, Heidegger believed that the individual is in a continuous process of openness to the world, of uncovering and illuminating which simultaneously establish him and the world as one—as reality.

of being. By his very structure, an individual is "there" in the sense of an illuminated space, a section of the world which is his immediate context. In this space, which is a kind of illuminated clearing (*Lichtung*), the world and others are revealed. *Dasein* is established in and establishes the clearing in which things appear to the individual. The person is "there" in a self-transcendent manner: incomplete and seeking completeness. Thus, Heidegger perceives the individual as only a *potential being*. As such, the individual always realizes his existence by his behavior in relation to something or somebody (Boss, 1963), and Heidegger emphasizes a person's concrete existence as caring for somebody or something other than himself: "*Dasein* must always be seen as *being-in-the-world*, as concern for things, and as caring for other [*Daseins*], as the *being-with* the human beings it encounters, and never as a self-contained subject" (1927, p. 159). Thus, an individual encounters/discovers beings "there" in the world in line with his intentionality, which illuminates beings for him. In Heidegger's words: "*Dasein* brings its realm of lumination, its 'there,' with it from the very beginning; neither does it actually exist without its 'there', nor is it this particular being [person] without its 'there'" (1927, p. 133).

According to Heidegger, the individual is therefore incomplete and aspires to a wholeness that lies beyond him, as a continuous process of coming into being. The individual is the source of light that uncovers being and so establishes himself and the world. In other words, *Dasein* as a space of uncovering, revealing, and perception delineates and embodies being as a wholeness that cannot be defined for all its endless modes of existence and behavior (Sigad, 1975). Thus, contrary to theories that define the essence of human beings in terms of certain characteristics, the above argumentation posits that the human essence is a *process*: we seek openness and transcendence from the moment of the actual existence in which we live; from the "here" (the current "there") toward the "there."

Heidegger explains that *Dasein* "consists of 'pure,' invisible, intangible capacities for receiving-perceiving what it encounters and what addresses it" (ibid.). This definition undermines and dismantles the traditional concept of the "subject," by portraying the individual as an entity whose existence is not enclosed within itself, but rather is the sum of all its potentialities for openness and uncovering. In summary, Heidegger rejects the concept of the human being as a subject with intrinsic substance and suggests viewing the individual as a process, a "being there." As paraphrased by Askay and Farquhar, *Dasein* would depict itself thus: "I am not a substantial subject or thing. I have no permanent essence that constitutes my core nature [...] I am merely a way of existing [...] a 'happening' in the process of realizing itself" (2011, p. 16). *Dasein* is the uncovering of a space of endless possibilities of an individual's real, directed, and concrete activities, which are reality.

At this point, we wish to focus on the concept of truth in Heidegger's philosophy. Heidegger argued insistently that the concept of truth was held hostage by traditional metaphysics (Quirk, 2016) and criticized traditionalist attempts to define truth in fixed and absolute terms, whether in the context of correspondence, coherence, or utilitarian theories of truth. For example, he viewed the "characterization of truth as 'agreement,' *adaequatio*, *homoiosis*" as being "very general and empty" (1927, p. 258). Heidegger opined that such definitions overlook the way in which the truth is uncovered and revealed to us as being. In addition, such a definition is entangled in the difficulty of explaining the connection between consciousness and beings (things), that is, the difference between idea and reality and subject and object. Heidegger sought to eliminate the subject/object and individual/world dualities and to overcome the gap between consciousness and the world. Thus, he wanted to explain the concept of truth in a way that included the ontological aspect of being and beings. For this purpose, Heidegger embraces the concept of "unconcealment" (*Unverborgenheit*), a translation of the ancient Greek notion of *Aletheia*.[35] *Aletheia* describes the revelation or disclosure of something that had previously been hidden, referring to the *process of disclosure* rather than the particular object or contents disclosed. *Aletheia* is therefore at odds with traditional models because it does not relate to truth as a matter of correspondence between mind and world, consciousness and things, or as a concept that could be supported by reasoned argument.

According to Heidegger, "the truth" is dependent on the individual and without him has no existence. This is because truth is the process of a person's disclosure to himself (Sigad, 1975). In other words, the truth is the disclosure of an individual as *Dasein*. As Heidegger puts it: "The most primordial phenomenon of truth is first shown by the existential-ontological foundations of uncovering. Uncovering is a way of Being for Being-in-the-world" (1927, p. 263). As derived from the definition of the human being as *Dasein*, the essence of an individual's being is the search for ways to reveal and uncover possibilities to transcend his concrete existence. The very acts of searching and uncovering denote that an individual is real, authentic: "Being-true ('truth') means Being-uncovering [...] Being-true as Being-uncovering, is a way of Being for *Dasein*. What makes this very uncovering possible must necessarily be called 'true' in a still more primordial sense" (1927, pp. 262–263). Truth is, in effect, an infinity of possibilities for the individual's existence—namely being; and the aspiration of reaching this truth is the essence of an individual's "being there" (*Dasein*).

According to Heidegger, the actual existence of being-in-the-world and of being-with-others confines a person, alienates and distances him from himself, and conceals the truth from him to the extent that he becomes inauthentic. Heidegger uses the term "fall" to describe a situation in which the other gains control over an individual and the truth about being remains concealed from him. This is a situation in which a person is seduced to give up on his singularity in favor of generalized reasoned objectivity, in other words, "an Other." This represents a sort of forgetfulness of oneself on the part of the subject, who possesses an infinity of possibilities (Sigad, 1975), and a "fall" into inauthenticity. This inauthenticity causes the individual to abandon his ability to create the world and confines him to being a witness who merely sees the world (Sigad, 1975). On the other hand, when an individual scrutinizes his existence by

[35]This notion appears in the Tragedies of that era, which precede Socrates. While this is usually translated as "truth," Heidegger chose to adopt the literal translation of non-concealment.

transcending his actual life, that is an act of revelation that uncovers the individual as authentic and singular. In other words, the act that simultaneously establishes both the individual and the world is *Aletheia*, which is essentially an act of uncovering the truth, of transcendence from a false existence toward an authentic one. This perception of the truth is implicit in the concept of "authenticity," which Heidegger drew from Kierkegaard's work and which principally means an existence devoid of any form of disguise. For Heidegger, the individual will be authentic when he ceases to disguise himself as a rational object and stop viewing the world as having intrinsic substance. He will then see himself and the world as a system of endless possibilities and as totally open. Such an existence relies on the concept of *Dasein*, that uncovers the individual's encounter with the potentially abundant possibilities in his existence and, in particular, with his incompleteness, his finality of being-toward-death and being "thrown" into a world not of his choosing. The authentic individual is one who takes himself out of himself, who transcends the "fall" into actuality, which is a "false existence" (yet another concept borrowed from Kierkegaard).

Heidegger emphasizes that he is in no sense passing a negative moral judgment through the concept of "falling," elucidating that "the entanglement of Da-sein" should not "be interpreted as a 'fall' from a purer and higher 'primordial' condition" (1927, p. 164). Moreover, for Heidegger, inauthenticity is a necessary aspect of *Dasein*'s existence and, as such, uncovers the truth of being to the same extent as authenticity. For the individual, the uncovering of his incompleteness is simultaneously an uncovering of completeness. A person's uncovering of his own finitude is at one and the same time the uncovering of infinite possibilities for his existence, just as the uncovering of a possibility is simultaneously the uncovering of an infinite and open system of possibilities.[36] Finally, in accordance with this, the uncovering of inauthenticity is at the same time an uncovering of authenticity.

Thus, in Heidegger's approach, the truth is an "illuminating concealment," a concealment that illuminates reality as a possible but not necessary option out of an infinity of such options (Sigad, 1975). In a revolutionary way, Heidegger links truth to freedom. As explained above, Heidegger is critical of metaphysical theories that neglect the truth of being. In his "Letter on Humanism" (1947), written as a response to Sartre's *Existentialism Is Humanism* (1946), Heidegger explains that any humanistic theories that rely on metaphysical theories are mistaken when they profess to define the authentic essence and nature of human beings as absolutely intrinsic and general. As he emphasizes: "In defining the humanity of the human being, humanism not only does not ask about the relation of being to the essence of the human being; because of its metaphysical origin, humanism even impedes the question by neither recognizing nor understanding it" (1947, p. 245).

---

[36] Heidegger offers the allegory of the flashlight: When a person in a dark room points the flashlight at one particular corner, the rest of the room remains obscured. Thus, any act of uncovering or illumination inevitably covers and eclipses at the same time.

In line with his general criticism of metaphysics, Heidegger accuses humanistic theories of ignoring the truth of being which is dynamic and coming into being, as well as for injecting into the definition of the individual's essence contents that are determined by time period, society, and ideology. In this sense, humanistic theories limit an individual's essence to particular contents; they promise the freedom to implement one's "true" essence, but in practice subjugate the individual to whoever and whatever dictate these erroneous metaphysical definitions of human truth and essence. As far as Heidegger is concerned, every attempt to discuss human freedom must begin with altering metaphysics so that it contains the truth of being *as a process*. "Being there" (*Dasein*), as seeking to discover and uncover the truth of being, that is, the openness of being, is a *hope for freedom*. Here would be a good point to share with the reader our feeling that it is so tempting for our minds to construe *Dasein* as a thing, as an object, but Heidegger's language and grammar constantly remind us that we must keep thinking of it as an ongoing process of "being there," which cannot be reduced into a confined entity or moment.

In summary, for Heidegger, the concepts of *Dasein* and truth are interconnected in that the essence of *Dasein* ("being there") is the attempt to uncover the truth in relation to being, which is the quest toward the openness of being. Heidegger draws on Plato's allegory of the cave to explain the essence of the relation between "being there" and truth:

> Man's existence, living on the disc of earth arched over by the sky, is like a life in the cave. All vision needs light, although the light is not itself seen. The *Dasein*'s coming into the light means its attainment of the understanding of truth. (1927, p. 284)

The person who is able to leave the cave and come into the light, that is, to uncover the truth, lives a life of authenticity, establishes himself and the world, actualizes his freedom and his humanity and can lead others toward such a truth (Sigad, 1975).[37]

Freud and Heidegger—a possible dialogue?

In this discussion we will be exploring differences and areas of convergence in the thinking of Freud and Heidegger, asking whether and in what way existential ontology can complement and inform psychoanalysis so as to achieve a broader and more complex understanding of human existence and, in particular, human suffering.

At first sight, comparing these two thinkers may appear to be a questionable undertaking. Freud was ambivalent in his view of philosophy in general and displayed a particular

---

[37] It is important to mention here the critique of this "different" existentialism offered by Heidegger, which we find justified. According to this critique, Heidegger falls into the same trap that he himself denounces: he also talks about an individual's essence. Although this is not a fixed essence or any actual contents but rather a way of possible existence, it is the necessary essence of human beings.

indifference to phenomenology. Heidegger, on his part, was highly critical of the attempt to study human beings using traditional positivistic scientific methods and was particularly critical of psychoanalysis which, in his view, exemplified this kind of scientific inquiry (Askay & Farquhar, 2011).[38] Despite these seemingly antagonistic positions, historical investigation reveals that both Freud's and Heidegger's renowned teacher, Edmund Husserl, was a student of Franz Brentano. Brentano was a philosopher and a psychologist devoted to building bridges between his two disciplines. Freud and Heidegger admired him and were greatly influenced by him. Freud described Brentano as a genius and Heidegger noted that Brentano's doctoral thesis, "On the several senses of being in Aristotle," kindled his own ontological research (Askay & Farquhar, 2006). Although Heidegger and Freud interpreted Brentano's ideas differently, the philosophical background they assimilated from his teachings is evident in their respective theories and may account for a certain affinity between their ideas.

On another level, both Heidegger and Freud characterize human experience and existence using similar concepts, as described by the aforementioned Medard Boss, who sought to intertwine Heideggerian ideas with Freudian practice and recognized the similarity between the two: "Both Heidegger and Freud talked again and again of 'understanding,' of 'meaningfulness,' 'openness,' 'clarity,' 'language,' 'truths,' 'die Angst' and 'freedom' [...] these two pioneers of the science of man are talking about exactly the same phenomena" (Boss, 1963, p. 61).

Another point of convergence is that the thinking of both Freud and Heidegger was molded by the horrors of the world wars. In effect, their thinking emerged from the same crisis of belief: It was felt that human existence was losing its meaning and that humankind was on the verge of forfeiting its core humanity. As Heidegger put it: "There is no foundation to the very being and yet we demand one [...] this is the burden of our existence" (Askay & Farquhar, 2011, p. 15). Both thinkers reacted to this crisis in a similar conceptual vein: In order to bring one's humanity into effect, *one must discover the truth about oneself.* Since these self truths are a burden, people tend to avoid confronting them.

While this affinity in terms of the importance of discovering the truth about oneself is significant, there is a fundamental difference between the two thinkers on this subject. Whereas Freud generally views the individual as a "subject," Heidegger insists that we should think of them as a "being"; this distinction directly affects their respective quest for truth. Freud's research focuses on an individual's inner experience and the way in which it is established in the depths of the psyche. Heidegger, on the other hand, explores being and its ontological and existential meaning and views Freud's use of concepts such as "truth" and "subject" as grounded in an unfounded metaphysical assumption. Namely, that they are construed, in the spirit of the Enlightenment, as objective, absolute, fixed, and universal.

Interestingly, for both thinkers the objects of their research and what they identify as the source of knowledge—respectively, the psyche and being—are inherently inaccessible.

---

[38] For more on Heidegger's critique of Freud and psychoanalysis see Askay and Farquhar, 2006, pp. 192–202, 212–223.

Freud argued that the id is "the dark, inaccessible part of our personality" (1957, p. xxii), while Heidegger described being in terms of "what manifests itself as the inaccessible is the mystery" (1927, p. 183). Freud attempted to provide a framework for conceptualizing, at least partially, the unconscious parts of the psyche, to which there is no direct access. Similarly, Heidegger attempted to describe "being" while fully aware that we will never be able to reach a final and exhaustive definition of it. Despite such inevitable inaccessibility, this is not the end of the journey for either thinker, but rather a challenging point of departure toward discovering what *can* nevertheless be said meaningfully about these realms. It is this search for meaning in the seemingly inaccessible that marks their respective doctrines as revolutionary.

According to Freud, the individual who engages in self-knowing directs his gaze inwards, to the truth that is in the deepest recesses of the psyche. In Heidegger's view, this process requires one to look beyond oneself, transcending oneself and, as a result, opening oneself up to the truth of being. For Freud, openness to truth means willingly illuminating the darkness of the depths of the psyche whereas, for Heidegger, a person who opens himself up to being is illuminating his personal "clearing," as a space of endless possibilities for his existence. To a great extent, Freudian psychoanalysis focuses on the conflict between knowing and not knowing and on the question of how one could open oneself up to the truth. This focus resonates the questions posed by Heidegger and parallels the importance he attributes to uncovering the truth of being through *Aletheia*. According to Freud, the individual is in a state of continuous inner conflict regarding truth, between the wish to know and discover the truth and the wish to ignore truth and hide it from oneself. Accordingly, the aim of psychoanalytic therapy is to develop an openness to truth. Since a person's relation to the truth about himself is essentially *intentional*, the work of psychoanalysis consists of an inquiry into intentionality; as Blass emphasizes, it seeks "to interpret the conflicted dynamic meanings, the underlying motives that stand in the way of knowing, that prevent seeing reality as it is and living in it fully" (2016, p. 314). Blass points out that, in Freud's view, whether the choice is made consciously or unconsciously, the responsibility for the choice rests with the individual. According to Freud, psychoanalysis directs the neurotic patient's ego to understand that:

> the blame [...] lies with yourself [...] Turn your eyes inward, look into your own depth, learn first to know yourself! Then you will understand why you were bound to fall ill; and perhaps you will avoid falling ill in the future. (Freud, cited in Blass, 2016, p. 308)

This formulation parallels Heidegger's claim that it is up to the individual to engage in a process of openness to the truth, by confronting and overcoming his "thrown-ness" into "being there" (*Dasein*) and his fall-into-the-world and thus to choose uncovering over concealment. Nevertheless, this notion is somewhat complicated in Heidegger's thinking, seeing as he views every uncovering as also a concealment, and even openness to truth, *Aletheia*, as signifying the uncovering of truth by way of disguise.[39] These notions very much resemble the psychoanalytic description.

Both Heidegger and Freud regard the consequence of choosing not to know in terms of a *fall toward inauthenticity.* Freud saw the choice of an individual not to know as causing him to become "ill" and to lead a false existence. Similarly, for Heidegger, a person who chooses not to know "falls" into the world of others and, since being is thereby concealed from him, he leads an inauthentic life. Accordingly, both thinkers believe that "truth" or "authentic being" are revealed through "liberation" or transcendence. For Freud, this is liberation from subjugation to the unconscious, whereas for Heidegger it is freeing oneself from the prison of "the others" ("the them," "the they"): the prison which is inauthentic life, daily life turning the individual into a social entity which is anesthetized, fed, and provided for as long as he turns his back on the uncovering of being.[40] The conclusion of both thinkers is similar: Through "uncovering," a free part of an individual becomes available for transcending oneself/others, creating oneself and the world, and so gaining a "shred" of authenticity.

Thus, for both Heidegger and Freud, the individual has to make a choice—to light the torch and illuminate the clearing or to let darkness rule. Thus, for each of these thinkers, responsibility rests with the individual alone. Nevertheless, for both Freud and Heidegger, the individual is determined by given structures and is not his own master. According to Freud, a person's everyday choices and actions are determined by his *psychic* structure, whereas for Heidegger they are determined by the conditions of *being*. In this sense, both thinkers exhibit deterministic outlooks. At the same time, both see the individual as regaining his "mastery" over himself in terms of an immanent conflict between knowing and concealment. In other words, a person chooses whether and to what extent he tries to open himself up to the (psychic or ontological) truth. Therefore, this intriguing combination between a deterministic setting and freedom of choice is uniquely shared by both thinkers.

From this resemblance, however, there also emerges the difference. As already said, in Heidegger's thinking, an authentic person and one who chooses not to be authentic are on an equal ethical footing: There is no moral hierarchy. Heidegger does not disparage someone who chooses not to open himself up to the truth of being, in the same way that he does not extol someone who does. Moreover, the two are interconnected in that one is a condition of the other's existence: Every concealment is also an uncovering and every uncovering is also a concealment. For Freud, on the other hand, a person who chooses not to know the truth is manifesting unconscious "resistance." He is responsible for this choice and is therefore

[39] In his essay "Language Closing and Disclosing," H. N. Bialik (1915) identifies the double meaning in language which reveals and conceals reality/truth at the same time.

[40] A similar idea is found in the writings of Hannah Arendt, who was a student of Heidegger. Arendt explains that it is as if a person who turns over his thinking and his judgment to another has turned from a "somebody" to a "nobody" (Arendt, 1973).

"guilty" of the development of his neurosis. Freud, unlike Heidegger, creates a clear hierarchy between sickness and health, that is, between a person who is prepared to know and acknowledge the truth and someone who refuses to do so. While Freud proposes a linear path of individual development toward authenticity, Heidegger states that a person can transcend himself and change, alternating between authenticity and inauthenticity and thus interchangeably approaching and moving away from being.[41]

Diving deeper into the intricacies of this choice, we also see similarities between Heidegger and Freud in terms of the reasonings and circumstances of a person's choice not to know and thus to live a false and inauthentic life. For both thinkers, the main factor is anxiety (*die Angst*) and both devote a central place in their thinking to the role of anxiety as a formative condition, though their respective understanding of it differs. Freud, the psychologist-scientist, understood anxiety as a psychic affect, which can be investigated by psychoanalytic tools. Heidegger, on the other hand, saw *die Angst* as a mood (*Stimmung*) which must be understood with the aid of phenomenological philosophical tools. Although Freud saw a measure of anxiety as part and parcel of being alive, he still regarded extreme states of anxiety as a source of illness which requires treatment. Heidegger, in contrast, regards anxiety as an opportunity for discovery.

In Freud's psychoanalytic theory, anxiety is discussed in three principal contexts: the anxiety of birth, signal anxiety, and castration anxiety.

According to Freud, a person's primary experience, the event of birth, is a very traumatic experience: The individual is pushed out of the womb, where he and the world had been one and the same, as he is confronted for the first time with his own limitations, partiality, and finitude. The infant experiences these sensations physiologically, as a barrage of unsynchronized stimuli (cold, light, noise, etc.). This is the individual's first and most formative experience and it is accompanied by feelings of extreme anxiety. Throughout life, in situations that arouse anxiety, the individual is confronted with internal anxiety which arises as a repetition of the initial traumatic anxiety of birth. Furthermore, Freud distinguishes anxiety from fear by indicating that anxiety, unlike fear, is not related to a specific object. Thus, anxiety occupies a central role in a person's psychic survival, by serving as a signal of some menacing threat, either internal or external, which is unknown and not understood. Anxiety signals the psyche to activate its defense mechanisms in anticipation of said threat. Thus, an individual's conduct in the world is mainly dictated by his way of coping with anxiety and the defenses he is able to mount against it. Finally, Freud discusses castration anxiety as a formative psychic event. As a main driving force in the resolution of the oedipal conflict, the identification with the father, and the internalization of parental figures as the foundations of the superego,

---

[41] In later developments in psychoanalysis, one can detect ideas that are more in line with Heidegger's concepts and thinking. Theoreticians such as Winnicott, Bion in his later writings, Kohut, and Alvarez offer a more compassionate approach than Freud's and believe that a certain degree of inauthenticity is part of being human. Although he was not a psychoanalyst, R. D. Laing, in his influential book *The Divided Self* (1960), refers to this position and defends it.

castration anxiety is closely linked to the capacity to acknowledge the differences between the sexes and the generations. Thus, it positions the individual in his intrapsychic, interpersonal, and cultural worlds in a very profound sense.[42]

In Heidegger's thinking, anxiety also has a constitutive significance and is endless: "what Angst is about is completely indefinite" (1927, p. 174). In his view, anxiety is a person's first and most fundamental adjustment to the world and to himself.[43] Heidegger explains that anxiety is an immanent opening to *Dasein*, to the very fact of one's existence as having been arbitrarily "thrown" into the world. As he stresses: "What *Angst* is anxious for is *being-in-the-world* itself" (ibid., p. 175). Since an individual is fundamentally and *ab initio* "thrown" into the world, his existence is from the very beginning a "being-in-the-world" and "being with other things/ with others." Heidegger argues that though the individual's "fall" into otherness (he/others/ world) makes him feel authentic and close to himself at the ontic level, at the ontological level he is in effect distancing himself from himself. He is submerged in "otherness" and does not feel "at home" ("not-being-at-home," *Entfremdung*, uncanny). In his words: "in *Angst* one has an *uncanny* feeling" (ibid., p. 176). Heidegger explains that this is the ontological indication that an individual can potentially choose to open up to the truth of being; in other words, to be individual and authentic, transcending himself as being-with-others. Therefore, anxiety is also an indication of one's responsibility for one's life and one's choices: "*Angst* reveals in Da-sein its *being-toward* its own most potentiality of being, that is, *being free* for the freedom of choosing and grasping itself" (ibid., p. 176).

This, according to Heidegger, is the burden of *Dasein* that awakens anxiety. Anxiety at the prospect of opening himself up to the truth and accepting responsibility is what usually leads a person to flee from himself toward "other ..."[44] As he puts it:

> It is not a flight *from* innerworldly beings [as in fear], but precisely *toward* them as the beings among which taking care of things, lost in the they, can linger in tranquilized familiarity. Entangled flight *into* the being-at-home of publicness is flight *from* not being-at-home, that is, from the uncanniness which lies in Da-sein as thrown, as being-in-the-world entrusted to itself in its being. (Ibid., p. 177)

Thus, anxiety moves a person closer to himself, in terms of his individuality and authenticity, and illuminates his freedom. Heidegger summarizes anxiety and its unique role in adjusting

---

[42] As discussed in *Civilization and Its Discontents* (1930a).

[43] Anxiety, in Heidegger's terminology, is a unique form of what he termed "*Stimmung.*" Translations of this term vary and include "state of mind," "mood," "existential," etc. In this context, *Stimmung* refers to a person's mode of adjustment to the world, one of several including boredom, care, and joy.

[44] Oscar Wilde quotes Emerson in saying that "Nothing is more rare in any man [...] than an act of his own." And then explains that "most people are other people. Their thoughts are someone else's opinions, their lives a mimicry, their passions a quotation" (1897, p. 30). This worldview resonates Heidegger's notion of how easy and tempting it is for every one of us to fall prey to "they," instead of being "oneself."

to the world as follows: "In *Angst* there lies a possibility of a distinctive disclosure, since *Angst* individualizes. This individualizing fetches Da-sein back from its falling prey" (ibid., p. 171). As said, at birth an individual is "thrown" into the world, into the "there"; which is to say that, from the outset, a person encounters himself as partial and limited and so aspires to achieve an unattainable completeness. The source of anxiety lies in this first encounter with oneself, when one's completeness is "there": "*Angst* provides the phenomenal basis for explicitly grasping the primordial totality of being of Da-sein" (ibid., p. 171).

For Heidegger, like Freud, anxiety occupies a primary, fundamental, and constitutive position in establishing the subject/*Dasein* and stems from the subject's encounter with the truth about himself and the world. Thus, it would seem that these two perspectives, the psychoanalytic one and the ontological one, enrich and deepen the analysis of the phenomenon of anxiety.

At this juncture, it is interesting to return to an additional meaning of the concept of *Aletheia*. In ancient Greece, the word also denoted the end of the phase of contractions in childbirth and the baby's arrival into the world.[45] If we take this meaning of *Aletheia* into account (even though Heidegger himself did not address it directly), we could attribute to Heidegger a link between birth, truth, and anxiety as we saw was the case with Freud. It is at birth, as *Aletheia*, that the truth of the individual as partial and limited, as having been "thrown" into the world, is exposed and that anxiety is therefore awakened. This is the immanent basis for the establishment of a person. Whereas for Freud this involves an exploration of causal psychic relations between the subject and the world, for Heidegger it is an ontological description of *Dasein* (being there) which emerges and establishes the world and the individual. Meaning that while anxiety for Freud is an *affect that exists in a person's psyche*, for Heidegger, anxiety (*Angst*) is a *Stimmung* involving *a way of becoming attuned to and involved in the world.*

We think it is fair to say that, for Heidegger, the *Stimmung* of *Angst* is a complex mood involving a mixture of dread, depression, alienation, and uncanniness. In a fictional dialogue between Heidegger and Freud written by Askay and Farquhar, Heidegger states:

> I do not evade the silent voice that attunes me toward the horror of the abyss. [...] There are times when I drift here and there in the abysses of our existence like a muffling fog. During [these] darker times, I hardly know anymore who and where I am. None of us knows that, as soon as we stop fooling ourselves. (2011, p. 15)[46]

For Heidegger, anxiety awakens and destabilizes a person (*Dasein*). Essentially, *Dasein* illuminates the choice of whether to open up and uncover the anxiety-provoking truth that it is

---

[45] It is conceivable that Heidegger had this in mind when he placed this concept at the center of his ontological treatise. We are grateful to Sharon Hass for bringing this point to our attention.

[46] This is taken from the play, *Of Philosophers and Madmen*, written by Askay and Farquhar (2011), in which they combine quotes from Heidegger's writings to create a fictional dialogue between him and Freud.

partial and limited and so move closer to itself and actualize its freedom, or to distance itself from itself as such and give in to calming and anesthetizing inauthenticity.

Excursion: existential/ontological anxieties

> *Imagine death: imagine nothing,*
> *And then imagine even less, imagine absolute darkness. Then imagine a darkness even darker, imagine that*
> *Which you cannot imagine, imagine everything you've known. The women, the rain, the bread-rolls, the sun*
> *And add to them the modifier "no,"*
> *No-rain, no-sun, no-bread-rolls and no-women, Imagine all of that and then erase imagination too,*
> *Because there are no more shapes, sounds and sensations are gone. Nor should you be afraid, for fear too, is erased*
> *And there are no more words, not even of negation. The word "no" is erased and so is the word "gone." Nothingness itself is gone and nothing is redoubled. You could not picture it until you arrive.*
> *And once you arrive you can no longer picture anything.*
>
> —Levin, 1999, p. 68; translation by the authors

This brief discussion of anxiety in Heidegger and Freud tempts us to explore, for a moment, a different approach to anxiety than the mainstream psychoanalytic one. As mentioned, Heidegger's chief reservation concerning the practice of psychoanalysis was that it operated on a medical model and was thus inapplicable to human beings. His close friend, Boss, described the dangers of this inevitably objectifying and dehumanizing model as follows: "The psychoanalytic lingo leads too easily to a hazardous and artificial subdivision of the human being into different 'things' or 'objects,' for example, in its terms of theoretic abstractions, such as *ego*, *id*, *super-ego*, and so on" (1949, p. ix). This problematic approach is alarmingly manifest in Bleuler's famous remark about his schizophrenic patients, as quoted by Laing, that "when all is said and done they were stranger to him than the birds in his garden" (Laing, 1960, p. 28). The spirit of Heidegger's insistence on a non-medical model has resurfaced in some psychoanalytic authors and in their efforts to humanize even the most dehumanized of pathologies and mental states, even those originally deemed untreatable and unapproachable by classical psychoanalysis. This spirit is most remarkably pronounced in Sullivan's famous dictum that even schizophrenics are "much more simply human than otherwise" (1953).

As mentioned above, for Heidegger, anxiety is one of the most basic experiences of human life and a most revelatory one, as it brings *Dasein* face to face with the nothing. In his lecture "What Is Metaphysics?" Heidegger describes anxiety as the moment in which "the nothing makes itself known [...] as a slipping away of the whole" (1963, p. 102). He views this experience as a necessary precondition for *Dasein* to be able to be aware of its unique relation to being and beings: The encounter with the nothing "brings *Dasein* for the first time before beings as such" and reveals the meaning of *Dasein* as "being held out into nothing." This places *Dasein* in a state of fundamental transcendence and openness because, as Heidegger puts it, "If it were not in advance holding itself out into the nothing, then it could never be related to beings nor even to itself " (ibid., pp. 103–104). As such, anxiety becomes an encounter with one of the hallmarks of our humanity and a constitutive and revelatory experience. Moreover, Heidegger asserts that anxiety is a relatively rare phenomenon and one that involves "a kind of bewildered calm" (ibid., p. 102).

But what of those of us for whom this experience of "being held out into nothing" is not so rare, or who, for whatever reason, cannot maintain a state of "bewildered calm" in its face? For them, this encounter with the basic elements of being there, of being human, can be something different entirely. Perhaps we can view this fundamentally human moment as the bedrock from which "anxieties of being" or "existential anxieties" draw their potency and their life-shattering force. In the following paragraphs, we have outlined several approaches that continue this humanizing approach that considers symptoms, experiences, and states that are often viewed as "beyond the pale" of humanness—as "much more simply human than otherwise."[47]

First, let us consider the contributions of the controversial R. D. Laing regarding ontological anxiety, which date back to 1960. Laing, who was much influenced by existential philosophy and most notably by Sartre and Heidegger, heavily criticized the dehumanization of psychotic patients and their exclusion from the "realm of interpretation" (see also Bakewell, 2016). As part of his efforts to make psychotic and schizophrenic patients more accessible to comprehension, he differentiated between people who are "ontologically secure"—having a sense of themselves and of others as real, alive, whole, and cohesive—and those suffering from ontological insecurity, in which all of these "assurances" have failed to emerge (1960, p. 39). As Laing puts it, the ontologically insecure individual "may feel more unreal than real [...] more dead than alive; precariously differentiated from the rest of the world so that his identity and autonomy are always in question" alongside his sense of temporal continuity, personal consistency, or substantiality (p. 42). Because such people have no solid sense of self that is capable of withstanding the ubiquitous "despair, terror and boredom of existence," they often experience everyday life as a deadly threat and as requiring a constant effort to preserve their fleeting identity (p. 41).

Laing lists three key types of anxiety encountered by the ontologically insecure individual. The first, *engulfment*, is the sense that any relatedness to others will result in the dissolution of one's autonomy and identity, creating a vicious dialectic between such dreaded "complete loss

---

[47] While the present exploration is inevitably limited in scope, we would nevertheless like to mention other leading authors who have recently advocated such an approach: Bergstein (2018, 2019), Symington (2006), Zaltz (2018), and Ferro (2019). Note also Civitarese's use of Heideggerian philosophy to contextualize the work of Bion (2019).

of being and absorption in to the other person" and total isolation (p. 44). The second, *implosion*, involves a sense that one is but empty, a vacuum, which is under constant threat of being impinged upon and crushed by external reality or an other, resulting in the obliteration of all personal identity. The third, *petrification and depersonalization*, involves the sense that the existence of the other as a full human being or subject inevitably reduces the fragile self into a mere object, robbing it of all its aliveness and being (pp. 43–48). Such individuals secure their survival in the face of these ontological dreads in ways that coincide with "traditional" perverse maneuvers, namely, the (preemptive) objectification and depersonalization of the other and the formation of pathological dependency and isolation patterns that preclude any mutual encounter.

Another example can be found in Durban's (2016, 2019) conceptualizations and depictions of a variety of "anxieties-of-being." Durban's work draws significantly on his work with autistic patients, demonstrating yet another realm that psychoanalysis has been successfully applied in, through the capacity to recognize and conceptualize the experience of very "other" patients. Durban describes "anxieties-of-being" as "unthinkable anxieties" (Winnicott, 1952) which "involve our threatened sense of existing as bounded, psycho-biological units" and include: "having no body, [...] having no inside and outside, leaking out and emptying, liquefying, freezing, burning, falling, dissolving and having no sensation of time and space" (Durban, 2016, p. 92). Patients experiencing such anxieties often resort to internal deadening autistic organizations, entering "pre-verbal, pre- or non-symbolic states of mindlessness: frozen, shattered, terrified and hateful of anything human" (p. 93). Such states are also related to attempts to destroy the mind of the other or to confusion between self and object as a defense against either symbiosis or separateness, both of which are experienced as equally annihilating (2016, pp. 88, 92; 2019, p. 923). These anxiety states thus constantly lead to the dehumanization of self and other. Durban describes one patient who was constantly preoccupied with the question "Am I a person?" (2019, p. 931) and another who declared that "It is either suicide or murder, that's all there's left to do!" (2016, p. 88).

In terms of therapeutic technique, Durban highlights the importance of acknowledging the different psychic strata at which different types of anxieties emerge. He suggests that analysts must focus on the detection of "the most urgent, deeper anxieties and [...] their interpretation in what might be considered their own language or syntax" (2019, p. 926). For example, when clients present with anxiety states related to disintegrated bodily state or the "repeated destruction of space and time," Durban recommends mainly relying on the "stability, continuity and boundaries of the setting" (pp. 935–936). Finally, seeing as such anxieties dismantle and disintegrate the psyche's "connective tissue" and the links between body, mind, and object, Durban suggests that the rehumanization of those dehumanized by anxieties-of-being can be effected by "*finding a 'real' development-promoting object to be gradually implanted within the mind*, which will supply the patient with his *total mind-body presence*" (2016, p. 93; emphasis in original).

These bold approaches, which dare to expand psychoanalytic terminology to recognize such extreme experiences at the phenomenological and experiential level, thus bring these mental states into the fold of what we view as human. They can be seen as following in the footsteps of such analysts as Frida Fromm-Reichman who, in her famous "Rose Garden" case, facilitated the patient's recovery by accepting her psychotic delusions as a valid human experience and existential option (H. Green, 1964). The need to encounter the patient and their psychic material at their level involves the perilous encounter with our own psychotic, perverse, and autistic parts and mechanisms and our own "anxieties-of-being." This gap is more easily bridged when we recognize that our and our patients's experiences are part of the same spectrum of human experience.[48]

Still, in a way, analysts must walk a fine line between two equally dangerous forms of collusion: first, by refusing this encounter and embracing the dehumanizing and objectifying aspects of the medical model in psychoanalytic discourse, we risk colluding with the dehumanizing mechanisms within the patient, actively joining those internal dynamics that seek to limit the patient's claim on and share in humanity. Second, too close an encounter with the patient's and our own psychotic, perverse, and autistic materials and states may deaden us, robbing us of the capacity to think and leading to repetitions and enactments that have no curative potential. By agreeing to meet the patients' existential anxieties at their own level and in their own language, while finding the balance between these two collusions, we may be able to facilitate what Loewald called "creative repetition" or "recreation" (1971).

Freud and Heidegger on death

Another subject that both thinkers address and that we have found suitable for comparison is that of death. For Freud, the subject of death is mainly discussed through its position as a basic component in the dualistic theory of the drives that motivate individuals (and societies): the life instinct and the death instinct (Freud, 1940a). Freud presents the death instinct as a wish to either nullify any tension or, alternatively, to return to an inorganic state. He views this return to the inorganic as one of the purposes or goals of all life, while the role of the life instincts is to attempt to disrupt this "natural" flow. His two papers, "Thoughts for the Times on War and Death" (1915b) and "On Transience" (1916a), are the only writings in which Freud deviates from this central thesis and relates to death as a human experience and to the

---

[48] Indeed, these existential anxieties or "anxieties-of-being" resonate—as a much more intense and debilitating version—more traditional psychoanalytic conceptualizations of anxieties surrounding merger or annihilation. For example, consider Otto Rank's "death fear" and "life fear," which respectively involve the fear of identity loss through merger into others and the fear of isolation and alienation due to one's autonomy (1945); or, Loewald's conceptualizations of paternal vs. maternal castration, which respectively entail separation from the mother-infant union and the engulfment of the ego into original unity (1951). It is interesting to note that Loewald, who was directly influenced by Heidegger, posited a direct and significant connection between these anxieties and the experience of reality (ibid.).

fear of death.[49] In the latter, Freud argues that the very recognition of the existence of death makes life more emotionally intensive, more valuable in the sense of evoking a desire to experience more and to make the most of life. Freud recalls a summer walk in a forest with Rilke, who expressed sadness and despondency at the prospect that the beauty surrounding them would be gone when winter came and began contemplating the transience of human beings, life, and the world. Freud presents Rilke with the opposing point of view, arguing that the fact that things change, beyond not harming their beauty, may even reinforce the secret of their fascination in the present. Freud also highlights the notion that death is not the end of everything, that there are spiritual possessions that transcend death (Razinsky, 2013). Emboldening himself and encouraging Rilke, he avows that not everything dies when the individual dies.

By discussing death from a metaphysical perspective, Freud relinquishes the opportunity to analyze death from an ontic point of view, as Heidegger does, that is, addressing the response of the living to the knowledge of imminent death, which is arbitrary and not in our control. It was Melanie Klein who rescued Freud's death instinct from its exclusive identification as a biological instinct to reach homeostasis and an inorganic state. Klein was clear about the existence of a fear of death and her view of life as led under the constant shadow of death, disputing Freud's choice to overlook the fear of death. Indeed, as we see it, death anxieties are so all-engulfing that more than a few people fight death or defend against death anxiety by bringing about their own death as well as that of others (Durban, 2016; Shoshani et al., 2021; Shoshani & Shoshani, 2021).

Heidegger, on the other hand, sees the whole voyage of life as a journey toward death and a preparation for that event. In this sense, the most profound truth for *Dasein* is being-toward-death (see also Becker, 2007). It is a kind of certainty and an objective, knowledge, and purpose; death is the end of the road, the possibility of no possibilities. Being changes all the time, it is in constant movement, never standing still, becoming toward death. It is conscious of its partiality and aspires toward completeness. Death is presented by Heidegger as the only situation of absolute completeness in *Dasein*'s being. One of the main sources of anxiety according to Heidegger is "*the understanding that we are being-toward-death*" and that *Daseins* examine their lives and existence in the shadow of death. This is the deepest meaning of one of Heidegger's greatest contributions—the notion that *being and time are inseparable.*

Summary

Heidegger's thinking is, in many ways, a turning away from classical philosophy and, as such, one can see its potential for a fruitful dialogue with psychoanalysis. Heidegger's view of human beings recalls subjects that, since Freud, psychoanalytic theory has addressed as central to psychic life.

[49] These two texts join the heroic and classical tradition which affords death a central role and view life as always in death's shadow, a theme that until Heidegger and Montaigne had received little attention since the Stoics. In his book *Life and Death in Psychoanalysis* (1970), Laplanche quotes Freud as saying that "Our unconscious is just as inaccessible to the idea of our own death, as murderously minded towards the stranger, as divided or ambivalent towards the loved, as was man in early antiquity" (p. 6).

Evidence of this tendency can be seen in Heidegger's claim that anxiety is the main characteristic of *Dasein*. This anxiety is linked to the uncovering of the truth of human existence as arbitrary, transient, partial, and aspiring to completeness; it is limited to the concreteness of its possibilities and is finite, advancing toward the completeness of its existence—death. The revolutionary way in which Heidegger replaces the *universality* stressed by classical philosophy with *particularity*, as well as *object* with *action*, represents the transition from objectivity to subjectivity in understanding human beings. This transition facilitates a sort of affiliation between Heidegger's philosophy and Freud's psychoanalysis and provides grounds for exploring their affinities.

Despite the gap between Freud's and Heidegger's metaphysical views in relation to the concepts of "subject" and "truth," a closer exploration of Freud's psychoanalytic theory and Heidegger's ontological ideas shows that *both stress the process of opening up to the anxiety-evoking truth and its disclosure, as well as the individual's responsibility to know the truth as a source of freedom*. Both theories illuminate and stress the person's potential for significantly establishing himself as *authentic, individual, and singular*. However, each of these theories approaches the matter from its own typical point of departure. In Freud, the stress is on the complexity of intrapsychic structures (id, ego, and superego) and the dynamic nature of the turbulent relations between them as they appear in the unconscious. Psychoanalysis is concerned with healing, asking the question "why?," and attempting to answer it through the exploration of the patient's emotional experience. In comparison, Heidegger's ontological existential investigation deals with *what is* through questions that in some ways precede the above *why*. Heidegger attempts to investigate the meaning of "what existing in the world is." While this investigation is aimed at facilitating processes of "opening up" and "disclosure" that are geared toward "being there" (*Dasein*) authentically, it seems to highlight dimensions of *creative becoming and intersubjectivity*, through an analysis of immediate and extensive phenomenological revelations. Nevertheless, the manner in which this investigation is conducted involves observing a specific individual. In addition, each of these explorations represents a dynamic space in which an individual has the opportunity to establish himself, even if he is not master of that space.

Thus, the two theories move toward one another. Despite Heidegger having started his inquiry from an entirely different point of departure, he eventually deals with basic questions that have a psychological meaning, such as anxiety, truth, and death—elementary questions about human beings with which psychoanalysis is also preoccupied. Risking oversimplification, one can say that Heidegger highlights the existence of *individual-world as a single unit*, whereas Freud's emphasis is on exploring an individual's unconscious motivations.

Canadian philosopher and psychoanalyst, Jon Mills, discusses Heidegger's thinking and its links to psychoanalysis. He argues that the Freudian "unconscious" is the layer in which the process of endless discovery and concealment with which Heidegger is concerned takes place. Mills (2014) believes that, from a Heideggerian perspective, the analyst's role is to be the discoverer of what is to be found in the unconscious. He characterizes the Freudian unconscious as the true home of the Heideggerian being. We also see the proximity between the "concealment" and "discovery" that Heidegger describes in the process of approaching the truth of being and Freud's notion of the unconscious and of the process of its uncovering as the central task of psychoanalytic work. Nevertheless, we have some reservations concerning Mills's claim that the unconscious is "the real home of the being (*Dasein*)." We wish to suggest the possibility of positioning the disciplines in a reverse order to that suggested by Mills. We would argue that *the process of being contains the unconscious*; in other words, *being is the "real home" of the Freudian subject*, including his unconscious. It therefore follows that the uncovering of truth on the ontological level is a fundamental condition that potentially facilitates the uncovering of unconscious psychic truth. Only by opening up to truth as a space of possibilities at the ontological existential level, will it be possible for an individual to open himself up to the deep recesses of the unconscious psyche. Moreover, a plausible way to describe the relation between ontological space and intrapsychic depths is as a dialectic of mutuality and dependence. The search for truth is simultaneously an individual's ontological condition and his psychological motivation. It is up to the individual to both search for and uncover his concealed truths (psychological motive), while simultaneously also discovering the truth of being (ontological condition). By the very act of opening up and uncovering, an individual can be said to be true, which is to say—authentic.

Further thoughts

As we reread this chapter, we find that rather than presenting our reader with a conclusion, we are hereby offering a beginning. After this discussion on Heidegger and Freud, we cannot help but feel that we are still only at the foot of this tall, intriguing, and inspiring mountain. The interface of psychoanalysis and Heidegger's philosophy is so fascinating and rich that we feel there are many more ideas to follow and explore. While we cannot, given the scope of this chapter, share with the reader all these strands of thought, we wanted to leave you with several ideas and intuitions, which may one day blossom into fuller explorations. As we continued to reflect on these ideas, we found that they capture many of the themes we have explored throughout this book and especially a crucial aspect of its spirit—the constant search for additional sources of insight and enlightenment into the human psyche, to enrich and inform our analytic theory and practice.

* * *

In exploring Heidegger's possible interface with psychoanalysis, we have come across Grotstein's (2007) discussion of the Heideggerian qualities of the late Bion, as discussed in his profound book, *A Beam of Intense Darkness*. Grotstein views Bion's "radical psychoanalytic metatheory" as "an ontological and phenomenological epistemology harvested from his experiences while treating psychotic patients" (p. 153). Furthermore, he identifies an affiliation between Bion's notion of "O" and Heidegger's notions of being and existence, arguing that Bion's discourse around transcendence and the use of the term "becoming" involves an attempt to steer psychoanalysis away from its *ontic* roots and toward an *ontological* perspective. Bion is portrayed as preoccupied with how the human being "seeks and hides from the ineffable" in a reality that has become so saturated as to constitute a "positivistic enclave" (pp. 129–130). In this context, his reformulation of psychoanalysis may be seen as striving "to help the analysand transcend the veils of illusion [...] that obtrude between him and the Other and between him and his Being-in-itself" (p. 123).

Grotstein's illuminating reading of Bion, as attempting to shift psychoanalytic technique from the scientific and deterministic ontic perspective to the ontological perspective, has highlighted for us our tendency as analysts to focus on the ontic in our clinical work to the exclusion of opening up for our patients the infinite possibilities of the ontological perspective. This brings to mind the case of a patient whose treatment Michael had supervised some ten years ago, that of a highly esteemed and brilliant surgeon in his forties. The analysis focused on his anxieties surrounding the fact that his father had been a "star surgeon" as well, trained in the very same surgical specialization. The patient was constantly anxious about metaphorically "killing his father" and taking his place. After two years of working through these issues, the patient terminated the analysis quite unexpectedly. Two years after that, he called the analyst in a state of panic and asked for an urgent session: The next day he was supposed to deliver a keynote lecture at an international conference. While this was not out of the ordinary for him, he was mortified at the possibility of failure and unsure about whether to attend or to cancel his lecture. His analyst, focusing on his patient's relationship with his father and on his grandiose narcissistic self, advised him to give the lecture, seeing as otherwise he might feel like an utterly worthless failure. The next morning, the analyst received a phone call from the patient's wife informing him that the patient had tragically died by suicide. In contemplating this case and the material that came up within the supervision, we wonder whether—in a Heideggerian sense—the analyst could have focused more on an ontological dimension—opening up to the potential possibilities that were unavailable in that patient's "clearing."[50] For example, the possibility that no harm would come from his not attending the conference. It is impossible to say whether such a course of action could have changed anything, but it is a powerful reminder that people in distress tend to see very limited possibilities, and that it is worth reminding them that there are other possibilities that are presently concealed from them. In this vein, perhaps the analysis could have focused, in addition to the envy, competitiveness, and guilt in the patient's relation to his father, on helping the patient search for his unique and authentic potential for being and for emerging as a person from under his father's shadow.

[50] Dreyfus and Wakefield present a notion of psychopathology that is grounded in Heidegger's notion of "clearing," While the traditional Freudian approach is a "depth psychology" that views psychopathology as involving repressed mental material, one could argue for adding a "breadth psychology" that relies on the ontological hermeneutic position: This means that unconscious material is not understood as fully having the character of an object in the clearing. Thus, "[I]t is something that exists everywhere and nowhere, like a theme imbuing all conscious experiences without itself necessarily existing as a specifiable mental content either in the conscious or the unconscious mind" (Messer et al., 1988, p. 19).

Perhaps the choice to avoid giving the lecture could have been a first step toward embracing a more authentic being, examining his career choices (as surfaced in his last sessions before leaving the therapy). It can be asked whether the choice to die by suicide was influenced by his sense of failure, or rather by the need to take a clear stand regarding his inauthentic existence. We believe that in this case, as in many others, had the analyst practiced the kind of binocular vision that holds both Freudian theory and Heideggerian ontology, side by side, perhaps other possibilities would have been open for understanding the patient's anxiety.

We have found that several of Heidegger's concepts, such as being, "being thrown into the world," "falling-toward-them," and especially "being-toward-death," add meaningful tools for addressing the experiences and suffering of patients on the perverse–psychotic spectrum. Our explorations into Heidegger's thinking have led us to wonder whether the existential distresses and anxieties expressed by both perverse and other patients are adequately described and addressed by classical psychoanalytic notions, which view human beings as distinct subjects, rather than in terms of being, or as subject-objects. Consider, for example, the following statements made by one of our patients depicted in a previous article (Shoshani & Shoshani, 2013)—David, the bottle man:

> As long as I am by myself, in my house, I know where I start and where I finish; I know my boundaries. I know, more or less, who David is. I have a grip on this "incommunicado," as Winnicott would say. But the second I step out of the door, whatever security I had evaporates. Even if I just meet someone in the lift for ten seconds, I get liquefied, and some other David is standing there, taking over. And this David is not real; he's just for show. You know what Sartre says? Hell is other people!

We feel that experiences such as those depicted here are better served by ontological conceptualizations rather than the deterministic and positivistic ontic formulations mentioned above. In this sense, Heidegger's insistence on exploring being, and his eventual influence on psychoanalytic discourse through his various disciples in psychoanalysis, are evident in a decades-long process that can be termed the phenomenologization of psychoanalytic language. This process, which is closing the aforementioned gap between "philosophy and life," is evident in Kohut's discussion of the notion of "selfobject," experience-near conceptualizations and interventions, and the hermeneutic focus on understanding instead of explaining. It is also evident in the conceptualizations of Laing (1960) and Durban (2019), as offering a humanizing outlook of pathology and our proposed conceptualization of perversion as an inability to think, love, and mourn. Such shifts of focus are bringing our discourse closer to the lived experience of our patients and further away from "scientific" terms. Today, we can approach perverse experiences through the experience-near conceptual contributions of Loewald, the late Bion, Meltzer, Tustin, Alvarez, Symington, Durban, and Bergstein, as well as other thinkers who discuss the primitive layers of the personality and primary mental states. We can talk about nowhere-ness, homelessness, and nothingness, which are in many ways akin to

Heideggerian "anxieties of being." The choice of such experience-near and even, in some ways, more poetic language over positivistic and scientific categorization, coincides with another of Heidegger's notions, namely, that one can never fully uncover being, that some aspects of being human will always remain hidden, mysterious, and ineffable. It could be argued that phenomenological, experience-near discourse is more attuned to minding these mysteries, and less inclined to foster the belief that existence can be exhausted by any terminology. This understanding that the mystery of being will forever remain far richer than any concept is manifest in many of our case presentations throughout this book and in our insistence on maintaining an experience-near position.

Finally, a note about Heidegger's view of modern life, overtaken as it is by technological innovation. Heidegger wrote extensively about the interaction between human beings and technology, and the way that technology affects our notion of being. Unlike the more common view that sees the realm of technology and the realm of human existence as separate but somewhat overlapping domains, formulated perhaps in terms of the distinction between technological *objects* and human *subjects*, Heidegger would argue that the relationship between human beings and technology is determined within a single ontological framework. Thus, as the modern world is becoming increasingly full of technology, the human experience of the world is increasingly reduced to technological terms. According to Heidegger, these are not separate domains that are in conflict with one another, but a single space in which our being is affected, distorted, and obscured by our recourse to technology.

In this technological day and age, our immersion in contemporary digital and virtual culture has left us untethered, loosening our hold on our tangible and concrete existence and giving rise to profound existential distress. The "short cuts" offered by technology seem to make all of us abandon the "long roads" of life, those that require effort, intention, and investment, that require us to mourn the limitations of reality and of being human, rather than find superficial ways to circumvent the inherent differences, difficulties, and limitations of our lives. For many years, one of the common litmus tests for perversion consisted of asking whether the person's reaction to the demands of reality manifested in adaptations that were creative and generative, or rather falsifying and destructive, such as resorting to manic solutions and illusions of satisfying liveliness instead of acknowledging limitations. In today's culture, it is sometimes hard to tell whether social and cultural changes are mobilized in order to creatively adapt to reality, or to destroy it. This is particularly poignant in our relation to time, which is an essential and inseparable aspect of our being: the omnipresent attempt to halt time, to live in an eternal and glorified golden age of youth, never growing old, gives rise to very intricate problems for beings which are, first and foremost, "being-toward-death."

When we practice psychoanalysis today, we must take into account this cultural setting, in which the patients coming to see us have been impaired not only by individual traumas, but also by a global context that has made tackling issues of existence, meaning, and relationships that much more complicated. It is not surprising to see that more and more patients with perverse organizations are voicing existential agonies and are inching closer and closer to the psychotic end of the spectrum. In our quest to augment our psychoanalytic toolkit with ontological insight, we would do well to remember that it is those patients whose self is impaired to begin with that have less capacity to deal with the problematic possibilities of modern life and its overarching theme of erasing differences and limitations.

Final remarks

We were very uneasy at times to be writing about a person who was a part of the Nazi party, however brilliant and inspirational his work may be. Since finishing the manuscript to the book, we came across a quote from Richard Rorty, the esteemed philosopher, that describes most accurately how we felt working on Heidegger's writings. We wish to leave this with you all to reflect upon:

> One of the twentieth century's greatest philosophers, without whom there would be no Sartre, no Foucault, no Frankfurt School, Martin Heidegger was also a man of great failures and flaws. A Faustus who made a pact with the devil of his time, Adolf Hitler. The story of Heidegger's life and philosophy, a quintessentially German story in which good and evil, brilliance and blindness are inextricably entwined and the passions and disasters of a whole century come into play … (Rorty, 1999)

CHAPTER SEVEN

Finding the truth in individual and large-group psychology

Vamık D. Volkan

In 1937, Sigmund Freud stated that an analyst's work is like an archeologist's excavation of an ancient dwelling place or ancient edifice that had been destroyed and buried. Analytic work brings into light what had been hidden in an analysand's mind. Freud added that for an archeologist the reconstruction is the aim; for an analyst the construction is only a preliminary labor. Further work is required for finding out if the construction is correct or not. This chapter examines *personal historical truth* in an individual's mind and how it is authenticated during the psychoanalytic process. It also describes how the *shared historical truth of ancestors*, whether it is correct or mythologized, impacts large groups. The term "large group" refers to thousands or millions of individuals, most of whom will never see or even know about each other, but who share many of the same sentiments. In everyday language, shared subjective experiences of large-group identities are expressed in terms such as "We are African Americans," "We are white supremacists," "We are Lithuanian Jews," "We are French," "We are Sunni Muslims," or "We are communists." A shared historical truth about ancestors, which I have named "chosen trauma," is utilized to protect and maintain large-group identity and also for political propaganda. No genuine societal efforts are made to verify its truth.

Personal historical truth

When I was asked to write for this chapter, what came to my mind was Andrew, a fifty-year-old successful business man, who had sought treatment from a newly graduated psychoanalyst, Dr. Hoffman. During his first visit with this analyst, Andrew loudly and aggressively demanded again and again to know the "*truth*" behind his inexplicable temper tantrums and wanted an answer from the analyst immediately. Dr. Hoffman, surprised and somewhat bewildered, called me for a consultation.

Andrew had managed to describe how he started having frequent temper tantrums without an appropriate reason after his second marriage two years earlier. For example, noticing a salt shaker empty during mealtime would drive him to smash plates in the dining room. He would scream and then go outside for fresh air to calm down. He had never had such temper tantrums during his first marriage and was experiencing guilt feelings for this behavior. He was also puzzled.

Andrew had married his first wife, a woman his age, when he was thirty years old. The couple had no children, and Andrew felt no passion for his wife. He had known his second wife, Emily, since her childhood because she grew up in his neighborhood. Andrew used to think of Emily, who is twenty-two years younger than he, as his "daughter." When he was forty-eight years old, he seduced Emily, quickly divorced his first wife, and married the much younger woman. His symptoms began soon after that.

When an analyst starts analyzing an individual, he or she wonders "What am I treating?" The analyst's assessment of a patient's psychological makeup is known as a "*formulation*." The *initial* formulation provides the analyst with a "psychoanalytic diagnosis" and also suggests ideas for the analyst about what to expect during the analytic process.

An initial formulation

De Masi (2019) reminds us what we learned from Freud's findings: "The kind of environmental response that the person received during the first part of his life lays the foundations for his later emotional disposition" (p. 391). Accordingly, when De Masi supervises a colleague's work, he firmly insists upon this so that the supervisee "can comprehend how the patient engages in the therapeutic task and with his analyst" (p. 391). When I begin supervising the treatment of a new case, I bring to the supervisee's attention the importance of studying the psychology of developmental ladders, and I specifically ask the supervisee to learn the patient's personal history, like De Masi would do, especially that of childhood. I insist that the analyst collect this data without machine-gunning the analysand with questions, but instead, psychologically speaking, walk with the patient and be curious about what is observed by both of them. When Dr. Hoffman called me for a consultation, I asked him to get in touch with me again after he received good-enough information about Andrew's developmental years. Soon Dr. Hoffman was able to collect satisfactory data.

Both of Andrew's parents had come from very rich families. Andrew was their only child. Andrew's father took frequent business trips away from home when Andrew was a child and was emotionally distant from his son. Andrew's mother had been raised by nannies. After her son was born, she also started hiring and firing caretakers for her son. When her husband was away she would often get drunk, sit on a couch in the living room and watch television. One day, when Andrew was a pubertal child, he found his almost-naked mother passed out in the living room with a bottle of bourbon next to her. Andrew described how he carried his mother to the parental bed. In a matter-of-fact way and without much affect, he added that he had an erection while carrying his mother's almost naked body.

When Andrew's father reached age forty-eight, he developed cancer and died. On his deathbed, he called his son and told him the following: "I had a huge business. I was like a king. I am now leaving my business, my kingdom, to you. Now you will be the king and take care of your mother." After his father died, Andrew indeed became a rich "king" at the age of twenty-two. His mother, who then was in her mid-forties, soon found a boyfriend. This boyfriend was the same age as her son. She told Andrew that her relationship with the young boyfriend was a platonic one; they were not having sex. Her son did not believe her.

Dr. Hoffman and I began to consider what might be the truth Andrew was demanding to know. First, we noticed that Andrew's father died when he was forty-eight and his son was twenty-two years old. Andrew divorced his first wife and remarried when he was forty-eight. We began wondering about Andrew's marrying a twenty-two-year-old woman whom he previously had considered a "daughter." We imagined that when his father died, Andrew replaced him as the "king"; in a sense, he had an oedipal triumph. By choosing a twenty-two-year-old boyfriend whom Andrew considered a displacement figure for himself, the mother actively stimulated her son's oedipal conflict over having suddenly reached such a triumph. Perhaps, in order to deal with her own guilt feelings, the mother presented her relationship with the young man as platonic.

Dr. Hoffman and I made the following *initial* formulation. When Andrew turned forty-eight years old, the age when his father had died and he had become a "king," he reversed the unconscious "mother–son" incestuous intimacy with a "father–daughter" incestuous intimacy that included actual sexual activities. This broke the incest taboo, increased Andrew's guilt feelings, competition (Andrew stated that he was afraid his wife would betray him with other men), and perhaps his castration anxiety. He responded to such conflicts with angry outbursts. Andrew's young second wife belonged to another race. Dr. Hoffman and I thought that this itself might provide a defense mechanism: a woman whose race is different from his mother's race would "fool" Andrew's unconscious mind, since he could not consciously be aware of the second wife as representing his mother; Abraham's (1913) notion of "neurotic exogamy" elucidates this very dynamic in detail.

Dr. Hoffman and I were aware that our initial formulation was only a *hypothesis* and that there would be much more data needed in order to make an authentic map of the patient's internal world. For example, Dr. Hoffman would wait to hear the stories of little Andrew's relationships with his nannies. Would he notice a link between the pre-oedipal Andrew's hunger for maternal care and his breaking plates while eating meals? If our initial formulation was correct, how would Andrew react to it when he learned the truth, and how would the analyst handle such a situation? I did not become a supervisor for Dr. Hoffman, and therefore I do not have information about what changes and additions might have been required for the *genuine* truth of Andrew's mind and its impact on him.

Making truth authentic

Analysands indirectly or directly describe the stories of their internal worlds, often without being aware of what they are doing, in many different ways. For example, sometimes such stories appear in fantasies or dreams, or a friend's recent adventures, or in a relationship with the boss at work. Other times we notice them in the theme of a film they watch or a novel they read. Some analysands know the truth about how a specific trauma in their lives has evolved, like asphalt paving on the sand at a beach in their mind. Known truth or initially constructed truth becomes authentic in a transference-countertransference development observed and worked through by the analysand. Only then can the analysand remove the asphalt paving and enjoy life on the beach.

Fuat was a twenty-seven-year-old, very bright Turkish man with a degree in molecular biology when he started his analysis in Istanbul a month and a half after the death of his father. His initial symptoms related to his ambivalent feelings for this father. Fuat had grown up in a house where the mother would not even cook meals, but would buy them from a restaurant or grocery store. The father was an educated man, but when at home, he would spend his time in a room watching television, eating, and gaining weight. When his son was a child, his father was already an obese man. He paid no attention to his growing son.

Fuat had a cousin who was five years older than he. This cousin noticed post-pubertal Fuat's difficulty in identifying with a strong father figure and his shyness around girls. This cousin, without informing Fuat's parents, arranged for fourteen-year-old Fuat to visit a prostitute. The prostitute repeatedly said "Hurry up! Hurry up!" to him, laughed and made humiliating facial gestures. He could not keep his erection. This became a major traumatic event for Fuat.

Afterwards, Fuat became preoccupied with fear that he might have contracted HIV. He told his mother what he had done. She took him to a physician and the HIV test showed that he did not have this infection. But his visit to the prostitute became the asphalt pavement in Fuat's mind, covering over other childhood traumas. He experienced depression on and off during the rest of his teen years.

While attending university, in spite of his great intelligence and good looks, Fuat would compare himself to other young men and feel that he was not as masculine as they were. He was shy around girls, but managed to have a girlfriend for a short time. When he had sex with her, he felt confused about how to use his hands, where to put them, and what to say and not say. Later, Fuat avoided developing close relationships with other young women, even though he was aware of his desire to have sex with a female partner. He knew the "truth" behind his symptoms—the impact of the trauma while visiting a prostitute at age fourteen.

Fuat's analyst, a woman, had not yet graduated from her psychoanalytic institute. I was her supervisor. For a year and a half on the couch, Fuat utilized intellectualization and often declared "I will not be able to do analysis," reflecting his recollection, "I will not be able to perform a sexual act." During the latter part of the second year of his analysis, his analyst, in transference, evolved as the prostitute who had humiliated young Fuat. Now, session after session on the couch, Fuat spoke of how he was imagining his analyst sitting behind him saying "Hurry up! Hurry up" and laughing at him. It was difficult for the inexperienced analyst, who came from a conservative family, to be perceived as a prostitute. As a supervisor, my role was to help her hold on to her psychoanalytic identity, and she became successful in maintaining the therapeutic position.

Details of the truth of fourteen-year-old Fuat's experience in a prostitute's bedroom and its associated emotions came alive with full force in the analyst's office. The truth became *authenticated*. After this, Fuat started coming to his session carrying a long red unopened umbrella. At first he would leave this umbrella outside the analyst's office door. Then one day, he entered the office holding the umbrella up. Symbolically he was showing the analyst that he possessed a penis capable of erection and was looking for her approval. His analyst did not even need to make an interpretation. Fuat no longer brought the umbrella to his session.

Fuat's analysis was one of the most successful cases I had supervised. Before he completed his analysis, Fuat was happily engaged to a young woman who had started living with him as his sex partner, and the couple already had made plans to get married.

Therapeutic play

Some analysands, especially those with a more primitive personality organization than a neurotic personality, often recall their personal traumatic historical truth, authenticate it, and render it harmless by becoming involved in what I have termed "therapeutic play" (Volkan, 1987). The "play" is expressed in activities that continue for weeks or months. It reflects a story of the patient's key mental conflict with associated pathogenic unconscious fantasies. It becomes the central focus of verbal communication from session to session. It takes place after an analysand crystalizes the analyst's representation as a "new object" (Loewald, 1960), also known in the psychoanalytic literature as "developmental object" or "analytic introject" (see for example: Baker, 1993; Cameron, 1961; Chused, 1982; Kernberg, 1975a; Tähkä, 1993; Volkan, 1976). The play comes to an end in a way that is a new experience for the analysand, which is shared with a new object. During the therapeutic play the analysand's personal traumatic historical truth becomes authenticated, and when the play ends the analysand can leave the pathological impact of a personal historical truth behind.

Jennifer's total analysis, from its beginning to its end has been previously published (Volkan, 2010). Here, I will summarize her therapeutic play. Jennifer's wealthy parents, living in a southern state in the United States, kept alive the racist traditions of the Old South. The racist tradition provided "two mothers" (Cambor, 1969; L. Smith, 1949; Volkan & Fowler, 2009) for Jennifer: the biological mother and the black nanny. Jennifer's biological mother treated Jennifer as if she were a beautiful doll, but did not provide good-enough motherly care and love. Jennifer was primarily raised by her black nanny who cooked food for baby Jennifer, fed her, sang songs to her, hugged and loved her. This all took place in the basement, as the nanny was not allowed to spend time in other parts of the house. When Jennifer was three and a half years old, the black nanny was ordered also to look after a newborn baby sister; Jennifer experienced rejection and loss of love. As an adult Jennifer filled her life with rituals in which she, as if a beautiful doll, would collect adoration from others. She was exhibiting an exaggerated narcissistic personality organization and hiding her loved and abandoned self-image.

One day during the beginning of the third year of her analysis, Jennifer attended a horse show in the Virginia countryside and noticed what she called an "ill-fed" (hungry for love) skinny horse at a stable and met Fanny, a black woman who was assigned the care of this animal. Then Jennifer's therapeutic play began. Previously, Jennifer used to come to her sessions in splendid dresses and lay on my couch like a "beautiful doll." Now, she began lying on my couch wearing wrinkled jeans. I learned that she had purchased the "ill-fed" horse and kept it at the same stable. She hired Fanny to look after it, developed an intense relationship with Fanny and started helping her bring the ailing horse back to health. Listening to Jennifer, I sensed that the animal represented the part of Jennifer that was hungry for maternal love, and Fanny stood for her childhood nanny. Jennifer, in her therapeutic play, went to her childhood and joined her "good" (not rejecting) nanny in order to have another opportunity to find love. Initially I did not tell Jennifer what came to my mind since I wanted to wait and see how this story would develop. While lying on my couch, Jennifer talked about almost nothing else but how she and Fanny looked after the horse.

After a month or so, I told Jennifer my idea about who the horse and Fanny represented: hungry (loved and abandoned) child/Jennifer and her nurturing black nanny. She did not respond to my explanation with any curiosity or verbalize any thoughts or feelings regarding her childhood. Instead, I became a spectator of her outside activities at the stables. Sometimes she came to her sessions wearing dirty jeans and a blouse soiled with animal feces. I wondered to myself if I stood for her white mother who did not know about her loving experiences with her black nanny in the basement. Then I sensed that I was a *different* white mother, a "new object/developmental object/analytic object." She wanted me to hear, learn, and appreciate her experiences with a loving black woman without interfering with her activities and without any racist attitudes. I did not interfere with Jennifer's relationship with her horse and Fanny. I tolerated her describing her actions in details on my couch four times a week without introducing new topics to wonder about. Jennifer's therapeutic play lasted for *nine months* before she had a "new beginning" (Balint, 1932), a "rebirth" (Rose, 1969).

Now, I will briefly describe Jennifer's new beginning/rebirth following her therapeutic play. After the horse was cured, Jennifer began behaving as if she were a tomboy. She began dressing like a man working on a farm, drinking beer with a bunch of young men, both white and African American, listening to their jokes and spending a great deal of time showing her horse to others and entering him in horse shows. Then she learned how to ride her horse. One day she had a dream in which her horse fell as he jumped a fence and bled from his neck. In spite of her conscious wish that her animal be protected from injury, she had another dream in which her horse was once more bleeding. I said to her, "In life, who does bleed regularly?" She looked dumbfounded. After remaining silent for a while, she responded: "A woman!"

Later Jennifer, who was married but never considered having children, became pregnant and then a good mother.

Total case histories

Since Freud's time, there have been different psychoanalytic "schools." Starting in the 1980s, an increase in new psychoanalytic theories and trends caused deep concern. In 1988, Wallerstein, during his presidential address to the 35th International Psychoanalytical Association Congress, expressed such a concern and wondered if we would have one psychoanalysis or many. In 2002, Leo Rangell, once president of the International Psychoanalytical Association and twice president of the American Psychoanalytic Association, also worried about a "growth of pluralism" (p. 1118) in psychoanalysis. Böhm (2002) stated that different ways of listening to the patient and different styles of handling clinical material were beginning to put analysts in different professions. In a book edited by Cooper (2006), thirty analysts considered a wide range of topics and shared their approaches to clinical conditions. While their differences appear profound, they also present new wine in old bottles.

Following these developments, I turned my attention to the benefits and pitfalls of this new growth of pluralism and wrote a textbook that includes ideas for psychoanalytic technique according to the level of the analysand's personality organization and describes new technical concepts, such as therapeutic play. I found questioning some classic assumptions and introducing new ways of understanding the truth about human psychology to be an enriching process. I also noted that some aspects of the pluralism supported resistances against examining unconscious material in depth (Volkan, 2010).

Besides writing a textbook, I began providing psychoanalytic case examples of individuals with different personality organizations spanning the first to the last days of analysis (Volkan, 2014, 2015a, 2015b, 2019, 2021; Volkan & Fowler, 2009). It is very difficult to measure scientifically the outcome of any type of psychoanalytic treatment since psychoanalysts deal with unconscious elements. The best way to describe changes in a person's internal world, I believe, is to recount *total* psychoanalytic processes without hiding behind psychoanalytic theoretical terms and without becoming a spokesperson for a specific psychoanalytic school. I believe that this is the best way to present the truth in an analysand's personal psychology and also to give the reader an opportunity to judge the authenticity of such a truth.

Shared historical truth

Freud was a discoverer of the internal world of individuals. His long dispute with Ferenczi, which started in 1925 about the influence of actual trauma—actual sexual abuse—on individuals' internal worlds, is well documented (for a review see Volkan, 2019). This controversy played a role in paths taken by other pioneer psychoanalysts as they continued to follow Freud's emphasis on the impact of seduction coming from the internal world. In 1932,

Freud's followers blocked Ferenczi from delivering a paper that focused on the truthfulness of seduction. During the same year Freud expressed pessimism about the role of psychoanalysis in wars or war-like situations in his correspondence with Albert Einstein (Freud, 1933b). While Freud and some well-known early psychoanalysts wrote about history, religious ideas, and arts, in the *clinical setting* external events shared by hundreds, thousands, or millions of persons were avoided.

Bowlby (1977) wrote that when he became a psychoanalyst in 1937, psychoanalysts in Great Britain were only interested in the internal worlds of their patients. Paying attention to historical events surrounding patients was considered inappropriate. Klein was treating a ten-year-old boy named Richard while World War II raged, literally overhead, during the London Blitz under which he and his psychoanalyst lived. It appears that throughout Richard's analysis, the terror of the war was not examined. After World War II, there was also silence about the Holocaust in analysts' offices (see for example, Blum, 1976). Even in 2002, Ira Brenner who, due to his personal history had studied and written a great deal about the impact of the Holocaust on affected individuals, stated how a number of "very talented 'outsider' analysts" challenged him by arguing that "analysis deals with the realm of psychic reality only" and that Brenner and his colleagues "were introducing an unnecessary element that only 'muddied the waters' and was unnecessary for successful treatment" (Brenner, 2002, p. xiii). I was born to Turkish parents on the Mediterranean island of Cyprus. I came to the USA in early 1957 a few months after I graduated from medical school in Turkey. When I was going through my personal analysis in the United States in the mid-1960s, a deadly ethnic conflict between Cypriot Greeks and Cypriot Turks was taking place on the island. I do not recall any serious focus during my entire analysis on this external event, which included the murder of my former medical-school roommate by an ethnic terrorist.

It is beyond the aim of this essay to review the changes in psychoanalytic practice during the last decades which have increased psychoanalysts' interest in the influence of shared historical, religious, and ideological events (for a review of this change see Volkan, 2019). Such events are linked to shared large-group identity issues. Now that the Covid-19 pandemic has made a big impact on psychoanalytic practices, most likely psychoanalysts' interest in shared external events will increase.

Shared identities

When Freud (1921c) imparted his theory of large-group psychology, he did not emphasize the importance of large-group identity; nor did he substantially use the term "identity" in this essay or elsewhere in reference to either individuals or large groups. It was Erikson (1956) who seriously focused on identity in psychoanalysis and defined it as "a sustained feeling of inner sameness within oneself … [and] a persistent sharing of some kind of essential character with others" (p. 57). In identity, the past, the present, and the future are integrated into a smooth continuum of remembered, felt, and expected existence for the individual (Akhtar, 1999).

Large-group identity can be defined as the subjective experience of thousands or millions of people who are connected by a persistent sense of similitude, even though they also share characteristics with individuals outside their large group. Though there are phenomenological differences between the various types of large groups since they may be focused on ethnic, religious, national, or ideological concerns, the focus here is on the psychodynamic factors common to all of them.

A child eventually stops being what Erikson (1959) called a "generalist" and develops a core large-group identity. Ethnic, national, religious, or ideological large-group identity becomes intertwined with the personal identity (Akhtar, 1992, 1999; Volkan, 1988, 1997, 2020). Scientific studies of recent decades illustrate that there is a psychobiological potential of "we-ness" and bias toward one's own kind (for example see Paul Bloom, 2010). As Freud (1940a) stated, parents represent the greater society to their children. The child's identification with them and other important people in their environment include elements of large-group sentiments and prejudices against the Other. Also, parents and other important people "deposit" images of past historical events, heroes, and martyrs into their children's minds. They give the child tasks in order to deal with such images. In a large group, thousands or millions of children also become receivers of the same or a similar deposited image and associated psychological tasks, and they begin to share the same "psychological DNA" (Volkan, 1988, 2020; Volkan et al., 2002). For example, after experiencing a collective catastrophe inflicted by an enemy large group, affected individuals are left with self-images similarly (though not identically) traumatized by the massive event. These many individuals unconsciously deposit such images into their children and give them tasks such as: "Put my mourning process on the right track"; "Regain my self-esteem for me"; and "Remain alert and be assertive."

Children in one large group also experientially learn how to share certain things, such as language or the design and colors of their large group's flag and become aware of how other things do not belong to their large group. Finnish children sense that having saunas is a "Finnish" thing to do, and Muslim children realize that eating pork is part of belonging to another large group. After age two, children begin mending their "good" (libidinally invested) and "bad" (aggressively invested) images of important objects and corresponding self-images (Kernberg, 1975a; Volkan, 1976). During this process, they invest both types of unmended images into what I call "suitable reservoirs of externalization" (Volkan, 1988, 2020) of shared common symbols of both their own and of the Other. Libidinally loaded unmended objects and self-images are invested in one's own large-group symbols, while aggressively loaded unmended objects and self-images are externalized onto shared symbols of the Other. Sophisticated thoughts, perceptions, emotions, and images of the history about one's own and the Other's large group develop later, without the children's awareness that the experientially learned symbol of the Other was also in the service of helping them avoid feeling object relations conflict.

During an individual's passage through adolescence, there is an unconscious review of childhood attachments—a "second individuation" (Blos, 1979). During this period, an individual's large-group identity that evolved during childhood also becomes a final identity (Volkan, 1988, 1997, 2020). If a person migrates or becomes a refugee, according to the age when going to a new place where another large-group identity prevails took place, he or she struggles in making a good or bad adjustment (Akhtar, 2014; Volkan, 2017).

There are also large-group identities that members assume in their adulthood, such as identities of extreme religious fundamentalist or terrorist organizations. Sometimes a political organization or party offers a new large-group identity for adults, as the Nazis did. These adults drastically change their investments in the core large-group identities that they developed in childhood. They may exaggerate selected aspects of their childhood large-group identities, and often they become believers of ideas that were not available in their childhood environments. In short, they give up sharing overall sentiments with people who had the same core childhood large-group identity but who have not made such specific new selections (Suistola & Volkan, 2017). During a psychoanalytic process, some analysands present issues regarding their large-group identity and work through such problems. I give examples of this below.

Avoiding or accepting the truth about large-group identity during the analytic process

In the 1970s, one of my analysands was a young woman whose Jewish parents used to live in New York. Just before their daughter's birth, they settled in Virginia. The father believed that in Virginia, as a Jewish man, he would not have enough customers for his business. He and his wife changed their names and pretended that they were not Jewish. They covered up the truth of their large-group identity. As their daughter was growing up, they shared their secret with her and asked her also to pretend to be a non-Jewish person away from home, a request she honored. When she grew up, a young man from a Christian traditional high-class Southern family fell in love with her, and they married. She could not tell her husband that she was raised as a Jew and that she was still not a Christian, because of her expectation that her husband would ask for a divorce if he knew the truth about her large-group identity. She became very anxious, and during the first year of her marriage sought psychoanalytic treatment. During her analysis, I maintained my psychoanalytic neutrality and gave her no advice. Before her analysis ended, she divorced her husband, became a very successful woman, and was comfortable with her Jewish identity. She continued to live in Virginia.

While supervising analytic processes in Turkey at a time when Turkish-Kurdish political issues were inflamed in this part of the world and had become deadly, I noticed on several occasions that anxiety would appear in cases when the analyst was a Turk and the analysand had a Kurdish background or the other way around. Also, in my book (2015a), *A Nazi Legacy: A Study of Depositing, Transgenerational Transmission, Dissociation and Remembering Through Action*, I supervised the total analysis of the grandson of a very high-level Nazi. One of the things his grandfather had done was to come up with the idea that putting Jewish people in a bus and gassing them to death would be financially advantageous. The parents of this analysand helped him to avoid the truth about his grandfather's Nazi identity. But his symptoms were linked unconsciously to the grandfather's terrible activities. For example, in a dissociated state he would break a bedroom window in order to have more oxygen. During his analysis, this analysand became fully aware of his grandfather's Nazi large-group identity and accepted the truth. In another book, *A Study of Ghosts in the Human Psyche: Story of a Muslim Armenian* (Volkan, 2019), I described the total analysis of a man in Turkey whose ancestors belonged to an Armenian tribe and whose treatment I supervised. Without paying attention to the truth of his ancestors' history, it would have been impossible to understand his internal world.

A special issue of the *Psychoanalytic Quarterly*, "Is Truth Relevant?" was published in 2016. In this special issue, Allison and Fonagy (2016) write that knowing the truth about oneself increases an analysand's learning about his or her social world and finding better ways to live in it.

Psychoanalysts' observations on large-group identity

In a well-conducted psychoanalysis, analysands on the couch do not lie. They may avoid telling the truth due to defense mechanisms they utilize, such as repression and denial, until such mechanisms no longer are needed. However, off the couch, often we notice how people, even those who are not actively involved in politics or diplomacy and who do not have racist attitudes, avoid or modify the truth while focusing on societal divisions and international affairs, with or without fully being aware of doing this, especially while referring to the Other.

Erikson (1956) theorized that primitive humans sought a measure of protection for their unbearable nakedness by wearing animal skins, feathers, or claws. On the basis of these outer garments, each tribe or clan evolved into *pseudo species* and behaved as if they were the real human beings or superior to others. Such postulations are supported by references to the Other in many ancient documents. Ancient Chinese regarded themselves as *people* and viewed the Other as *kuei* or "hunting spirits." The Munducuru in the Brazilian rain forest divided their world into Munducuru, who were people, and non-Munducuru, who were *pariwat* (enemies), except for certain neighbors who they perceived as friendly (Murphy, 1957). The names of Sudanese Dinka and the Arctic Yupiks refer to their being "real people" (Harari, 2014). The late psychoanalyst, Boyer (1986), who spent considerable time with Apache Indians, reported on how this tribe considered themselves to be *indeh*, the people, and everyone else as *indah*, the enemy. Humans continue to modify the truth in order to invest narcissism in their large-group identities. Loewenberg (1995), a historian and a psychoanalyst, in his well-known book, *Fantasy and Reality in History*, informs us about the irrationality and anxiety in history and their expressions in racism, anti-Judaism, and nationalism.

My observations on the role of large-group identity in international relations and domestic politics started after Egyptian president Anwar Sadat went to Israel on November 19, 1977, and at the Knesset referred to a "psychological wall" between the Israelis and the Arabs—a wall that, he stated, accounted for seventy percent of the problems between them. In response, the American Psychiatric Association's Committee on Psychiatry and Foreign Affairs, of which I was a member, brought influential Arabs and Israelis together for unofficial dialogues for six years to study this "wall." After this time I worked in many different countries examining large-group conflicts and also, with my interdisciplinary team, which included a historian, bringing together influential representatives of opposing large groups for unofficial dialogues. During these activities I met and worked with some well-known political and religious leaders (Volkan, 1988, 1997, 2004, 2006, 2013).

My work off the couch allowed me to focus on large-group psychology *in its own right*. This means studying the conscious and unconscious shared past historical/psychological experiences that exist within a large group in order to enlarge our understanding of the emergence of present-day societal-political-religious-ideological events and leader–follower relationships. This is similar to a psychoanalyst making formulations about his or her analysands' developmental histories associated with various conscious and unconscious fantasies in order to understand what motivates certain behavior patterns, symptoms, and habitual interpersonal relationships. "Chosen trauma" and "chosen glory" are crucial concepts in large-group psychology in its own right.

The truth about ancestor's histories and collective responses

As the dissolution of the Soviet Union began, my interdisciplinary team and I brought together influential Estonians and Russians for years-long dialogues in four-day meetings a few times per year. Our aim was to help the Estonians and Russians have a peaceful divorce. During one session, which was focusing on then-current problems between the two opposing large groups, an Estonian complained about the Russians' past treatment of his people. A very high-level person from the Russian parliament, who was a member of the Russian dialogue team, very loudly began talking about events that took place from the thirteenth to the fifteenth centuries: Tatar and Mongol lords' occupation of many parts of today's Russia, including Moscow. My facilitating team members and I were surprised. The Russian parliamentarian could not stop talking about what has become known to historians as "the Tatar-Mongol yoke." He wanted us to realize that the victimized Russians had stood between the Tatar and Mongol perpetrators and the Europeans. If Russia had not existed, the Europeans would have been devastated by the Tatars and Mongols. He was upset that the Europeans did not acknowledge how Russian suffering had saved them. He focused on why Russians had an entitlement to rule over other large groups, while being at the same time different than the Tatars and Mongols due to Russian behavior that protected the Others under their rule. How dare the Estonians not appreciate living under Russian rule, which had brought "good" things to Estonia! (Volkan, 2020). This event and similar ones that arose as we conducted unofficial dialogues between representatives of other opposing large groups led me to the concept I called "chosen trauma."

A chosen trauma refers to the shared mental image of a traumatic event at the hand of an enemy in a large group's ancestors' history. A chosen trauma is not an image of a rather recent historical event when photographs and belongings of the lost ones are still in their descendants' homes, and survivors' stories are still "alive," such as the Holocaust. Over many generations, over centuries, an individual, his or her parents, grandparents, other relatives, and friends will have no actual memory of the ancestors' trauma. The truth about the ancestors' trauma exists, but it is modified and mythologized. It undergoes a process which Waelder (1936, p. 48) named "change of function." Now it is perceived as a most significant symbol that psychologically links the large-group members together. It also becomes a source, to one degree or another, of an "entitlement ideology" (Volkan, 2013, 2020) in which the members feel entitled to regain what their ancestors lost decades or centuries ago and, as Freud (1916d) noted, can regard themselves as exceptions to conventional norms.

For example, the fall of Constantinople (today's Istanbul), the capital of the Byzantine Empire, in 1453, is the Greeks' chosen trauma, and the Greeks' entitlement ideology is called *Megali Idea* (Great Idea) (Markides, 1977; Volkan & Itzkowitz, 1994). A "chosen glory" refers to the shared image of a historical event that is a significant ethnic, national, religious, or ideological large-group identity marker. This time the image is linked to the ancestors' realistic, fantasized, and mythologized great accomplishments in dealing with another large group and the ancestors' heroes. Sometimes a chosen glory and chosen trauma are linked. For example, I noted that the Russian parliamentarian not only talked about the Russian chosen trauma, but also glorified victimized ancestors who, he believed, had protected the Europeans from disaster. Many times during the unofficial dialogues I observed the emergence of chosen traumas and chosen glories that influenced and modified the current truth between opposing large groups.

Humans everywhere behave the same in killing or loving the Other. Sometimes, under certain circumstances including those that are initiated by inflaming a chosen trauma, the destruction becomes a new huge tragedy. I studied how Slobodan Milošević (president of Serbia within Yugoslavia from 1989 to 1997 and president of the Federal Republic of Yugoslavia from 1997 to 2000) and the political circle around him, reactivated the image of the Serbian chosen trauma, the Battle of Kosovo, which took place in 1389 between the Ottoman Turks and Serb forces and how the entitlement ideology called "Christoslavism" was inflamed. My study included conducting interviews with people who knew Milošević. Here I will not tell the full story of my study (for a detailed version see Volkan, 1997, 2004). Briefly, as the six-hundredth anniversary of the Battle of Kosovo approached in 1989, with the permission and encouragement of Milošević, the 600-year-old remains of the battle's martyred hero, Prince Lazar, which had been kept north of Belgrade, were placed in a coffin. This coffin was then taken over the course of the year to almost every Serb village and town, where it was received by huge crowds of mourners dressed in black. Repeatedly during this long journey, Lazar's remains were symbolically buried and reincarnated, until they were buried for good at the original battleground in Kosovo. The inflammation of the Serbian chosen trauma and entitlement ideology led to new war including mass murder in Srebrenica. As Serbians were killing Muslim Bosnians, they called their victims "Turks." Truth was modified.

Most recently, Finnish historian Suistola and I (Suistola & Volkan, 2017) examined how the so-called Islamic State of Iraq and the Levant (ISIS) attempted to "reestablish" the Caliphate and turn their chosen trauma of losing the Caliphate into a new glory. The political propaganda ISIS openly used was an image of this chosen trauma. We can often observe references to somewhat truthful and even fantasied chosen traumas in other political propagandas as well. From August 11 to 12, 2017, a rally occurred in Charlottesville, Virginia where I have been living since the early 1960s. Marchers from other locations in the United States chanted racist and anti-Semitic slogans and carried Nazi and neo-Nazi symbols. I imagined that they shared a delusional chosen trauma of losing a United States that was only for white persons whose ancestors had come from selected countries and that now they were wishing for an America dominated only by such persons. Truth held no interest for these demonstrators.

Last words

In the clinical setting, there is a need to go beyond what a large group means for an individual and to study and pay attention to large-group identity and its place in creating symptoms and pathological behavior patterns. I hope that there will be interest in studying large-group psychology *in its own right* at psychoanalytic institutes. In making professional statements about societal/political and international themes, I am mindful of how and why knowing the truth is complicated, and I share Freud's pessimism about psychoanalysis playing a role in preventing wars. This does not mean psychoanalysts should be uninvolved when there is an opportunity to provide information on large-group identity and related concepts that can be used by diplomats and other authorities or to help large groups strive for more peaceful coexistence. I am most grateful for having had such opportunities.

Part III

Clinical realm

CHAPTER EIGHT

Narrative truth and theoretical truth

Donald P. Spence

I

The force of psychoanalytic argument has traditionally relied rather more on rhetorical persuasion than on appeal to the data. This tradition was heavily influenced by Freud who never felt it necessary to reveal all the evidence for a particular interpretation. Whatever the reasons for his reluctance, he later rationalized this tendency by stating that if the reader was not inclined to agree with his formulation, then additional data would scarcely change his mind (Freud, 1912e, p. 114).

Largely as a result of his initial decision, a custom has grown up which gives contributors to the literature the right to allude to the facts rather than state them in full. Because the evidential basis for any statement is only partly open to public inspection, the criteria for conviction are necessarily softer than they would be in a field where all the evidence must be presented. Precisely because the evidential domain is partly closed, the skeptical reader of the psychoanalytic literature is in no position to challenge any conclusion he may come across. For the same reason, agreement among readers can never be complete or compelling; acceptance of an interpretation or theoretical conclusion always reduces to agreement on faith.

Whether or not this tradition *must* be observed in just this way, the fact that not all the evidence is ever available for public scrutiny must necessarily affect the standards of argument and debate within the field. Just as Freud was unwilling to accept a patient who would not report everything (because, as it happened, he was bound to keep certain professional secrets)[51] so the field cannot function in an ideal manner so long as its reasoning *rests* on only

[51] See Freud, 1913c, p. 136.

partial data—and for exactly the same reasons. Just as the reluctant patient would be able to reclassify all his difficult moments as somehow secret and therefore exempt from analysis, so the reluctant author, faced with a piece of fuzzy reasoning or doubtful logic, is able to simply omit the embarrassing details from publication; given the tradition just cited, he does not even need to supply an explanation for the omission.

A further consequence of this tradition bears on the matter of generalizing from clinical particulars to the larger theory. If the full details of a given happening are never cited, then it becomes impossible to challenge the category formed from these details; if a given clinical happening, for example, is used as evidence for the return of repressed oedipal strivings, the assertion can only be taken on faith because the outside reader is never in possession of all the facts. As a result, clinical observations can be rather easily turned into far-reaching generalizations. The generalization, because of its greater visibility and rhetorical appeal, takes on an importance that goes far beyond the merits of its data base. In many cases, the generalization may be completely unwarranted.

To take a homely example from another field—suppose I give you a brief description of a cottage I just bought by saying that it has four walls and a roof. I choose not to provide further details. You hear my description, match it with a description of your own cottage, and conclude that yours is exactly like mine—even though yours is a modern beach house and mine is a made-over garage. In a similar way, incomplete clinical data lend themselves to premature labeling, unwarranted categorization, and give rise to theoretical concepts which are more metaphor than construct because of their largely nonexistent data base. As a result, conceptual agreement is much greater than the data justifies, and the theoretical state of the field seems more advanced than is actually the case.

If all the data for a given formulation are not available for independent examination, there is no possibility for the gradual refinement and clarification of theory. Rather than a particular formulation serving as a tentative and provisional arrangement of data, subject to subsequent test and cross-validation, the formulation tends to become substituted for the data. Despite Freud's proviso that his theoretical concepts were meant to be taken as only temporary scaffolding subjects to subsequent reformulation (Freud, 1914c, p. 77), the concepts have proved to be the most enduring parts of the clinical adventure; the relevant data are either incompletely reported or, even when made public, essentially inaccessible to anyone with only normative competence.[52] With the exception of a relatively small number of recorded cases, there is no clinical archive; most utterances exist only in memory, and in a form that is more distorted than veridical.

As a result of this one-sided arrangement, the path from observation to theory can never be retraced. Not only does this fact place a heavy burden on the original discoverer; it also makes

[52] Elsewhere I have discussed the distinction between normative and privileged competence: "Normative competence belongs to all members of the psychoanalytic community ... privileged competence belongs to the analyst at a specific time and place in a particular analysis" (Spence, 1981, p. 114).

it difficult to try out other formulations because the data can never be looked at twice. Given the lack of public findings, the theory has necessarily grown in largely individual fashion, with separate investigators each contributing his own set of concepts drawn from his private set of observations (Freud, of course, leads the list). Assuming the usual level of erroneous observation and faulty logic, there would seem, however, to have been surprisingly few conceptual mistakes. How has this high standard of performance been maintained?

Part of the answer lies in what we have identified as the tradition of incomplete data. If the grounds for a general proposition are incomplete, then there is no way for a critic to claim that a particular set of findings did *not* support the concept because the original discoverer can argue that the missing pieces of this set, had they been seen, would suffice to complete the puzzle. On the other hand, it is still possible to support the concept if and when the available findings happen to fit into that particular pattern. Thus, the missing data allow occasional support of theory but make falsification impossible. Given this state of affairs, no proposition will ever be disconfirmed. (It should be pointed out, of course, that the apparent confirmation is also suspect because it does not happen in every instance; but since we never have access to the full range of findings, we can never be sure of just what proportion of cases fails to fit.)

A second part of the answer is based on the difference between *the context of discovery and the context of justification* (see Reichenbach, 1951). A given theoretical proposition may, in the context of given clinical encounter (the *context of discovery*), provide necessary and sufficient reasons for a given piece of behavior; because it allows all pieces of the encounter to be fitted into a continuous narrative, it gives a sense of satisfaction and closure and the feeling that now at last a new understanding has taken place. Both patient and analyst may be convinced that an explanation has been found for an anomalous piece of behavior. This kind of "aha" experience seems to be central to the process of therapeutic change; narrative fit permits certain kinds of formulations to "become true" (see Viderman, 1979) and thereby to become an accepted part of the patient's contents of consciousness.

But even though an explanation may be perfectly adequate within the therapeutic hour, it does not instantly qualify for the status of a general law. To reach that level, it must meet other kinds of tests, usually carried out in what is known as the *context of justification*. To become a part of our theoretical system, the proposition must not only suit the individual case, where it was first discovered, but meet the requirements of *all other cases* which share the same characteristics as the target case. When we move from the single case to the larger sample, we need to see all the data—but as already noted, this wish is defeated by the system.

We now begin to recognize the need for two standards of reporting. When the clinician is reporting on a new piece of clinical insight, he has no need to convince his readers; his mission has already been accomplished, so to speak, with the conviction of his patient. He is speaking within a particular context of discovery. Any further reporting is probably after the fact; whether or not his readers agree, the clinical discovery has already taken place. But when he is attempting to justify his concept, the new readers *must* be convinced, and conviction, as we have seen, can only take place when we have access to all the data. This kind of argument requires a different kind of presentation.

Freud never made the distinction between the two kinds of reporting. When describing a new piece of clinical insight, he found it sufficient to present only what he *thought* was sufficient, and he was rather scornful of the need to provide all the evidence; as in telling a joke, if it does not seem funny the first time, telling it in more detail will usually not help. And his aim in his case histories was more to share than to convince; the clinical work had already been accomplished, and he only felt that others might be interested. For the purpose of initial reports, the tradition of incomplete data is perfectly adequate. But when he turned to a more general formulation, Freud needed to present a more complete analysis in order to bring about conviction. He never saw the need to provide a more elaborate presentation, and the failure to distinguish the two kinds of reporting has remained with us to the present.

How, exactly, do we go about finding confirmation? In the context of discovery, we seem to depend heavily on narrative fit and on the extent to which a given formulation or interpretation lends coherence and continuity to a particular set of happenings. Narrative coherence ranks as one of the four essential criteria used by Ricœur (1977a) to validate psychoanalytic facts: to "explain here is to reorganize facts into a meaningful whole which constitutes a single and continuous history" (p. 861). Narrative fit has been described by Sherwood (1969) as a critical feature of the clinical explanation. But while narrative fit can be highly persuasive in the immediate clinical situation, its compelling quality does not necessarily indicate the presence of more general truths. And it should be borne in mind that narratives are notoriously accommodating because they are almost infinitely flexible and because they usually depend on a rather simple chronological syntax ("and then … and then … and then");[53] as a result, they can almost never be used to *exclude* particular happenings. Thus, a narrative is not well suited to disconfirm a particular hypothesis; I can hardly say, except in a very small set of cases, that Event A could *not* have happened before Event B.

As a result of its flexibility, a narrative cannot be used to make a definitive test between two formulations. It therefore follows that we can hardly ever use narrative fit as a test of historical truth (and, as we will see later, of theoretical truth). True and false happenings (in the sense of historical truth) can both be smoothly fitted into a patient's developing story, and the goodness of fit be used to distinguish the first from the second. A good narrative explanation may be useful because it brings together disparate pieces of a patient's life in an appealing way, but what might be called its narrative truth may depend more on its aesthetic properties (which stem from matters of timing and phrasing) than on its historical validity. This state of affairs has an ironical consequence. If we were able to know, by some kind of magic, which pieces of the narrative were historically false and could revise our narrative to leave them out, we might seriously jeopardize its aesthetic appeal, just as a painting might be seriously flawed by turning it into a strict representation of realty.

[53] See Atkinson, 1978, p. 129.

In what way does narrative truth differ from historical truth? Consider a specific interpretation about how the patient might conceivably have felt at a certain time in his life. Proof that he actually had these feelings is probably out of reach because feelings and attitudes leave few traces—thus the historical truth is always in doubt. But to the extent that the interpretation explains many subsequent aspects of the patient's behavior and to the extent that it completes the unfinished clinical picture in just the right way, it acquires its own truth value, and no further checking is necessary. To the extent that an explanation is persuasive and compelling, it acquires features of what might be called narrative truth.

The contrast between the two kinds of truth is highlighted even further when we look at the nature of autobiography. Gusdorf (1980) tells us that:

> In autobiography the truth of facts is subordinate to the truth of the man, for it is first of all the man who is in question ... The significance of autobiography should therefore be sought beyond truth or falsity, as these are conceived by simple common sense [an apparent reference to historical truth]. It is unquestionably a document about a life, and the historian has a perfect right to check out its testimony and verify its accuracy. But it is also a work of art ... The literary, artistic function is thus of greater importance than the historic and objective function in spite of the claim made by positivist criticism both previously and today. (p. 43)

At first glance, the contrast between narrative and historical truth may seem equivalent to the contrast between psychic and external reality. In fact, however, the terms have quite different meanings and should not be confused. External reality, first of all, is not the same as historical truth. We are coming to be skeptical of Freud's far-reaching positivism and are discovering that in many ways external "reality" is very much a construction of the perceiver and thus contains large portions of narrative truth. My account of yesterday's football game is undoubtedly a mixture of what really happened and what I wanted to happen, a mixture of the objective physics of the game and its subjective meaning. *Conversely*, psychic reality may often be securely grounded in historical fact, and one of our tasks as analysts is to increase the historical truth of the patient's inner world in whatever way we can. At the same time, however, we are also interested in enlarging its narrative base and providing more complete access to fantasy when this seems appropriate. Thus, psychic reality may, at any one time, contain elements of both historical and narrative truth, and its power to persuade is apparently independent of which truth is represented. In similar fashion, external reality is usually composed of both fact and fiction, and one consequence of analysis is to make the patient philosophically more sophisticated and less of a naïve realist.

If narrative truth differs from historical truth, how does it compare with theory? We can say that a narrative account derives its appeal from the particular; theory, from the general. Among the elements of the narrative account, some may be true in the sense of having actually happened (historical truth), and others may be true in a narrative sense, but false from the standpoint of history. In a number of places in his writing, Freud admitted that both true and false fragments could be contained within a particular reconstruction, but he claimed (somewhat optimistically it would seem) that this was no problem because it was the "kernel of truth" (Freud, 1937d, p. 268) that made all the difference. But it is by no means clear how the "kernel of truth" can be identified and separated from the set of equally likely fabrications which make up the patient's life story, and if we have no sure way of identifying historical truth, we are seriously handicapped in our attempt to frame theoretical laws. This is not to say that narrative truth is an unimportant aspect of the true or to deny that it contributes significantly to therapeutic success; it is only to point out that narrative truth is not always success; it is only to point out that narrative truth is not always equivalent to "the whole truth" and to make clear that we cannot use therapeutic success to validate our general theory.[54] This very success may be an important reason for taking a proposition seriously in the first place, but to rest a general theory on the results of one patient (or even one hour) is to seriously restrict our data base and to ignore the importance of individual differences. Once again, context of discovery should not be confused with context of justification.

But this would seem to be an unfair accusation; confirmation of theoretical constructs always seems to rely on more than one patient, and we can find countless examples in our literature of new clinical findings which seem to support established theory. The trouble lies in the nature of the confirmation, and this problem brings us back to our tradition of incomplete data. As we have seen earlier in this chapter, when all the facts are not presented, loose confirmation can be rather easily achieved. Precisely for this reason, the fit between theory and findings can never be more than preliminary when not all the facts are available, and particularly good fits are special causes for alarm because of the possibility that the good fit is achieved by judicious selection and arrangement of the findings.

It would seem as if the apparent validation of theory by clinical data, because it is necessarily based on incomplete evidence, must necessarily depend on "soft" pattern matches. If all the facts were known, many of these matches would not stand up to scrutiny. But because the large store of clinical utterances disappears as soon as they are uttered, there is no going back; thus, the validity of a pattern match can never be tested, and with the authority granted by printer's ink, it comes to take on a status which it probably does not deserve. Soft pattern matches turn into hard confirmations, without our ever being quite aware that the change is taking place.

Another reason for the general belief in confirmation stems from a second aspect of narrative truth. We have seen that narrative truth can be distinguished from historical truth in the analytic hour and that the former may contribute significantly to the effectiveness of an interpretation. But there is a second kind of narrative truth which lies at the heart of the way each of us thinks about the general theory. We are always constructing a conceptual narrative from a combination of clinical experiences and theoretical exposure, fitting together into a coherent whole our sense of psychoanalytic theory and psychoanalytic process. We bring to this task

[54] See Hartmann (1964) and Eagle (1980a) for similar cautions.

criteria which are relevant to the problem of narrative fit. As a result, we are more than usually tolerant of soft pattern matches and incomplete evidence because we aim to construct a coherent theoretical "story," not an ironclad account of the facts.

This attempt is good enough to provide us with a usable narrative which is always being reinforced by our ongoing clinical experience. Matches between clinical happenings and our developing narrative provide us with the sense that we are privy to a certain part of the truth; what we never stop to examine, of course, is the fact that the matches are often selective and that our theory never accounts for all of the data. We are also inclined to remember the positive and ignore the negative matches because we are searching for coherence and continuity; as a result, we tend to minimize anything which interrupts the "flow" of the narrative. Because we are searching for narrative truth, we are always attempting to write the best possible "story" from all available data; we are not attempting to keep careful track of matches and mismatches.

It could be argued that the very reasons that allow us to construct a usable narrative prevent us from generating a valid theory. As the history of science makes clear, theory building is discontinuous, episodic, and often marked by critical reevaluations; at certain points along the way, old paradigms must be dismantled and replaced by substantially different worldviews. To build good theory, we must be prepared to give up a familiar formulation and return to the data of observation until a new explanation is discovered. But such a step not only requires access to the original observations (many of which are permanently out of reach), but also a readiness to throw away large parts of the enabling narrative which help us to make sense out of our day-by-day clinical encounters. Even though it may not make sense of everything, this narrative is still better than nothing and, as a result, tends to remain in place despite any number of disconfirming observations. Even though wrong in parts, it is also true in parts; enough confirmation is provided by our daily encounters with our patients to convince us that we are on the right track. If we assume, in addition, that the correct theory is only waiting in the wings, then we may find it even less necessary to carry out a critical review of all the evidence—assuming we could somehow make it reappear.

II

In our general satisfaction with our private narrative as a predictor of behavior, supported by confirmations from our daily clinical encounters, we have tended to lose sight of the fact that everyone—you, I, and the man on the street—operates in a roughly comparable fashion. Some theories are better than others, but in every case the theory user always believes that his system is true enough and gives a sufficiently good account of the facts to justify continued use. This state of affairs comes about because of what might be called the ambiguity of everyday life, a lesson well taught by Freud. Since any piece of behavior can be looked at from several vantage points, we can produce any number of pattern matches simply by choosing the piece which best fits our particular theory. To complicate matters further, this ambiguity is composed of two different types: the multiple meanings of events as they actually exist in the real world (a dream, for example, can be seen as both a source of information and a protector of sleep; a symptom as both an inconvenience and an appeal for sympathy); and second, the multiple meanings which we choose to project onto the world as we see it, meanings which are often guided by unconscious and preconscious fantasies (see Jacob Arlow, 1969). It is the second sort of ambiguity that is used to confirm the private theory of the paranoid and the mystic; the picture would be much clearer if these projected meanings could be simply set aside. But the difficulty seems to be that there is no easy way to discriminate the first set from the second—and therefore, all the more reason to be wary of private theory and subjective confirmation.

The problem is further complicated by language and the way it functions. In many situations, particularly when reality is unambiguous, it works as simple pointer. If I say, "Look at the aardvark," I have both given you an order and, assuming you had never seen an aardvark before, a lesson in identification. But when reality becomes more ambiguous and we move from simple objects to complex relationships, then language can open the way to a great deal of mischief. Suppose I describe the case of a student who just failed an examination and say wisely, "It looks like *castration* anxiety." Language is pretending to be a pointer, as before, and you may hear me telling you something veridical about the student. In fact, however, I am not making an observation at all—or at least, not an observation that can be checked by a random set of other observers. On the contrary, I am invoking a piece of theory without saying so; I am making it appear as if the theory were proven rather than problematic: and by using the word *castration* in such an offhand fashion, I am giving you the feeling that *everyone* believes that castration fears have rather profound and long-lasting effects on behavior, and that this belief has been supported once again. In short, I am mischievously using language to make it look as if we have found a confirmation of a general law—when, in fact, the notion of castration anxiety is at best a rather weak hypothesis of rather restricted scope.

How much of this mischief comes from my own projective system and how much is the sentence a valid description of the student's behavior? The answer depends on your own set of beliefs, your own theory of the world. If you are a Freudian, you will tend to hear the statement as a simple observation, a statement similar to my saying, "There is an aardvark." If you are not, you may hear it as a whimsical comment, as a metaphor, as an outrageous and unfounded accusation, or as a mixture of all these and more. If you are a Freudian, you will tend to hear my statement as an example of what Quine would call an observation sentence, defined as a sentence which does full justice to its stimulus meaning,[55] Observation sentences are the datum sentences of science; they can be described as "the bottom edge of language, where it touches experience: where speech is conditioned to stimulation" (Quine & Ullian, 1978, p. 28). Observation sentences produce agreement in all observers exposed to the same situation.

But while all observers would probably agree when I say, "There is an aardvark," a much smaller sample would agree with my statement, "It looks like castration anxiety." The non-believers might have been exposed to the same stimulation—the failing student—but choose to describe him in other ways. If the disagreement is large enough, we would have to call my

[55] In Quine's (1960) language, observation sentences "wear their meaning on their sleeves."

statement something other than an observation sentence; as a result of this relabeling, it would not be used in the formation of a larger theory.

Now here is where our particular troubles begin. The bulk of putative observation sentences in our literature can never be checked because the utterances giving rise to these sentences have disappeared. As a result, their status can never be challenged, and the way is open to using them in a theory where they probably do not belong. Because of our language habits, statements which are cast in the form of observation sentences tend to be taken as valid observations; in the absence of primary data, this tendency becomes all powerful and, as noted earlier, random comments may be elevated to the status of theory; with repetition, they are advanced to the level of eternal truths. A given proposition may be completely unfounded and yet every time it is invoked, even in the absence of any kind of confirming evidence, it carries the impression that the proposition has once more been confirmed. In the example just given, to invoke the concept of castration anxiety is to make the claim that it has once again been supported. Frequency of use breeds familiarity, and familiarity breeds persuasion. Just as a general law is strengthened with each new piece of supporting data, so a tentative proposition such as castration anxiety can be mistakenly supported simply by being invoked. Each usage may be completely without foundation, but the power of language is such that when I use words in a pointing fashion, you assume that I am being truthful and telling you something veridical about our shared world. You assume, in other words, that I am making a valid observation.

Here then, is another way by which our theory becomes wrongly confirmed. Because it depends on incomplete data, it lends itself to pseudo-observation sentences which carry the conviction of confirmation. Because the data tend to disappear as soon as they are conceptualized, the statements about the data tend to take their place; the statements become the core of our literature and, because they are publicly accessible, they tend to function as evidence. What began as a tentative observation may be prematurely cast as a theoretical statement (see Esman, 1979) and becomes invested with authority and finality; given a certain frequency of appearance, it becomes established as tested theory. As the literature takes the place of the primary data, disputes are referred to specific papers when they should be referred to the original evidence, and concepts remain current so long as they are published and tend to drop into disuse when they are no longer cited. With attention shifted to the literature, we no longer notice the absence of primary data, the small numbers of recorded cases, or the gap between what can be understood from a recorded case and what was available to the treatment analyst when he was treating the particular patient.

III

In one of his papers to a more general audience, Freud (1933a) stressed his interest in building a general theory.

> I have told you that psychoanalysis began as a method of treatment; but I did not want to commend it to your interest as a method of treatment but on account of the truths it contains, on account of the information it gives us about what concerns human beings

> most of all—their own nature—and on account of the connections it discloses between the most different of their activities. (p. 156)

Freud always wanted to go beyond interpretation and use the clinical material to establish general laws. He gained his insights from the individual case but hoped to avoid circularity by confirming them with other cases. His successors have tried to carry on this tradition by testing what might be called the working theory against the new circumstances of each ongoing case.

We speak and write as if this tradition was flourishing—and yet, as I have tried to make clear, on only a very few occasions is a general proposition ever confronted by the underlying evidence. The data are conspicuous mainly by their absence, and what confirmations we have are almost incomplete and essentially private, inaccessible to the outside critic. We have no tradition which requires an assertion to be backed by all the evidence; on the contrary, as we have seen, Freud emphasized the right of privileged withholding, and we have followed in his footsteps. In similar fashion, we have no tradition of what might be called the loyal opposition, no forum for well-intentioned disbelievers who are not satisfied with a given set of conclusions. It may be that the lack of legitimate opposition is closely tied to the tradition of incomplete data, because so long as there is a possibility that the data are confirming but simply being withheld, the critic tends to suppress his criticism. But as in other arenas, the absence of dissent does not always indicate agreement.

I have tried to argue that narrative truth must be distinguished from theoretical truth. An interpretation may be useful because it brings together disparate pieces of a patient's live, because it reduces many pieces of behavior to one underlying cause, and because it finds a "narrative home for an anomalous happening" (Spence, 1982b)—all of these satisfactions depend on the narrative and aesthetic truth of the interpretation, but they have no necessary bearing on its place in the larger body of theory. Narrative truth is useful—indeed, essential—for generating our understanding of the particular case we are treating but significantly incomplete for generating laws. We tend to lose sight of this conclusion because we keep having experiences which seem to prove the opposite. Every day, some part of our clinical experience seems to support one or more pieces of our general theory, and in the face of these accumulating confirmations, we continue to think that the clinical happening does, after all, provide the basis for sound theory. But as we have seen, the confirmations tend to be piecemeal and can never be checked by others; and because we are working toward building up a private narrative of the theory, we tend to emphasize coherence and continuity rather than mismatch and surprise. (If there were surprises, they might never be remembered; and if they were remembered, where would they be published?)

I have argued that each of us is constantly developing his own version of the received theory—our subjective narrative. Because it is based on private data and never made public, it can never be compared with the working theory of another analyst. Nevertheless, we all believe that our own private theory is essentially the same as that of our colleagues; and furthermore, that they all correspond almost exactly to the developing general theory which will someday appear. But this assumption needs to be challenged. The working hypotheses of any particular analyst may have no necessary connection with the general theory or with any other private theory; so long as they do not violate the narrative truth of the analyst's experience, they can range over a broad landscape of ideas, some true, others not so true; and so long as the large majority of clinical happenings are never recorded, there is little likelihood that his private hypotheses will ever be tested against another set of data.

Public theory is just as much protected—because of the tradition of incomplete data. Not only does a pseudo-observation statement derive authority by simply being stated; the more often it is used, the better its credentials seem to become because it takes on the character of a general law. As I have argued above, each particular use of a proposition may be based on only soft data, but the accumulation of many soft instances builds up an air of infallibility and general truth.

Most in need of examination is our general theory. It may be necessary to recognize the unpleasant fact that Freud was being somewhat wishful in his assumption that his theory contained a body of general truths, just as he was somewhat frivolous in his approach to confirmation. Discussing the problem of corroborating an interpretation, Freud (1923c) writes that

> what makes him [the analyst] certain in the end is precisely the complication of the problem before him, which is like the solution of a jig-saw puzzle. ... If one succeeds in arranging the confused heap of fragments, each of which bears upon it an unintelligible piece of drawing, so that the picture acquires a meaning, so that there is no gap anywhere in the design and so that the whole fits into the frame—if all these conditions are fulfilled, then one knows that one has solved the puzzle and that there is no alternative solution. (p. 116)

But because of the elasticity of narrative fit, there is any number of good arrangements; and as we have noted, what suits the context of discovery may not fit the context of justification. Freud was too ready to generalize from the single case—too excited, perhaps, by the rapture of discovery to realize that one swallow does not always make a summer.

We may have to reconcile ourselves to the possibility that a general theory may be a long time coming—because of the particular nature of our clinical operation which is based on narrative truth. As I have argued elsewhere,

> If the analyst functions more as a pattern maker than a pattern finder, then we may be faced with a glaring absence of general rules. What rules there are, moreover, may pertain mainly to the more trivial aspects of our clinical material. If the impact of a particular interpretation is contingent ... on the specific texture of time and place, the rules for it being true are just as much out of reach as the rules for any other kind of artistic masterpiece. (Spence, 1982b, p. 71)

Each time a particular interpretation is followed by more insight or a new set of associations, the analyst is apt to draw the mistaken conclusion that its historical truth is also being confirmed; from this, it is but a small step to conclude that something of theoretical importance has been established. But implicit in the notion that narrative truth can be distinguished from historical truth is the conclusion that narrative truth can be based on nonhistorical premises (see Viderman, 1979 and his conception of an interpretation as a creative act). To the extent that interpretations work for nonfactual reasons (in the usual sense of the word), it is obviously a mistake to use clinical data as the main ingredient in a general theory. Some parts may indeed be relevant, but we are faced with the problem of never knowing, in any particular instance, which pieces of data have general relevance, and which are specific to the hour and patient and analyst in question. We can imagine situations in which the persuasive power of an interpretation stemmed largely from the particular shape of the transference: the analyst, vested with all of his transference power, was more important than what he said. It would clearly be a mistake to use the content as the basis for some general theory of behavior. At other times, the content might be more relevant to the effect and could be considered as the "kernel of truth" that produced the effect. If seems clear that we have no reliable way of distinguishing the first case from the second, and the same could be said of Freud. By failing to draw the distinction, he tended to raise all significant clinical happenings to the level of theoretical propositions. By failing to distinguish narrative from historical truth, he tended to confuse the specific effects of the treatment situation with the generality of the clinical happening.

IV

What, then, are the prospects for a general theory of "what concerns human beings most of all"? I have talked about the tradition of incomplete evidence and how this has stood in the way of critical thinking and vital theory. Is there a prospect for change? The answer, it would seem, must depend on how we move from description to explanation (see Hartmann, 1964).

Because we are working with complex patterns of form and content, it often becomes difficult to identify the relevant data. More than the wording of an interpretation needs to be known, but how much more? We would like to know something about the state of transference, about the history of that particular interpretation, about the additional meanings suggested by the wording but not made explicit—but in every case, we need to know how much ground to search, and we have no precise guidelines. Each investigator tends to use his own standards, and as a result, what is data for one researcher may be skeletal evidence for another.

A second reason to be dubious about whether we can gain access to all evidence bears on the problem of privileged context. The visible text of the session under study is always being heard—by patient and analyst—against the background of what each of them is thinking (see Spence, 1981). Once again, we are confronted with a complex mixture. Does conviction come from the wording of a specific interpretation or from the meshing of its lexical content with the patient's hopes and fears? In many cases, a particular interpretation gains extra force from the private meanings read into it by the patient, meanings which are invisible to the outside observer (we are back to the distinction between normative and privileged competence). The reason for giving a particular interpretation may often depend less on the demands of the analytic "conversation" than on the inner experience of the analyst who, because of some series of subjective feelings, decides that now is the time to speak; once again, this inner experience is inaccessible to the outside observer. Yet it is clearly part of the data, because without knowledge of this inner context, we can never "hear" the analytic conversation with the correct "phrasing" and "accent."

The problem of privileged context carries with it a formidable challenge. The more subjective the experience, the more difficult it is to reduce it to a set of general laws—and we might argue that any such attempt could lead only to sterile theory. We not only have the problem of how to translate a highly individual set of meanings into some kind of general formulation, but we must also find an answer to the question of how much context to include. To interpret a given session, do we need to know the detailed experience of the analyst during the preceding twenty-four hours? Forty-eight hours? Three months? Six months? The questions are endless because we have no systematic way of approaching the problem.

Thus, it would appear that we will always be hampered by the tradition of incomplete data. Even with the best of intentions, there seems to be no systematic method for defining the proper size of the search space and gathering a proper context for each visible utterance. And note the irony—even with an awareness of what is missing and the knowledge that all the evidence must be searched, we are still helpless in formulating the next step. Perhaps Freud took his privileged stance for a reason!

As we discover that narrative truth lies at the heart of insight and therapeutic change, we are also learning that historical truth is less accessible than we are taught to believe. Toward the end of his life, Freud seemed to accept this verdict and argued for *construction* (a partly creative endeavor) over *reconstruction* (an attempt to resurrect a piece of the past); the former concerns itself with narrative truth whereas the latter is an attempt to find historical truth. In recent papers (see David Shapiro, 1981, in particular), we have again heard increasing doubts[56] about the possibility of ever uncovering what "really" happened during the early years of a patient's life, and a recent series of studies by Loftus (1979) has shown how easily memories can be influenced by leading questions, making us necessarily skeptical about the effect of the treatment process on the patient's associations. From every side, there seems reason to doubt the historical truth of our evidence, and we are learning to treat even fairly "hard" memories with a certain skepticism. As a result, we have tended to see more and more significance in the narrative truth of a formulation and in the central position of narrative appeal in the treatment process.

But narrative truth brings with it its own set of problems. It is first and foremost highly relative; each story is different, and what makes a particular formulation persuasive and

[56] For an example of earlier doubting, see Kris (1956b).

compelling is precisely the fact that it is carefully tailored to the patient's life. (If all our interpretations were the same, word for word, they would quickly lose their power to persuade.) But if each piece of narrative truth is relative, how can we build it into a general theory? Each piece of narrative explanation tends to be somewhat ad hoc, drawing its power to persuade from an accumulation of individual details which we can never hope to replicate in any other situation. Given the explanation and given its clinical effect, how do we go about expressing it in some more general manner so that I can compare my narrative with yours and ultimately develop some general laws of what makes a good narrative? The study of literature has traditionally been concerned with what might be called the theory of the good story; we know certain things about form and content, about some of the transformations necessary to turn the chaotic details of reality into the smooth form of a persuasive story. We can also learn from the hermeneutic tradition something about how to go about finding the ingredients for our narrative—how to sift through the ambiguous material of dreams, memories, and fantasies to find the particular meanings we need. But neither storytelling nor hermeneutic discovery will teach us much about the science of man, and here is where the primary drawback of the narrative tradition comes home. If the bulk of historical "findings" are in some way biased in the telling, we have inevitably restricted the scope of our theory. We may have to recognize that the past is essentially out of reach and that our data are relevant mainly to understanding the here and now of a particular hour. We are in a privileged position to report on the here and now, but in only a weak position to report on the past. The difference may be described with the use of Russell's (1912) famous distinction between knowledge by acquaintance and knowledge by description. We are privileged observers of the data within the session and in a position to observe how a particular interpretation, let us say, is heard by the patient and how the hearing (or mishearing) can be understood in light of the transference neurosis. Experiences of this kind lead to knowledge by acquaintance. But reports of the past are a kind of hearsay with the referent permanently out of reach, and although we may make a genetic interpretation, it is always based more on knowledge by description (theoretical knowledge). An explanation rooted in the transference and reinforced by the countless details of the immediate context is always more persuasive than an explanation based on a hypothetical construction of the past.

But more than persuasion is at stake; there is also a certain respect for the evidence. By prematurely reducing a clinical observation to some earlier, hypothetical event (a primal scene, for example), we may have convinced ourselves that we have explained the observation, but once labeled in this manner, it is never looked at again. Multiply this tendency by thousands of hours across thousands of analysts and we can see the waste of data. All the time we were settling for doubtful explanation, rooted in the past, we were being exposed to thousands of clinical events which contained significant amounts of unmined clinical information about the present. But because we had less interest in what was in front of our eyes, the significant data often slipped through our fingers as we continued to confirm doubtful propositions about the past.

We can put the matter more precisely by looking again at the conflict between public and private theory. Each analyst is continuously engaged in updating his private narrative, adding the latest examples of good and bad interpretations to his accumulating store of clinical wisdom. He is always trying to *assimilate* the evidence to his working hypotheses. But it would be a mistake for the field in general to take this approach; on the contrary, it must put the emphasis on *accommodation* and find ways in which the received theory must be changed to conform to the evidence.

To this end, it might be useful to separate journal contributions into two categories: the clinical discoveries (narrative truth) and the more abstract formulations (theoretical truth). Papers in the first category might serve as the archive from which general conclusions could be drawn; formulations drawn from these cases would appear in the second category. Papers in the first category would emphasize the clinical context of a particular happening; this would include (in much more detail than is currently found) a detailed exposition of the context of the case along with an account of the privileged context of the treating analyst. If enough detail were provided, in the appropriate context, it would be possible for an outside reader (someone with only normative competence) to understand and integrate the information and be in a position to compare it with other accounts of similar events. The clinical evidence would then become publicly accessible, and theoretical discussions could be referred to one or more specific specimens, making it possible to generate public discussion and, even more important, to be able to retrace at will the path from data to construct. A new concept (e.g., "splitting") could be defined by reference to a particular sample of clinical accounts, and its evidential basis would be available for all to consider. For the first time, analytic data would become public property, publicly discussed.

If clinical detail is appropriately presented against the right kind of context, it should be possible to bring about conviction based on narrative truth alone. For almost the first time, an outside reader would be able to sense the excitement of a bona fide clinical discovery—rather than be told that such things exist, to be taken on *faith*, he would experience the conviction as it occurred. What has been knowledge by description would thus turn into knowledge by acquaintance. While it may be necessary to develop a mixture of literary and dramatic expertise to properly present a clinical happening in a way that can truly convince the reader, if this goal can be achieved, we will be able to capture a critical feature of narrative truth and build this into our theory.

The contents of these vignettes would be analyzed and discussed in the second category—the theoretical papers. Here the aim is to convince as well as discover; the specific reason of the particular instance would give way to the formulation of general laws (see Eagle, 1980b). Argument about formulation could thus be kept separate from argument about particulars, and a given piece of the clinical archive could be discussed by any number of authors (in contrast to the current practice of supplying new examples for each new discussion). Theoretical papers might also be judged on more general grounds; ad hoc arguments would give way to more general kinds of reasoning; and the detail of the case could be kept separate from its larger meaning. Unresolved disagreements might lead to a call for new clinical instances (rather than the formation of new institutes); new additions to the archive would generate new discussions and further clarification of theoretical issues. (One is reminded of the case system in law and the way in which new cases lead to new decisions.)

To close with a specific example of how such a scheme might work, consider a paper by Langs (1981) on modes of cure in psychoanalysis. He proposes the idea that only interpretations based on the here-and-now context of the hour are curative in any significant degree, and that other kinds of interpretations, based on manifest content or genetic formulations, may actually reinforce the resistance. *Only* interpretations which take account of the interaction between patient and analyst "can offer the patient adaptive structural change and insightful symptom resolution" (Langs, 1981, p. 212). Strong claims, one would think—where is the evidence? Unfortunately, it is largely invisible, and once again, the claims must be taken largely on faith. Whether or not the argument is true, there is no way in which it can be fairly evaluated. Think how much more convincing the argument would have been—and how much more lasting its consequences—if supporting data were available. Under those conditions, it would move from an interesting speculation to a matter of public record—from a matter of narrative truth to (if confirmed) a piece of theoretical knowledge. Very likely the original formulation would undergo several stages of modification; significant conditions might be uncovered which would increase or decrease the general effect; certain exceptions to the general rule might be discovered as it was challenged by new pieces of clinical evidence. But the end result would produce more general conviction than is possible in the absence of evidence; by embedding the rule in a context of particulars, we would move from knowledge by description (which comes cheap) to knowledge by acquaintance (which is significantly more lasting).

CHAPTER NINE

What is true and whose idea was it?

Thomas H. Ogden

The practice of psychoanalysis is, I believe, most fundamentally an effort on the part of analyst and analysand to say something that feels both true to the emotional experience of any given moment of an analytic session and utilizable by the analytic pair for psychological work. In this chapter, I entertain a number of ideas related to the question of what we, as psychoanalysts, mean when we say something is true and what one person's thinking has to do with that of another with regard to what is true. I am not laboring under any illusion that I am doing anything more than raising questions and suggesting directions in which these questions might lead. My intention is to begin to explore the paradox that human emotional truths are both universal and exquisitely idiosyncratic to each individual and are both timeless and highly specific to a given moment of life. As will become apparent, the various questions that I raise spill into one another and, as a result, the discussion often doubles back on itself as I rethink, from another perspective, matters addressed earlier.

Many of the ideas in this chapter are responses to concepts discussed by Bion. I attempt to locate the source of the ideas I present, but it is difficult for me to say with any confidence where Bion's ideas leave off and mine begin. Since the matter of "Whose idea was it?" is at the core of this contribution, it seems only fitting that it be faced in the experience of writing and reading the text that follows.

The question of whether an analytic exchange achieves an articulation of something that is true—or at least "relatively truthful" (Bion, 1982, p. 8)—is not an abstruse theoretical matter best left to philosophers. As analysts, we are at almost every moment of an analytic session asking ourselves and tentatively answering (or, more accurately, responding to) this question. I present a detailed account of an initial analytic meeting in which I illustrate some of the ways

I approach both the question of what is emotionally true at specific junctures in the session and the question of who is the author of the idea that is felt to be true.

Whose idea was it?

In asking, "Whose idea was it?" I am inquiring into what it means for a person to claim, or to have attributed to him, original authorship of an idea regarding what is true to human emotional experience and how those ideas serve as an influence on the thinking of others. In reading Freud and Klein, for example, how are we to determine who is to be credited with original authorship of the concept of an unconscious internal object world. In "Mourning and Melancholia" (1917e), Freud introduced what I view as the essential elements of what would later be termed by Fairbairn (1952) "object-relations theory" (see Ogden, 2002, for a discussion of the origins of object-relations theory in "Mourning and Melancholia"). However, many of the components of Freud's theory of internal object relations, contained in "Mourning and Melancholia" are presented only in rudimentary form and often, in all probability, without Freud's awareness of the theoretical implications of his ideas. In considering the question of how one person's ideas concerning what is true influence those of others, we routinely adopt a diachronic (chronological, sequential) perspective in which the thinking of one person (for example, Freud) is seen as influencing the thinking of contemporaries and those who follow temporally (for example, Klein, Fairbairn, Guntrip, and Bion). Despite the seeming self-evidence of the merits of such an approach, I believe it may be of value to call into question this conception of authorship and influence. In reading "Mourning and Melancholia," if one listens carefully, I believe one can hear the voice of Klein in Freud's discussion of the "internal world" of the melancholic. Freud posits that the structure of the unconscious internal world of the melancholic is determined by a defensive dual splitting of the ego leading to the creation of a stable unconscious internal object relationship between the "critical agency" (later to be termed the superego) and a part of the ego identified with the lost or abandoned object:

> The melancholic's disorder affords … [a view] of the constitution of the human ego. We see how in [the melancholic] one part of the ego sets itself over against the other, judges it critically, and, as it were, takes it as its object … What we are here becoming acquainted with is the agency commonly called "conscience." (1917e, p. 247)

In saying that the reader can hear Klein's voice (her concept of internal objects and internal object relations) in this and many other passages of "Mourning and Melancholia," I am suggesting that influence does not occur exclusively in a chronologically "forward" direction. In other words, influence is not only exerted by an earlier contribution on a later one; later contributions affect our reading of earlier ones. One needs Klein to understand Freud, just as one needs Freud to understand Klein. Every piece of analytic writing requires a reader who assists the author in conveying something of what is true, something that the author knew, but did not know that he knew. In so doing, the reader becomes a silent coauthor of the text.

While this form of mutual influence of earlier and later contributions (mediated by the reader) is undoubtedly important, I would like to focus for a moment on another sort of influence that ideas exert on one another—often spanning great stretches of time, both chronologically forward and backward. Turning once again to the example of the influence of Klein's ideas on Freud's and vice versa, I am suggesting that the ideas Klein formulated in 1935 and 1940 on the subject of internal object relations may already have been available to Freud in 1915[57] and were utilized by him (unwittingly) in writing "Mourning and Melancholia." Though he used the ideas, he could not think them. To say this is to entertain the possibility that the ideas that we think of as Klein's and as Freud's are creations of both and neither. The ideas that each articulated are formulations of the structure of human experience, a structure, a set of truths, which psychoanalysts and others attempt to describe, but certainly do not create.

Bion, I believe, held similar views on the question of the temporal bidirectionality of influence of ideas on one another and articulated "his" formulations with far greater grace than I have achieved:

> You can look at this [the inconsolable cries of a baby in his mother's arms immediately after his birth] as you like, say as memory traces, but these same memory traces can also be considered as a shadow which the future casts before [an anticipation of the future in the present as opposed to memories of the past] ... The caesura that would have us believe [Bion is quoting Freud's clause here—word for word—on the way in which the caesura of birth seems to speak for itself in an effort to convince us of the power over us]; the future that would have us believe; the past would have us believe—it depends on which direction you are traveling in, and what you see. (1976, p. 237)

The future, for Bion, is as much a part of the present as is the past. The shadow of the future is cast forward from the present and is cast backward from the future on the present, for example, "it depends on which direction you are travelling in." (A great many questions regarding the relationship of an author to "his" ideas, and of the relationships among past, present, and future ideas, will have to be left in a suspended state for the time being, pending a discussion of what we, as psychoanalysts, mean when we say something is true.)

What's true?

The foregoing discussion of temporal bidirectionality of influence ("Whose idea was it?") is inseparable from the question "What's true?" I will take as a premise for my discussion of this question the idea that there is something true to human emotional experience which an analyst may accurately sense and communicate to a patient in words that the patient may be able to utilize. In assuming that there is something potentially true (or untrue) about psychoanalytic

---

[57] Although "Mourning and Melancholia" was written in 1915, Freud, for reasons that remain a mystery, chose not to publish this paper until 1917.

formulations and verbal interpretations of human emotional experience, it follows that emotional experience has a reality, a truth,[58] to it that is independent of the formulations or interpretations that the patient or the analyst may impose (Bion, 1977).

The idea that the truth is independent of the investigator lies at the core of the scientific method and is taken for granted in natural science. In molecular biology, for example, it seems self-evident that Watson and Crick did not create the double helical structure of DNA. That structure preexisted their formulation of it: DNA has a double helical structure regardless of whether they or any other scientific investigator discern it (and provide evidence for the formulation).

The double helix is a structure that can be "seen"—albeit by inanimate objects (machines) that offer us the illusion that the human eye is capable of seeing the structure itself. In psychoanalysis, we do not have machines with which to see (even in illusory ways) psychological structures; we have access to psychological "structures" only in so far as they are experienced in the medium of unconscious, preconscious, and conscious dreaming, thinking, feeling, and behaving. We give shape to these structures in the metaphors that we create (e.g., the archaeological metaphor of Freud's topographic model or the metaphor constituting Freud's structural model which involves an imaginary committee comprised of the id, the ego, and the superego attempting to deal with external and internal reality). And yet, there is something real (nonmetaphorical) that psychoanalytic formulations—whether they be in the realm of metapsychology, clinical theory, or interpretations offered to a patient—are measured against and that "something" is our sense (our "intuition" (Bion, 1992, p. 315)) of what is true to a given experience. In the end, it is emotional response—what feels true—that has the final word in psychoanalysis: Thinking frames the questions to be answered in terms of feelings.

The analyst's feelings regarding what is true are mere speculations, however, until they are brought into relation to something external to the psychic reality of the analyst. The patient's response to an interpretation—and, in turn, the analyst's response to the patient's response—serves a critical role in confirming or disconfirming the analyst's sense of what is true. This methodology represents an effort to ground psychoanalytic truth in a world outside the mind of the analyst. It takes at least two people to think (Bion, 1963). The "thinking" of one person on his own may be interminably solipsistic or even hallucinatory, and it would be impossible for a solitary thinker to determine whether or not this is the case.

Nevertheless, despite the analyst's effort to ground what he feels to be true in a discourse with others, human beings are highly disposed to treat their beliefs as if they were truths. So, who gets the last word on what is true? How are the various "schools" of psychoanalysis to be differentiated from cults, each of which is certain it knows what is true? I will not attempt

---

[58] Absolute (and unknowable) truth, referred to by Bion (1970) as O, roughly corresponds to Kant's "thing-in itself," Plato's "Ideal Forms," and Lacan's "register of the Real." Bion, at times, labels it simply, "the experience" (1971, p. 4). In this essay, I am almost exclusively addressing humanly apprehensible, humanly meaningful, relative truths concerning human experience (as opposed to absolute truth).

to address directly these questions concerning how we develop some degree of confidence regarding the question of what is true. Instead, I will respond indirectly by offering some thoughts about what I think we, as analysts, mean when we say something is true (or has some truth to it). If we have an idea about what we mean when we say something is true, we may gain some sense of how we go about differentiating what is true from what is not.

As a starting point for thinking about what we mean when we say an idea is true, let us return to the idea that there are things that are true about the universe (including the emotional life of human beings) that preexist and are independent of the thinking of any individual thinker. In other words, thinkers do not create truth, they describe it. Thinkers from this perspective are not inventors, they are participant observers and scribes.

A comment made by Borges in an introduction to a collection of his poems comes to mind here.

> If in the following pages there is some successful verse of other, may the reader forgive me the audacity of having written it before him. We are all one; our inconsequential minds are much alike, and circumstances so influence us that it is something of an accident that you are the reader and I the writer—the unsure, ardent writer—of my verses [which occasionally capture something true to human experience]. (1923, p. 269)

Borges and Bion are in agreement: truth is invented by no one. For Bion (1970), only a lie requires a thinker to create it. What is true already exists (e.g., the double helical structure of DNA) and does not require a thinker to create it. In Bion's terms, psychoanalysis prior to Freud was "a thought without a thinker" (p. 104), that is, a set of thoughts that are true, "waiting" for a thinker to think them. Psychoanalytic conceptions of what is true to human emotional experience were not invented by Freud any more than the heliocentric solar system was invented by Copernicus.

Nonetheless, from a different vantage point, thinking thoughts that are expressive of what is true alters the very thing that is being thought. Heisenberg brought this to our attention in the realm of quantum physics. It is equally true in psychoanalysis and the arts that, in interpreting or sculpting or making music, we are not simply unveiling what has been present all along in latent form; rather, in the very act of giving humanly sensible form to a truth, we are altering that truth.

Shapes in nature do not have names; they do not even have shapes until we assign them visual categories of shapes that we are capable of imagining. Entities in nature simply are what they are before we assign them a place in our system of symbols. So, despite (or in addition to) what was said earlier about the independence of the double helical structure of DNA from those who formulated it, Watson and Crick did alter the structure of DNA—they named its structure and, in that sense, gave it shape. The truth of the name of the shape was borne out by its power to give humanly sensible and humanly comprehensible organization to what had formerly lacked coherence. However, the fact of the creation of coherence is not a sufficient basis for establishing the truth of an idea. Religious systems create coherence. The truth of an idea, both in natural sciences and in psychoanalysis, rests on evidence brought to bear on an idea. Evidence consists of a set of observations (including the emotional responses of participant observers such as psychoanalysts working in the analytic setting) of the way things work (or fail to work) when one applies the idea/hypothesis to actual lived or observed experience.

In summary, we require what Bion refers to as "binocular vision" (1962a, p. 86)—perception from multiple vantage points simultaneously—to articulate what we mean by the truth in psychoanalytic terms. What is true is a discovery as opposed to a creation, and yet, in making that discovery, we alter what we find and, in that sense, create something new. Nothing less than the psychoanalytic conception of the therapeutic action of the interpretation of the unconscious depends on such a view of the truth and the transformations effected in naming it. The analyst in making an interpretation (which has some truth to it and is utilizable by the patient) gives verbal "shape" to experience that had been nonverbal and unconscious. In so doing, the analyst creates the potential for a new experience of what is true which is derived from the patient's inarticulate unconscious experience.

Saying something one believes to be true

Let us pause a moment to take stock of what has been said thus far. Aside from issues of an author's narcissism, it is immaterial who it is that articulates something that is true—what is important is that a thought that is true has "found" a thinker who has made it available for a patient or a colleague to use. Neither does it matter, or even make sense to ask, "Whose idea was it?" What does matter in psychoanalysis—and it matters greatly—is finding words with which to say something that has quality that is true to lived experience (whether it be an interpretation offered to a patient or a contribution made by an analyst to the analytic literature).

In this effort to say something that is true, the analyst must overcome Freud and the entire history of psychoanalytic ideas as well as the history of the analysis of the patient with whom he is working. In a somewhat whimsical aside made during a consultation, Bion spoke of the role of preconception in his clinical work: "I ... would [rely on theory only] if I were tired and had no idea what was going on" (1978, p. 52). For Bion (1975), every session is the beginning of an analysis with a new patient. He was fond of saying that a patient may have had a wife and two children yesterday, but today he is single.

An analyst must also overcome himself in his written communications of ideas that he feels may have some truth to them. When analytic writing is good, the author is able to avoid getting in the reader's way by being too much of a personal presence in the writing. It makes for a very unrewarding experience for the analytic reader when the real topic of the paper one is reading is the author himself and not what the author is saying or what is being created by the reader in the act of reading.

Borges said of Shakespeare that he had a capacity equaled by no other writer to make himself transparent in his poems and plays. In his work, there is no one between the art and the audience. Borges wrote in a parable about Shakespeare,

> There was no one in him; behind his face ... and his words, which were copious, fantastic and stormy, there was only a bit of coldness, a dream dreamt by no one ... History adds that before or after dying [Shakespeare] found himself in the presence of God and told Him: "I who have been so many men in vain want to be one and myself." The voice of the Lord answered from a whirlwind: "Neither am I anyone; I have dreamt the world as you dreamt your work, my Shakespeare, and among the forms in my dream are you who like myself are many and no one." (1949, pp. 248–249)

This rendering of Shakespeare as "a person with no one in him" is a harrowing picture of a human life, and yet I find that this portrayal of Shakespeare's relationship to his writing offers the psychoanalyst something to emulate in the sense of making himself available to becoming everyone in the patient's life (transferential) and no one (a person who is content not to be noticed, not to be attended to). Borges's depiction of Shakespeare captures something of the task faced by an analyst in not inserting himself—his cleverness, his agility of mind, his capacity for empathy, his unerring choice of *le mot juste*—between the patient (or reader) and the interpretation.

In trying to stay out of the way of patients (or readers) in their efforts to discern something true, the analyst strives in his use of language and ideas to be both emotionally present and transparent. There was little that Borges more deplored in literature than "local color" (1941, p. 42) and little that Bion more deplored in analytic interpretations that the analyst's explicit or implicit claim that the interpretation reflected the unique qualities "of *his* knowledge, *his* experience, *his* character" (1977, p. 105)—his own "local color."

Literary critic Michael Woods, speaking of the place of the writer in his writing, observes, "The writer is not to be absent, but to become absent; to be someone and then go away, leaving traces" (1994, p. 8). How better to describe what we, as psychoanalysts, strive for in making interpretations? We offer interpretations not for the purpose of changing the patient (which would be to attempt to create the patient in our own image), but to offer the patient something that has some truth to it, which the patient may find useful in doing conscious, preconscious, and unconscious psychological work. Accompanying any psychological growth achieved in this way, we find not the signature of the analyst (i.e., his presence), or his absence (which marks his presence in his absence), but traces of him as someone who was present and has become absent, leaving traces. The most important traces the analyst leaves are not the patient's identifications with him as a person, but traces of the experience of making psychological use of what the analyst has said and done and been.

What's true and for whom?

What is true to the relatively stable structure of human nature in general, and to an individual personality in particular, is bound not by time or place or culture—even allowing for the influence of a wide range of value systems, forms of self-consciousness, religious beliefs and customs, forms of familial ties and roles, and so on. For example, there are no political or cultural borders separating human beings in the experience of the pain felt following the death of a child, the fear of bodily mutilation, the anguish of recognizing that one's parents and ancestors do not have the power to insulate themselves or their children from life's dangers and the inevitability or death. A culture may afford forms of defense against (or ways of evading) the pain of loss; or may provide traditions, myths, and ceremonies that facilitate grieving; or may create rituals that help (or interfere with) efforts to loosen one's hold on infantile wishes. Whatever the cultural influences may be in a given instance, our responses to the basic human tasks of growing up, aging, and dying take place in cycles of love and loss; of dreaming oneself into existence and confronting the full force of the constraints of external reality; of feats of daring and the search for safety; of wishes to identify with those one admires and the need to safeguard (from one's own wishes to identify) the undisrupted evolution of one's self; and on and on.

These human tasks and the cycles in which they are played out contribute to a body of experience that I believe to be true of all humankind. It seems that paradoxically what is true is timeless, placeless, and larger than any individual, and yet alive only for an instant and unique to the set of circumstances constituting that moment of lived experienced by one person. In other words, in an analysis, what is universally true is also exquisitely personal and unique to each patient and to each analyst. An analytic interpretation, in order to be utilizable by the patient, must speak in terms that could only apply to that patient at that moment while at the same time holding true to human nature in general.

I am reminded here, of another comment by Borges: "Though there are hundreds and indeed thousands of metaphors to be found, they may all be traced back to a few simple patterns. But this need not trouble us since each metaphor is different: every time the pattern is used, the variations are different" (2000, p. 40).

Borges's observation is itself a metaphor suggesting that there are only a handful of qualities that make us human and that every person who has ever lived or whoever will live is an absolutely unique being made up of variations on a very small number of human qualities. And, in that sense, we are all one.

What's true and whose idea is it in an analytic session?

What has been said thus far concerning what we, as analysts, mean when we say something is true, remains pure abstraction until it is grounded in the lived experience of analytic work. As an analyst, I am not striving for absolute truth in what I say to a patient; I consider myself fortunate if once in a great while the patient and I arrive at something that is "very close/to the music of what happens" (Heaney, 1979, p. 173). The relative truths arrived at in poetry (and in psychoanalysis) represent "a clarification of life—not necessarily a great clarification, such as sects or cults are founded on, but a momentary stay against confusion" (Frost, 1939, p. 777). In the following account of a piece of analytic work, the patient and I strive to make psychological use of such momentary stays.

Mr. V phoned me asking for a consultation concerning his wish to begin analysis with me. We set up a time to meet and I gave him detailed instructions about how to get to the waiting room of my office suite, which is located at the ground level of my home. Just before the appointment time we had agreed upon, I heard a person (whom I assumed to be Mr. V) opening the side door of my house. There is a short passageway between that door and a glass-paned interior door, which is the entrance to the waiting room. I anticipated hearing the waiting room door open, but instead I heard the person walk back to the outer door, which was followed by a period of quiet lasting a minute or two. He—the footfalls sounded like those of a man—repeated this pattern of walking to the waiting room door and then returning to the outer door where he remained for another couple of minutes.

I found this man's movements distracting and intrusive, but also intriguing. Ms. M, the patient who was with me in my consulting room, commented that someone, probably a new patient, seemed to be pacing in the hallway. Immediately after Ms. M left my office by a door that exited into the same passageway in which the man had been walking, I heard the shuffling of feet and the voice of a man mumbling words of apology. I quickly went to see what was going on and for the first time encountered Mr. V, a tall man of stocky build in his early forties. I said, "Mr. V, I'm Dr. Ogden," and, motioning toward the glass-paned door, "Please have a seat in the waiting room." He had a sheepish but slightly bemused expression on his face as I spoke.

Then, about five minutes later, when it came time for Mr. V's session, I went to the waiting room and showed him to my consulting room. Once he was settled in his chair and I in mine, Mr. V began by telling me that he had been thinking about beginning an analysis for some time, but "one thing and another" had caused him to delay. He then began to tell me about how he had been referred to me. I interrupted saying that there was a great deal that had already occurred in the session and that it would be important for us to talk about it before he and I could meaningfully talk about anything further. He looked at me with the same bemused expression I had observed in the passageway. I went on to say to Mr. V that of all the ways he might have introduced himself to me, the one he had arrived at took the form of what had occurred in the passageway. So, it seemed to me that it would be a shame not to take seriously what he had been trying to tell me about himself in that introduction.

There was a short pause after I finished speaking during which I had a fleeting memory (in the form of an emotionally intense series of still images) of an incident from my childhood. A friend, R, and I were playing on a frozen pond imagining ourselves to be Arctic explorers—we were both about eight years old at that time. The two of us ventured too close to an area which unbeknownst to us was not solidly frozen. R fell through the ice and I found myself looking down at him floundering in the freezing-cold water. I realized that if I were to get down on my hands and knees to try to pull him out, the ice would probably give way under me, too, and we both would be in the water unable to get out. I ran to a small island in the middle of the pond to get a long branch that I saw there. When I got back to R, he took hold of one end of the branch and I was able to pull him out of the water.

In the reverie, I pictured us (in a way that felt like peering intently into a photograph) standing there silently on the ice, R numb in his cold, wet clothes. As this was occurring, I felt a combination of fear and guilt and shame about his having fallen through the ice. The pond was much closer to my house than to his and I felt I should have known the signs of weak ice and should have protected him from falling through. The shame was in part connected with the fact that I had run away from him (the reality that I was running to get a branch with which to try to pull him out did not diminish the shame). But for the first time, it occurred to me on looking back on this event that there was shame felt by both of us about his being dripping wet as if he had wet his pants.

It had been years, perhaps a decade, since I had thought of that incident. While recalling these events in the session with Mr. V, I felt sadness in response to the image of R and me becoming so separate and alone in the fear and shame that I assume he had felt, and that I know I had felt, after the accident. This had been no Tom Sawyer–Huck Finn adventure. R (I imagine) and I experienced our fear as well as our shame separately: we each felt stupid for having walked on the thinly frozen section of the pond and cowardly for having been so afraid.

He and I never once mentioned the incident to one another afterwards, nor did I ever tell anyone other than my mother about it. These fleeting thoughts and feelings occupied only a moment of time but were an emotional presence as I went on to say to Mr. V that, from the sound of his footsteps in the passageway, I suspected that he had been in some turmoil as he approached our first meeting. (Even as I was saying them, these words particularly "turmoil" and "approached"—felt stiffly "therapeutic" and lifeless to me.)

Mr. V responded by telling me that when we spoke on the phone, he had written down the directions I had given him about how to get into the waiting room from the outside of the house, but on arriving he found that he had forgotten to bring the scrap of paper on which he had written the instructions. When in the passageway between the door to the outside and the door to the waiting room, he was not sure whether the door with the glass panes was the waiting room door. He vaguely remembered my having mentioned a glass-paned door, but there was another door (the exit door from my consulting room) so, not knowing what to do, he went back to the outer door. The door to the outside has an opening in its upper third which is divided by vertical wooden spindles with wide spaces between them. Mr. V said that, as he stood inside the passageway peering out through the "bars" of the door, the daylight seemed blinding. He had felt as if he were in a prison in which, over a long span of time, his eyes had become so acclimatized to the dark that he could not tolerate daylight. So, he turned and went back to the glass-paned door and stood in front of it uncertain as to whether or not he should go in.

He then returned to the outer door and stood for a while more, looking from what felt like a great distance at the people outside who had lives they led in ways he could not imagine.

I told Mr. V that I thought that he had not had a way, other than through his actions in the passageway, to convey to me what it felt like to him to be coming to meet me. I said that without words he had told me how alone he felt in the no man's land of the passageway. He felt barred both from coming in to see me to begin analysis and from going out and living as he imagined the people outside were able to do. The patient responded in a strikingly monotone voice, "Yes, I feel like a visitor everywhere, even with my family. I don't know how to do and say what seems to come naturally to other people. I'm able to keep that fact a secret at work because I am very good at what I do [there was a note of haughtiness in his voice here]. People are afraid of me at work. I think it's because I am abrupt. I don't know how to chat."

The patient, in the first part of the hour, tended to move to generalizations about experience outside of the session, while I periodically redirected his attention to what had occurred and what was in the process of occurring in the session. About halfway through the hour, Mr. V seemed to become interested in, and less fearful about, discussing what had occurred at the very beginning of the session. He said he had felt startled, first by the woman and then by me, as she and I came out of my office into the passageway. "I felt caught doing something I shouldn't have. No, that's not right … I felt caught at being weird and clueless about what everyone else knows."

After a brief pause, Mr. V went on to say with little feeling in his voice, "I've learned to use my detachment from other people to my advantage in business because I can see things from an outside point of view. Being removed allows me to be ruthless because I say and do things to people that other people don't do in business. Either they don't think to do it or they don't want to … I'm not sure which. In a stand-off, I'm never the first to flinch." I said to the patient in a series of short comments that I thought he was telling me that he was afraid his extraordinary capacity for detachment and ruthlessness would make it impossible for him to be present in his own analysis; in addition, I said I thought he was suggesting that it was very likely that I would be frightened and repelled by him to the point that I would want nothing to do with him.

There was then another silence of several minutes' duration which felt like a long time at such an early stage of the work. But it did not feel like an anxious silence, so I let it go on. During this silence, my mind "returned" to the reverie concerning the incident from my childhood. This time I experienced the childhood scene quite differently—I had a far greater sense of seeing and feeling things from inside the two of us (R and me). This reverie experience was not that of a series of still images, but of a lived experience unfolding. I felt a good deal more of what it had been for me to be an eight-year-old boy on that frozen pond in winter. It was a state of mind that was living in a daydream made up of a combination of sensations that have such great immediacy that there is no room (or desire) to think. Things just happen, one after another. The events on the pond now had the emotional impact of a balloon exploding—not only had R fallen through the ice, we both were hit in the face with a blast of reality that annihilated the dreamy aspect of exploring on the frozen pond/Arctic Circle. It felt to me in the reverie that I had no choice but to become in an instant someone who could do the things that had to be done. R was in the water. I had to become someone I feared I could not be, someone more grown-up than I was. I did not feel the least bit heroic in the experience constituting this (second) reverie; I felt a bit disconnected from myself, but mostly I felt keenly aware that I was in over my head.

By this time Mr. V had broken the silence and had begun to tell me about having been in therapy when he was in college. He had not been able to make friends and felt terribly homesick. The patient said that it had been a real stretch for his parents to pay for the therapy. After some time, I said to Mr. V that I thought that, when he realized in the passageway that he had forgotten the directions he had written down, he felt embarrassingly childlike and that for him to behave or even feel like a child is a very shameful thing. The patient said nothing in response to my comment, but the tension in his body visibly diminished. We sat quietly for a while. (It seemed to me the Mr. V was worried that being in analysis would be a stretch for him—in a great many ways.) He then said, "Outside there, I felt so lost." There was softness to Mr. V's voice as he spoke these words, a quality of voice that I had not heard from him, a softness that would prove to be a rarity in the course of the next several years of his analysis. (I was aware that the patient's feeling that there was an "outside there" was also a feeling that there was beginning to be an "inside here"—inside the analytic space, inside the relationship with me—in which he did not feel as lost.)

Discussion

Mr. V's initial analytic meeting began in earnest about ten minutes before we actually met for the first time. His communications were made in the medium of sounds that echoed through the rest of the initial meeting and from there down the labyrinthine corridors of the analysis as a whole.

In my first interaction with Mr. V in the passageway, I responded to his anxious nonverbal communications by identifying myself as Dr. Ogden, thus naming not only who I was, but also what I was and why I was there. I firmly, but not coldly, directed him to the waiting room. The effect of my intervention was to both interrupt Mr. V's communications in the medium of action (over which he appeared to have little, if any, control) and to define the geographic space in which analysis was to take place.

In his manner of speaking to me once he was in the consulting room, Mr. V seemed to ignore—and seemed to invite me to ignore—the events that had transpired in the passageway. I soon interrupted Mr. V's second introduction of himself. In telling him that I viewed his actions in the passageway as a way of telling me of his fears about beginning analysis, I was conveying to him the fact that I took him seriously in his unconscious efforts to be heard. My interpretation represented a continuation of my introducing myself to him as a psychoanalyst and my introducing him to psychoanalysis. Implicit in what I was doing and saying was the idea that the unconscious speaks with a quality of truthfulness that is different from, and almost always much richer than, what the conscious aspect of our selves is able to perceive and convey. I was also introducing myself to the patient as a psychoanalyst for whom his behavior in the passageway did not represent an infraction of "analytic rules"; rather, it represented intense, urgent communications of some things he unconsciously believed to be true about himself which he felt were important for me to know from the very outset.

Mr. V's reflexive response to what I said was to give me the sheepish, bemused smile I had noticed in the passageway. He seemed to be showing me in his facial expression a mixture of what felt like abject surrender and arrogant defiance, a particular mix that I would learn over time was characteristic of the patient as a response to certain types of narcissistic anxiety. A brief silence followed in which I recalled a series of still images, my boyhood experience with R when he fell through the ice. Particularly vivid in this reverie were feelings of fear, shame, isolation, and guilt. A component of the shame in this reverie experience seemed new and very real to me: the idea/feeling that R's pants were wet because, in his fear, he had soaked them with urine.[59] Just as immediate, for me, as my image of R (with whom I thoroughly identified) in his shamefully soggy clothes, were my feeling of sadness concerning the isolation from one another that R and I had felt.

The emotional field of the session was changed in ways that I was only beginning to understand by my having lived the experience of this reverie in the context of what was occurring at an unconscious level between the patient and me. Following my reverie, Mr. V gave a detailed, but affectively muted, account of his experience in the passageway. He recounted having forgotten the scrap of paper on which he had written the directions I had given him; he went on to describe his inability either to enter the waiting room or to leave the passageway (which felt like a prison) and enter the blindingly lit world outside. My response to Mr. V's depiction of himself in the passageway involved an effort to restate what he had said in slightly different language and with expanded meaning. My intention was to underscore the ways in which the patient knew, but did not know that he knew, about another level of the experience he had just described. My use of the phase "no man's land" in retelling the story Mr. V had told me suggested that he not only felt alone, but also unmanly and like no one. Moreover, in my making explicit that entering the waiting room was, for him, emotionally equivalent to beginning analysis, I was also suggesting that entering the waiting room posed the danger of entering

[59] My "new" thought/feeling (that R's water-soaked pants were emotionally equivalent to urine-soaked clothing of a baby) did not necessarily represent an unearthing of a repressed aspect of my childhood experience. Rather, I conceive of the experience at the pond as having generated elements of experience (Bion's (1962a) "alpha elements") which I stored and later "recollected" in the context of what was occurring at an unconscious level in the session. My "recollecting" elements of my boyhood experience was not the same as remembering that experience; in fact, it is impossible to say whether the newly recollected aspect of the childhood experience had actually been a part of the original experience—and it does not matter. What does matter is that elements of experience (past and present) were available to me in the form of reverie that was true to the emotional experience that I was having with Mr. V at that moment.

into the potentially crazed world of the unconscious. (The patient's fear of the out-of-control world of the unconscious was already alive in me in the form of the frightening reverie image of R falling through the ice.)

An important shift occurred midway through the session, when Mr. V, on his own, returned to the experience in the passageway. He made a delicate, yet critical, emotional distinction in saying, "I felt caught doing something I shouldn't have," and then corrected himself: "No, that's not right ... I felt caught at being weird and clueless about what everyone else knows." There was a sense of relief in Mr. V's voice in being able to say something that felt true (and significant) to his emotional experience. The patient then quickly retreated to the familiar ground of reliance on defensive omnipotence in asserting that he could be more ruthless in business than others dare to be (or even aspire to be) and that he was never the first to flinch.

The long silence that occurred at that juncture was a period in which it felt to me that the patient and I were able to do a good deal of unconscious psychological work that had not been possible up to that point in the session. My reverie during that silence was one in which the memory of the incident on the pond was reworked in the context of what had transpired in the session in the interval between the first and second reverie. In contrast with the first reverie, which I experienced as a series of still photographic images, the new reverie was an experience of an unfolding event that felt much closer to and more alive with the feelings of an eight-year-old boy. In that sense, it was a far more understanding, more compassionate rendering of the event. *I* was less fearful of experiencing the feelings that the reverie involved.

At the heart of the second reverie was a feeling of myself as a boy being called upon (and calling upon myself) to do something that I was afraid was emotionally and physically beyond me. This feeling of shameful immaturity was a new version of a feeling I had experienced in the earlier reverie in identifying with R as an eight-year-old boy who was behaving like a baby (who, in fantasy, had peed in his pants).

The more emotionally accepting affective state generated in the second reverie allowed me to listen differently to Mr. V. I heard his reference to his parents' financial "stretch" (in paying for his therapy while he was homesick at college) as a comment on how he was feeling at the moment in the analysis. I told him that I thought he had felt painfully and embarrassingly like a child when he was in the passageway and that for him to behave like or even feel like a child was a very shameful thing. He did not respond with words, but there was visible relaxation in his body. Not only my words, but also the feeling-tone of my voice reflected my own experience in the reveries in which I had felt painfully over my head and shamefully infantile.

Mr. V then said, "Out there I felt so lost." These words were alive in a way that was different from anything that the patient had previously said or done, not only because of the softness of his voice as he spoke these words, but also because of the words themselves. How different it would have been if he had said, "In the passageway, I felt lost," or "Out there, I felt very lost," instead of "Out there, I felt so lost." There is something unmistakable about the truth when one hears it.

In closing this clinical discussion, I would like to address briefly the question of who it was who came up with the ideas that felt true in the analytic session I have described. As I have previously discussed (Ogden, 1994, 1997, 2001), I view the analyst's reverie experience as a creation of an unconscious intersubjectivity that I call "the analytic third," a third subject of analysis, which is jointly, but asymmetrically, created by analyst and patient.[60] It would make no sense to me to view the reveries involving my boyhood experience on the pond solely as reflections of the work of my unconscious or solely as a reflection of the unconscious work of the patient.

From this perspective, it is impossible (and meaningless) to say that it was my idea or the patient's that was conveyed in the interpretation of Mr. V's feeling shamefully infantile and over his head when "caught" being clueless both about how to enter analysis and how to be present and alive in the world. Neither Mr. V nor I alone was the author of this and the other understandings (relative emotional truths) that were spoken and unspoken during this initial session. If there was an author, it was the unconscious third subject of analysis who is everyone and no one—a subject who was both Mr. V and myself and neither of us.

---

[60] I view the cocreated unconscious analytic third as standing in dialectical tension with the unconscious of the analysand and of the analyst as separate people, each with his own personal history, personality organization, qualities of self-consciousness, bodily experience, and so on.

CHAPTER TEN

Truth heals, if one can tolerate it

Cobi Avshalom and Gila Ofer

Psychoanalysis views truth as a basic human need and associates it with both developmental challenges and changing self-states (Bion, 1965; Freud, 1911b; Kohut, 1959) and the quest for the truth has remained one of the driving forces of psychoanalytic practice and theory (Bromberg, 2009; Hanly, 1990; Yadlin-Gadot, 2017). Nevertheless, the current psychoanalytic zeitgeist views truth in terms of a psychic experience or a psychic reality rather than as a shared objective reality (Yadlin-Gadot, 2016).

Freud noted that the desire to know has to do with the child's initial curiosity about how children are born and the concealment or the enigmatic messages with which this curiosity is answered (Ofer & Durban, 1999). As Freud (1909b) argues in his introduction to the case of Little Hans: "Thirst for knowledge seems to be inseparable from sexual curiosity" (p. 9). Jean Laplanche (1995) emphasized that the key precondition for the development of the desire for knowledge is the temptation evoked by concealment. The enigmatic signifier expresses a secret, a riddle that the child seems compelled to solve.

The interpretation of the oedipal myth highlights various themes that concern different attitudes toward truth: the wish for truth versus denial of truth, blindness and enigmatic messages, arrogance as a fundamental obstacle for uncovering the truth as well as the quest for truth as the subject's process of becoming. In his reading of the Oedipus myth, Bion (1958) viewed the core of the myth as a quest to uncover the truth at all cost. He believed that the most powerful human need, that which surpassed all other human aspirations, was the need for truth. But he also developed the notion of intrapsychic conversations taking place between different parts of the personality. While some of these parts are capable of thinking, others hate thinking and fear it. In this context, avoiding thinking is tantamount to avoiding one's duty to accept what is truly happening. Thus, Bion viewed the figure of Oedipus as representing the attempt to come in contact with reality and acknowledge it; while Teiresias, the blind prophet, represents the attempt not to know, because of the anxiety and the danger knowledge involves, as a position that fears knowing or fears having to face the consequences of potential knowing (Bion, 1963, pp. 48–49). Bion saw the conflict between these two approaches as an essential dynamic that is characteristic of the psychoanalytic encounter per se. Bion conceptualized this state of affairs as an instance of *reversible perspective*, which expresses the activity of the psychotic part of the personality in defending itself against knowing and pain. Therefore, our psychic substrate entails both the wish to know the truth and the fear of the pain such knowledge brings.

Steiner (1985) used the oedipal myth to demonstrate his concept of "psychic retreat": a powerful defensive system, which serves the individual as a shelter from internal and external reality, when these are experienced as too threatening or painful. The protection offered by the psychic retreat grants psychic equilibrium at the price of forgoing one's potential for growth. Steiner's reading of the myth unfolds a downward psychic spiral, from being entrenched in a perverse retreat in *Oedipus Rex* to being entrenched in a psychotic one in *Oedipus in Colonus* (Steiner, 1993).

In this context, Ofer et al. (2021) discussed the various ways in which the film *Incendies* (2010), which alludes to the oedipal myth, highlights the intrapsychic conflict between the desire to know and the desire not to know. The film offers its own version of the oedipal myth, deeply resonating the intricate quest for knowledge and truth, alternately driven by love or hate or, in Bion's words, by the life or death instincts: "In the personality where life instincts predominate, pride becomes self-respect, where death instincts predominate, pride becomes arrogance" (1958, p. 144).

The conceptualization of truth and reality in psychoanalytic theory has undergone many changes over the years, gradually shifting from an epistemology of a unified reality to a relative, intersubjective, existential-subjective truth (Yadlin-Gadot, 2016). While it is not the aim of the present chapter to review these changes, we will note that the truth and reality relevant to psychoanalysis are not absolute, but experienced ("O," in Bion's case). The process of reaching the truth is utterly subjective and experiential. In addition, knowledge is inherently intersubjective and thus it exists subjectively.

Each person, from infancy, through childhood to adulthood, undergoes various life events and experiences the world around them through their five senses. Their emotional system reacts to these sensory experiences and, over the course of their life, they can work through their emotional reactions to these events: the subject's emotional reactions to life events experienced through the senses (Ogden, 2009). The subject also perceives the emotional reactions of the people around him, registering these as impressions throughout his life. Bion calls such sense impressions with potential emotional reactions "beta elements." While these sense impressions serve as our psychic connection to reality, they must be processed by the alpha function in order to become dream-thoughts, which are the symbolic representations of the abovementioned unsettling experiences (Bion, 1962b; Ogden, 2009). These impressions also create different self-states (Bromberg, 2000, 2009). Bromberg's view suggests that opposing self-states impair emotional regulation and lead to dissociation.

The potential for acknowledging reality and sense impressions is dependent on one's ability to contain one's emotional reaction to said events. One might say that when certain life events or ongoing relationships are traumatic, when emotional responses to stimuli are too powerful or painful and the subject is unable to contain that amount of pain or does not have anyone to help him do so, these events are erased from one's memory or retained in a way that does not contain their emotional meaning.

These states, which are not experienced and are not processed by the psyche, remain in one's implicit sensory memory and become dissociated self-states. Often enough, they are inscribed as symptoms. The symptom is meant to stop an emotional response that the subject is unable to stop and to prevent the encounter with a subjective truth, an encounter that Ogden (2005, 2016) describes as an undreamt dream or an interrupted cry.

These states can be described as intolerable emotional reactions. There are many reasons for such inability to tolerate the emotions that arise in emotionally loaded situations, including constitution, cultural context, the object relations in which the person grew up and the nature of the traumatic event. When the individual can no longer tolerate his emotional reactions, he becomes detached, much like an electric short circuit that shuts itself off in order to protect the system when the electric current flowing through the system becomes excessive. It is a kind of biological mechanism through which the neurons in the brain bar passage to keep intolerable pain from reaching consciousness, in an attempt to remain unaware of psychic reality. Winnicott (1974) called the same maneuver "fear of breakdown."

The analyst should meet the patient first on a level in which that patient is capable of dwelling in his experience, and to the extent that he is able to experience his emotional meaning. The analyst must recognize the potential of his future growth. As Bromberg states:

> The analyst must accept the patient on his own terms, and at the same time not settle for them. If he does not accept the patient on his own terms, it is *as though he is asking him to be someone else*, the patient will not have cause for hope and he will not recognize the analyst's vision. If the analyst settles for the patient's terms, he is ignoring the concealed part of the personality and betraying the patient's wish for greater fulfillment. (Friedman, 1988, cited in Bromberg, 2009)

In analysis, the patient's growth depends on facilitating the mutual structuring of a transitional space in which questions of objectivity versus subjectivity and, similarly, true versus false, become insignificant. As Winnicott (1951) put it: "No decision on this point is expected. The question is not to be formulated" (p. 12). In such a space, reality is an unconscious relational mental state that is shared by both analyst and patient. The boundary between analyst and patient becomes permeable so that their relationship creates a therapeutic environment in which old truths can become reorganized in new patterns of meaning. The more the analyst allows for communication which is more significantly grounded in the sharing of the patient's subjective experience—because the analyst wants and enables its revelation, rather than introducing a preexisting truth—the more the patient will surrender himself to the process of shared discovery and structuring. When the patient becomes able to tolerate the emotional reaction to the truth he has experienced, subjective truth will be revealed and even revealed to be an objective reality.

Bromberg (2009) opens his paper, "Truth, Human Relatedness, and the Analytic Process," with the following quote from Laurence Sterne:

> For all this, I reverence truth as much as anybody; and when it has slipped us, if a man will but take me by the hand, and ... search for it, as for a thing we have both lost, and can neither of us do well without—I'll go to the world's end with him. (p. 347)

Difficulty in tolerating the truth

Gidi, who had been in his early thirties when he first started analysis, came to see me because he felt lost: He was looking for love and could not find it; he was confused about his professional future. Gidi completed his mandatory military service and then went to university, but found academic learning difficult. Feeling that he was not cut out for higher learning, he took up an administrative position at a company that organized nature tours. In the first two years of analysis, Gidi found it very difficult to talk freely about himself. Most of what he said was harsh self-criticism about not using the analysis adequately, about how he acted, about not being efficient enough, not thinking things through. He told me that he made himself lists of assignments and ideas to develop or test. He would prioritize these lists every hour, reprioritizing or checking off assignments he has completed and then reordering the list—all the while subjecting himself to constant self-criticism about not being efficient or good enough. Even when he brought other materials to analysis, he occasionally interrupted the flow of his words to berate himself, accusing himself of introducing material that was unimportant and contributed nothing to the therapeutic process. Every now and then, his criticism and his anger at himself gave rise to difficult feelings of wanting to drop everything and run away. He would go out to nature, off on a hike, without any assignments or commitments, even in the hopes of finding romance, of feeling that a woman loved him in a way that would be a comfort and an escape. He did not really know how to describe what went on during those love-seeking excursions to nature. His words suggested that he found himself on a bus headed back home, feeling lost, frustrated and unable to fully recall what happened on the trip. These depictions felt like an alarming dissociative state, but Gidi was able to assure me that nothing dramatic happened on those trips, he just could not remember exactly what he had done and where he had been.

Whenever I offered interpretations of the material Gidi brought up, including his dissociation, he would often say: "Sorry, I wasn't listening to you, my mind wandered off to thoughts about work and errands." Meaning, he was busy mentally revising and reprioritizing his to-do list, thus keeping himself from hearing what I had to say. He accepted the interpretation that he might be using this mechanism to keep himself from feeling difficult or painful emotions. Alongside this, another symptom came up in the analysis. Whenever Gidi entered the room, he experienced difficulties breathing; he felt his chest tightening and a lack of oxygen: "This only happens when I come in here, never anywhere else." He accepted the thought that this was a manifestation of anxiety that arose in relation to our session, and he thought that this anxiety had to do with certain thoughts that scared him. Because of the difficulty of making room for his thoughts and Gidi's wish not to give in to this fear, we began meeting four times a week instead of three.

It took several long months of complex analytic work—under the thick cover of Gidi's blurring thinking, which sometimes reached the level of falling asleep and which expressed his fear and reluctance to know things about himself—until we finally clarified what it was that Gidi called "looking for love" and then failed to recall what had happened. He would frequent places where he could meet girls who were by themselves and create intimate situations that were initiated by the girl. For example, at the beach on a grey, wintery day, he would make tea on his portable stove, not too far from a girl whom he had already spotted sitting alone. She extends a longing look at the boiling tea and he generously offers her a warm cup of it—seduction ensues. Gidi speaks openly about himself and his troubles, the girl talks about herself. He talks about feeling that there is a special emotional bond between them and physical intimacy is initiated by the girl, after Gidi has given her some clear signs that this is what he wants but is unable to initiate because of his own difficulties in that area. Once the sexual encounter is over, Gidi cuts the girl off completely, not answering her calls or texts, and moves on to look for the next girl. In the analysis, we named these events "the hunt"—hunting for girls. Gidi made it clear that it is not about being sexually attracted to a certain girl: "Every girl, young or old, thin or fat, ugly or pretty will do for the hunt"; "Most of them do it because they're lonely." It turned out that a considerable part of Gidi's assignment calculations were plans for how and where to hunt girls.

As our work progressed, these wanderings grew less frequent and, most of all, the dissociated sensation that accompanied them had disappeared. Gidi entered into a romantic relationship that looked serious, while secretly keeping up his hunt for girls. Around that time, Gidi shared a dream in which he was in the consulting room, lying on the analytic couch. I'm inviting Gidi's younger brother to join the session. Gidi finds this unusual, but agrees to it. In the session with his brother, I tell Gidi that part of the therapy involves preparing him for a good sex life and, to do so, I have to masturbate him. He recoils at the thought but accepts my professional authority and agrees. I then propose the same "treatment" to his brother. When, in response to this dream, I said that what he was describing was sexual abuse, Gidi mentioned in passing that he might have been the victim of such abuse but he does not remember anything and if anything had actually happened, it had no effect on his life whatsoever, because it happened when he was four. He had no memories of this event in which he was sexually abused.

Gidi grew up in a small rural village, where everyone knew everyone. Everyone was very neighborly and friendly and children often stayed the night at the neighbors' rather than at home. Gidi was sexually abused by the Bible teacher who worked at the regional school. They both lived in the same small village. When this started being addressed in analysis, Gidi was astounded to realize that the abuse took place when he was fourteen and fifteen years old, not four, as he initially thought. He had and still has no memories of the abuse. There is not a single trace of any recollection of these events. He found out about it at eighteen, when another boy from the same village filed a complaint against the teacher. Under interrogation, the teacher confessed to sexually abusing him as well as Gidi and Gidi's brother, who is two years younger than him (the same brother who appeared in the dream about sexual abuse in analysis). Next, a trial was held, in which the teacher offered a detailed description of how he sexually abused those boys. Although Gidi has the trial records, he is incapable of remembering any of the events depicted in them and does not actually believe that he was abused himself, because: "I have an excellent memory and I can remember quite a bit from my childhood, so maybe this whole story never happened and that teacher just added me to the list for no reason?" When Gidi showed me the records, it turned out that the teacher hurt the boys in the exact same manner described in Gidi's dream—by offering to prepare them for adult sexual intercourse by masturbating them. Every time Gidi read the courtroom transcripts, he promptly forgot them and was unable to recall what they said, how the abuse took place and how old he was when it happened. Even bringing the records to analysis and asking me to read them to him had no effect. Gidi kept forgetting every single time.

I raised the question of why Gidi repeatedly forgot the events of the abuse. One time when we discussed the matter, Gidi said that knowing what had happened there gives rise to emotions that he could not contain: "How could I have let him do that to me? Why didn't I stop him? I should have beaten the shit out of him! How could I have been so naïve and stupid?" He felt rage and a desire to avenge the humiliation he had suffered rising in him. He said that if he could actually remember what the teacher had done to him, he might not be able to control his rage and murder that teacher; so, in order to keep from spending the rest of his life in prison, he is better off forgetting what happened.

Such talk about the danger of potentially murdering the teacher did not repeat itself. Instead, it was followed by renewed forgetting and an uncertainty about whether anything of this sort had really happened. I thought that this forgetfulness was protecting Gidi not only from his fear, but also from the actual possibility of not being able to control his rage and murdering the abusing teacher. It should be noted that Gidi's father was prone to frightening outbursts of rage, during which he was violent, broke things, and even severely beat his children. Even working on the fear of not being able to control his rage and turning violent to the extent of committing murder did not weaken the mechanism of dissociation that made Gidi forget his sexual trauma. I often mentioned to him that he was repeating the trauma through his "girl hunt," where he became the perpetrator who left those women feeling deceived, humiliated, guilty (for having initiated physical contact with him), and taken advantage of, and that he thereby seemed to evacuate into them those emotions that he could not tolerate in himself. Even this kind of work failed to allow him to contain the feelings of humiliation and rage that he suffered when he had been the victim.

Analytic work brought many good things to Gidi's life. He married a woman with whom he established a powerful loving bond and also made significant steps toward professional success. The girl hunt became less frequent and Gidi often confined himself to merely fantasizing about such situations rather than going out on actual hunts. Nevertheless, actual girl hunting stayed a part of his life, even after he became a father. He knew full well that his marriage was at stake, if his wife ever found out about his actions, but the urge to keep hunting was more powerful. After hunts, he would agonize over having cheated on his wife and risking the loss of "everything good and hard-won in my life." By the time analysis was terminated, Gidi was still not able to keep the memory of having been sexually abused in mind and doubted that it had truly taken place.

Tolerating truth

Amir was twenty-three when he came to therapy, seeking to address various somatic symptoms for which repeated medical examinations had ruled out any underlying physical pathology. His main difficulty involved his digestive tract and many types of food caused him intense stomach aches, constipation, and acid reflux. He also suffered from painful sensations during urination and complained that, when passing stool or urine, "My penis and my ass burn." Amir had spent a few years in a previous therapy, but his physical symptoms persisted.

Amir had lost both his parents under tragic circumstances. When he was seven, his mother died in a car accident while driving alone to work. His father, a devoted caretaker, raised Amir and his sister, who is two years younger than him. Amir's grandparents on both his father's and his mother's side were also significantly present in his life. The father never reentered into any new meaningful intimate relationship. Eleven years after his mother's death, when Amir was eighteen, his father went by himself on a two-week trip to Italy, during which he was murdered. The killer was caught and is now in jail. Amir and his sister chose to stay in their parents' apartment on their own and take care of themselves. Their grandparents were too old to help with their everyday needs. Amir had no intention of joining the army and the death of his father allowed him to avoid being drafted.

Despite his tragic life, Amir was always a happy child. He was socially and physically active, creative, and had a good sense of humor. His sister developed a kind of dreamy new-age attitude that went with the flow of whatever happened in a somewhat detached manner. Amir turned their home into a nonstop party center for his large circle of friends. They took drugs, danced, made music, enjoyed free sex, and celebrated their parentless life. Because their parents had left behind quite a bit of money, Amir and his sister did not have to worry about earning a living. Amir stayed unemployed, did not enroll in any study program, and spent most of his time partying. His physical symptoms brought him to his first therapy and, later on, to me.

We began analysis. Amir was full of stories, adventures, and jokes in a way that was understood as an extension of the same party that kept him detached from any psychic pain or anxiety, which ended up being expressed through his physical symptoms. Part of his party-narrative involved telling me about his numerous sexual partners and his many sexual exploits. After about a year in analysis, during which we worked through his need for partying as an "anesthetic," his need for this good-time defense mechanism decreased. Amir shared that every time he hit on a girl, he was worried about not getting an erection and not being able to function sexually. When he knew that a sexual encounter was about to take place, he got anxious and tried to calm himself down in various ways and to arouse himself before engaging in any sexual act. He felt tremendous relief when he was able to function sexually. One of the reasons he kept changing partners was the need to make sure that he could still function and that it was not "just a fluke and because I turned myself on in advance." His anxiety rendered Amir incapable of breaking this "loop." Any attempts to understand why Amir was afraid that he would not be able to function sexually, that he was not "man enough," led to no further insight. Every now and then, the hypothesis that he was latently homosexual came up, seeing as Amir was preoccupied with the sexual conquests of his male friends and with comparing the sizes of his and their penises, but this direction failed to resonate with him.

Some three years into the analysis, he shared a series of dreams in which he was at a drug party, completely stoned and going into the shower with some hot girl; as they were taking off their clothes, it turned out that she was a guy, who got very angry that Amir was a man and tried to kill him. It came to me that when he had told me about his father's murder, I asked him if he knew what had happened and why his father was killed. He had answered that he did not really know and that he had the transcripts from the killer's trial. Because these were in Italian, he did not know what they said. "I really should get these translated," he had said at the time, but he never did. Following our discussion of the matter, he also noticed that he was avoiding asking his father's parents if they knew why his father had been murdered. Around that time, he complained that his feelings of "my butt is burning" were becoming worse, after a long time in which his digestion problems disappeared almost entirely and his pain during urination or bowel movements significantly decreased.

When Amir shared yet another dream from a long line of "man/woman in a sexual situation who gets angry and wants to kill him" dreams, I asked, "Could it be that your father was a homosexual and that he was murdered by a raging guy in that context and that you are keeping yourself from thinking it?" Amir froze on the couch and went silent. The air in the room became intolerably tense; it felt like a disaster had struck. I felt like I had done something terrible. After long minutes had passed, I started asking Amir how he was feeling. Amir raised his hand to signal that I should stop talking. I grew silent. After several more minutes, which were saturated with the sense that some disaster has happened, Amir got up and said that he felt that he should leave now, even though we still had twenty more minutes to the end of the session. I nodded and he left.

I spent two very difficult days until our next session, not knowing if he was going to come back. At the next session, he came in and said that it was very, very hard for him to hear the hypothesis I made. He also felt that linking these two new thoughts together—his father being a homosexual and being murdered in that context—made things much more difficult for him. He was not angry at me, but he said that avoiding these thoughts in the past felt right to him. He told me that his friends always made fun of him about his father being gay and he would get very worked up and upset and insist that it was not true. He also said that he came across certain "wicked" rumors about his father having been killed because he was gay—rumors which he immediately rejected as "a nasty piece of gossip." He remembered certain events from his childhood that made him think that his father never touched his mother, even though he and his sister are his father's biological children because they resemble him physically.

The process of working through these memories and the thought that the murder happened in this particular context took several months and was very painful. Having avoided finding out why his father had been killed for such a long period of time, Amir read the transcripts from the murder trial, which had finally been translated from Italian. They described how the father had tried to ask a local man to have sex with him; the man reacted to being approached as a homosexual with terrible anger and he stabbed Amir's father with a knife and ran away. The medical report indicated that his father had not died on the spot. Because it was nighttime and there were no people around, no one came to his aid and he eventually died from his injuries. This difficult description gave rise to both pain and shame. Amir felt bad about not having gone to Italy with his father, even though his father had invited him and his sister to come along. The working through of this information was complex and, during this process, we discovered that Amir's anxiety about not being man enough and his need to repeatedly put his masculinity to the test with more and more women stemmed from his unconscious thought of his father's "impaired" masculinity and the anxiety that something might have gone wrong with his own masculinity, perhaps also as punishment for "having forsaken my father." This also rendered the burning sensations in his intimate parts intelligible and, as the analysis progressed, these disappeared entirely. Amir significantly cut down on the parties, which were designed to keep himself from thinking. He no longer chased after women in order to put his sexual prowess to the test. He learned a profession and started working in that field; he established a good intimate relationship, got married and had children. He tried to help his sister, who remained zoned-out and detached, also by sharing with her the information about why their father had been killed. This did little to improve her condition and Amir keeps caring for her and helping her.

Discussion

Both Gidi and Amir came to analysis with physical symptoms that indicated that they were in emotional pain and unable to contain their emotional reactions to events in their lives, which had remained as beta elements. Alternately, as Ogden (2003) puts it, they were unable to dream about their pain—the pain of the traumas they had suffered: sexual abuse, in Gidi's case; and the mysterious and unclear murder of his father, in Amir's.

The two cases mentioned above show that Gidi was unable to dwell in knowing the truth, while Amir was able to work through, in a way that added even more pain, the knowledge that came to him in his dream and "cry out" through his knowledge of the truth. One wonders why Amir was able to cope with knowing his subjective/real truth, while Gidi was left with dissociation, which kept him detached, at least emotionally, from his painful experiences. When Gidi shares his dream in which the analyst masturbated him in the presence of his younger brother, that is the beginning of a process of symbolization of the experience he would rather forget. The analyst offers him an interpretation which turns out to be factually correct, but Gidi himself is still unwilling to encounter this truth. Whenever the threat of encountering the truth grows imminent, he simply "forgets." He cannot emotionally contain the pain and the humiliation this truth entails. The pain is too great to bear. He cannot, recalling Sterne's words as quoted by Bromberg, "go to the world's end with the analyst." Moreover, it appears that the intensity of his rage, aggression, and need for revenge frightens Gidi and deters the analyst from being present with the full force of his emotions.

At the end of the day, Gidi's solution is to maintain his perverse behavior in the context of his relation to women, though in secret. Thus, this symptom helps him keep his truth at arm's length and without any permanent symbolic representation. He cannot confront this immutable truth from his past and denies it through partial remembrance and immediate forgetting as well as through the internalization of and identification with the aggressor, in an attempt to control the source of the abuse.

One might say that Gidi has shifted from the state of an undreamed dream, meaning, a state in which there was no mental representation of the sexual abuse he had suffered, to that of an interrupted cry (Ogden, 2005): whenever his memory of the sexual abuse resurfaces, along with the emotions it entails, the dream, the emotional working through, is interrupted. In other words, Gidi too is able to make use of the analysis, though partially, given his interrupted ability to tolerate the truth.

Amir brings to analysis a series of dreams which indicate to the analyst that the alpha function capable of containing an interpretation that will bring him closer to the truth has indeed developed in him. He comes closer to full symbolization of the understanding of the "unthought known." These dreams enrich his world with meaning that he had once understood but subsequently lost (Meltzer, 1984). This series of dreams allows him to gradually approach his psychic/external reality while regulating his emotional pain. When working with Amir, the analyst dares to speak out and offer a full interpretation, having realized that Amir is able to receive it. The meaning of such interpretation is, of course, understood by both the analyst and the patient. There is no need to "short circuit" one's emotional reactions. As a result, the symptoms Amir had suffered from—which served to protect him from knowing the truth and to punish him for not having protected his father—can now be replaced with the establishment of a loving intimate relationship. One might say that, for Amir, dreaming in analysis was not interrupted but ran its course, leading to the disappearance of all his symptoms and more complete healing.

There are, it seems, certain differences between Gidi and Amir which led to their different capacities for tolerating the truth. Some of these reasons are congenital: Amir had a winning sense of humor and creativity when he came to analysis, as well as basic *joie de vivre.* In contrast, Gidi's personality had a more significant depressive streak and he made little use of humor or playfulness. These differences may be congenital, meaning that some people are born with greater capacities for dealing with difficult events in their lives.

Other reasons are cultural in nature: Gidi was born and raised in a small rural village, where most of the people were national-religious in their views; they upheld the ethos of the Zionist project and had rather fixed notions of masculinity. A real man is supposed to be a combat soldier, unemotional, and anything but weak. For Gidi, having been abused, having been a weak, defenseless victim, was unforgivable in the terms of the social milieu he grew up in. Amir, in contrast, was born in Tel Aviv, the big city, where masculinity was not necessarily equated with machismo or power and homosexuality was not socially unacceptable. The environment he grew up in included masculine ideals that were more sensitive, attentive, and capable of expressing weakness. This means that, for Amir, homosexuality was not a source of intolerable shame or an unforgivable weakness.

Other reasons entail childhood object relations. Amir remembers his late mother as a hard, career-oriented woman, who demanded high function and high achievement. However, he remembers his father as a warm, caring, and loving emotional presence. He was able to share the feelings of guilt he had when his mother died—guilt over not having loved her so much—with his father. His father's reaction was comforting, accepting, and soothing. As mentioned, Gidi grew up with a frightening father, who had severe outbursts of rage that stemmed from the strict demands and expectations he imposed on his children. Gidi's mother was paralyzed with fear during her husband's outbursts and was unable to offer her children any support or protection. Perhaps the ability to tolerate the emotional truth related to the traumatic experience had to do with different levels of emotional resilience, which had been established as a result of good experiences in early object relations.

Moreover, the nature of the trauma also played a role. It appears that the trauma Gidi had suffered, sexual abuse which gave rise to intolerable feelings of humiliation and rage, along with the impact of his early object relations—the fear that Gidi will take after his father and will not be able to control his rage—was so difficult because Gidi lived through it himself, it had happened to him directly. Amir's trauma, in addition to losing his father, who supported him, and, at a younger age, losing his mother, involved the enigmatic nature of his father's death and the secret hidden in his father's life and death. It appears that the trauma of this enigma and its resolution was less severe than the one Gidi suffered.

Finally, the analyst also plays a role in the patient's ability to work through the emotional truths of their life and the extent to which such working through is made possible. It seems that each psychoanalytic school of thought—maybe even each analyst—has their own answer about what curative factors come into play in the analytic process or about what is required of the analyst in order to facilitate progress toward growth and healing in the analytic process. Readers with different analytic perspectives may find good reasons as to why Gidi's and Amir's analyst had been able to allow Amir to fully work through the emotional experiences related to his trauma, while his work with Gidi had only achieved partial working through. The question of what elements of the analyst's conduct facilitate or hinder the development of the analytic process is beyond the scope of this chapter. Our claim is that when the patient is able to come in contact with emotional truths arising from events in his life and to begin or continue to work through these emotions, in a way that allows him to remember both the events and the emotions in a livelier fashion, his growth and healing become more complete. One might say that this claim resonates that of Freud (1914g) in his paper, "Remembering, Repeating and Working-Through": "The aim of these different techniques has, of course, remained the same. Descriptively speaking, it is to fill in gaps in memory; dynamically speaking, it is to overcome resistances due to repression" (pp. 147–148). Such filling in of gaps in memory is made possible when the patient encounters and experiences, within the analytic process, those emotions that originate in "gaps in memory." These emotions had hitherto been intolerable, meaning that the patient had not been able to face the truth—that these emotions exist within him—and tolerate it.

CHAPTER ELEVEN

Seven types of truth and their clinical relevance

Salman Akhtar

The first thing I note in approaching the topic of "truth" is the absence of clarity and consensus about its definition. Dictionaries seem to fumble, fudge, and fail to come up with a simple and straightforward statement. *Webster's* (1998), for instance, includes words or phrases like "fidelity … constancy … sincerity … in action, character, and utterance … a transcendent fundamental or spiritual reality … a judgment, proposition or idea that is true or accepted as true … the property of being in accord with fact or reality" (p. 1269). Clearly, this has wobbly foundations (e.g., do we really know what is a "fact"?) and circular reasoning (e.g., "truth is what is true or accepted as true"). The difficulty in arriving at a precise definition arises from the inherent duality, in the English language, of the meanings subsumed under the term "truth." On the one hand, it refers to faithfulness, fidelity, and sincerity while on the other it tips its hat to consonance with reality. This duality seems to have arisen because of the origin of the word. Derived from Old English, *tréowe*, the word remained closely tied to fidelity and faith while also acquiring a sense of loyalty to facts.

Three other prevalent languages of the world, namely Spanish, Chinese, and Arabic, perpetuate the same Janus-faced conceptualization or create a linguistic bifurcation of the essence of the "truth." The Spanish word for "truth" is *verdad*. It is derived from the blending of Proto-Indo-European *ros* with Proto-Italic *weros* and subsumes both "factual" and "genuine"; it thus closely resembles the English word "truth." Chinese, however, distinguishes between *zhēnxiang* standing for the actual state of affairs, *zhēnli* denoting truth, and *zhēnqing* describing real feelings or sentiments. Arabic also contains a distinction along similar lines and uses *haqeeqat* for actuality and *sadaqat* for truthfulness.

Such a dizzying romp through four demographically dominant languages leaves me well-informed but unsatisfied and unclear. Must there be an accord between "truth" and "fact"?

Do demonstrations of "sincerity" and "genuineness" on an individual's part assure us of his or her "truthfulness"? And are "real feelings" always true? Where does "authentic" falsehood emanating from having been "gaslighted" (Barton & Whitehead, 1969) fall on this spectrum? What is the relationship between plausibility and truth? And between provability and factuality?

Bombarded by such questions, I seek refuge in the established canon. Philosophers come to our help but even they seem divided and end up serving us the sumptuous, if intimidating, banquet of five theories of truth. Summarized with an unjust brevity, these are (i) *correspondence theory* (Aristotle, *c.*340 BCE) which tells us that what reflects the observable reality is true, (ii) *coherence theory* (Spinoza, *c.*1660) which says that what "hangs together" well is true, (iii) *pragmatic theory* (Pierce, 1901) which declares what is useful and beneficial to be true, (iv) *redundancy theory* (Frege, 1918) which states that the concept of truth is only needed as an indirect reference and otherwise is superfluous, (v) *semantic theory* (Tarski, 1944) which proposes that truth can only exist in small declaration segments that are subject to logic; broader, complex, and generalized statements cannot be declared as being true or untrue, (vi) *consensus theory* (Lakatos, 1976) which declares that what most people agree upon is true.

Not well-versed in philosophy, I return to the comfort of daily language only to find that many new words and phrases have been coined pertaining to truth in relatively recent times. These include: truth-value (1903), truth-table (2016), truth-serum (1925), and post-truth (2016). These denote, respectively, the proportionality of truth vs. falsehood in a given statement, an algorithm to "calculate" the truth value of a compound statement, an intravenously administered chemical substance that overcomes resistance to speak truthfully, and circumstances when objective facts pale in comparison to emotions when it comes to shaping public opinion. Armed, or shall I say, unarmed, with all this knowledge, I arrive at a new awareness about truth and find at least seven varieties of it waiting to greet us at this juncture. These are (i) physical truth, (ii) historical truth, (iii) narrative truth, (iv) poetic truth, (v) judicial truth, (vi) manufactured truth, and (vii) existential truth.[61] Brief notes on each of these categories and its clinical relevance follow.

Physical truth

Mundane and self-evident though it might sound, one does need to recognize the category of physical "truth," an alternate designation for which might be "organic" truth. This denomination applies to matters of physical reality. For instance, right this moment I am using a paper and pen (I still handwrite everything!) to give expression to my thoughts. Or, you are reading

[61] Since it seems possible to extend this list by adding other categories (e.g., divine truth, evolutionary truth, moral truth), my classification must itself be regarded as a form of narrative truth or, if you will, an earnestly intended "didactic truth."

these words printed on a sheet of paper or, if you are using Kindle, on a screen. I am sitting on a chair and, as usual, working not on my study desk but on my dining table; its maternal generosity contains not only various books, sheets of paper, pens, and xeroxed essays but also the scatter of my thoughts.

Away from such a self-referential beginning, my term "physical truth" refers to what Frosch (1964) has called "reality constancy" which may be "shifting and yet permanent and continuous in time and space" (Goldfarb, 1963, p. 51). Thus a tree is a tree, a car a car, and a tree does not become a car. Streets, buildings, rivers, mountains, birds, frogs, spaceships, boats, motorcycles, skis, bottles of gin and whiskey, keys, eyeglasses, condoms, coffee tables, and mailboxes—to name but a few among the multitude of things that surround us—also remain persistently loyal to their forum and nature. Indeed Spinoza (*c.*1660) asserts that a tiger wishes to remain a tiger and a rock a rock. These are "physical" truths.

To be sure, such truth can come into question as the gap between the observer and the observed increases and as the unit of observation becomes smaller. "Truths" about planets, solar systems, and distant galaxies lack the solidity of "truths" about the chair I am sitting on right at this minute. Truths about my beloved dogs, *Jackie* and *Majnun*, seem clearer than those about microorganisms, neural pathways, and chemical transport across cellular membranes. Such relativity, however, does not eliminate the existence and necessity of physical truth. The following terse reminder by Frankfurt (2006) provides invincible support to this point: "No one in his right mind would rely on a builder or submit to the care of a physician who does not care about the truth" (p. 14).

Extrapolating the thread running through the foregoing assertions to clinical psychoanalysis reveals that physical truths are of extreme, if silent, importance to its therapeutic framework and boundaries. Take the following questions, for instance. Is the patient young or old? In good health or bad? Biologically male or female? Rich or poor? Tall or short? Does he or she arrive on time or is chronically late? Are the payments made in time? Is the patient lying on the couch, sitting in a chair, or pacing around the office? Can the patient, medically speaking, hear the analyst or is he or she somewhat deaf? What is the patient's blood alcohol level? Is the analyst available or is he or she on vacation? And, so on and so forth. Such physical truths can have direct (distortion of frame) or indirect (transference resistance, and acting out) impact upon the progress of clinical work. The work of psychoanalysts might be focused upon fantasies and imagined manuscripts of object relations but it is conducted with firm boundaries that are anchored in reality and are forever mindful of physical truths.

One clinically inescapable physical truth is the reality of the analyst's office itself. Its location, authenticity, and constancy can all have a powerful impact on the analytic process that unfolds within its four walls (Akhtar, 2009; Gerald, 2021). More specifically, the placement of the couch, the wall next to it, and the sundry knickknacks, paintings, statuettes, rugs, and lamps in the analyst's office perform significant "holding," evocative, and containing functions which become dramatically evident when such objects are removed, replaced, or altered in any manner. While understanding the intrapsychic meanings of such physical changes is paramount for analytic work, the reality of their existence seeking such projections cannot be denied. The office and its contents constitute the physical truth of our clinical work.

Historical truth

The foregoing "anatomy" of truth paves the way for us to consider the "physiology" of truth. Here, I am referring to the "historical truth" which claims to recover old and buried facts from the moth-eaten register of memory (recorded or orally transmitted, personally accrued or received in a handed down manner, true or false, consensual or contested). Freud's (1907a) "archaeological metaphor" sums this notion up by comparing the human mind to a layered geography in which traces of older civilizations lie buried underneath the current cities and their customs. Digging the surface would therefore reveal different and temporally older material. This is the essence of historical truth which asserts that such and such event took place, at such and such time, under such and such circumstances, and with such and such individuals or groups as its prime participants, actors, motivators, beneficiaries, perpetrators, or victims. Claim is made for its veracity either by the authorial prestige, by its palatability to the audience/readership, or by enlisting "confirmatory" evidence. The enterprise, as one can readily discern, is not easy. Questions such as who has prepared and propagated the narrative, when, and why, are not the only ones muddying the waters here. Issues of motives, blind spots, deliberate omissions, and purposive miscommunications also enter the picture. Take, for instance, the issue of Hindu–Muslim relations in India over the last one thousand years. As I have noted elsewhere (Akhtar, 2005), there are two distinct narratives here. One highlights strife, the other synchrony; one underscores hatred, the other harmony; and one unmasks conflict, the other cooperation. In my reading of pertinent history, both narratives contain elements of truth. However, "which facet of this history gets highlighted, under what circumstances, by whom, for what purpose, and with what consequences" (p. 91) makes an assessment of historical truth in this context exceedingly elusive.

The situation in the clinical encounter is not different. A case in point here is the fate of Freud's (1893, 1895d "seduction hypotheses" and the controversy that still surrounds that fate. Essentially, this proposal viewed the symptoms of hysteria and obsessional neurosis as resulting from sexual overstimulation of children by adults. The "seduction" involved in such scenarios ranged from verbal and visual intrusion to actual sexual molestation. Neurotic symptoms resulted from the revivification of this early trauma by later life events that did not have to be sexual in nature themselves. However, within a year of its last iteration, Freud began to doubt the veracity of his "seduction hypothesis." He questioned his patients' reports and declared that "I no longer believe in my *neurotica*" (Freud, letter to Fliess, September 9, 1897, p. 223, italics in the original, in Masson, 1985). A few years later he added that "these fantasies were intended to cover up the auto-erotic activity of the first years of childhood" (1914d, p. 17). Concepts of infantile sexuality, erotic life of children, Oedipus complex, and so on thus came to the foreground and eclipsed the earlier "seduction hypothesis." Consequently, the enterprise to unearth historical truth in psychoanalysis gave way to making a plausible "construction" (Freud, 1940a).[62] Freud's change of mind received three kinds of critique: (i) the first was based upon the assertion that he denounced the "seduction hypothesis" due to the fear of retaliation by the Viennese bourgeois society (Masson, 1984), (ii) the second asserted that while Freud, in his later work, reduced paternal incest largely to fantasy and nullified the distinction between real and imagined seduction, he never disavowed the occurrence of sexual abuse (Ahbel-Rappe, 2006), and (iii) the third stated that Freud moved away from the "seduction hypothesis" to avoid the full impact of discovery that he might have been sexually abused by his childhood nursemaid and that he himself might have inflicted the same trauma on his younger siblings (Peter Rudnytsky, personal communication, June 10, 2018; see also Rudnytsky, 2022).

This narrow slice of vision regarding the fate of historical truth in psychoanalysis does not do justice to the conceptual challenges and nuances added to this realm by Freud's (1899a) own concept of "screen memory" and by the later emerging notions of "personal myth" (E. Kris, 1956a), "gaslighting" (Barton & Whitehead, 1969), "false memories" (Loftus & Palmer, 1974), "co-created facts" (Mitchell, 1988), "narrative truth" (Spence, 1982a, 1982b), and so on. Together, these concepts challenged the veracity and value of historical truth, pointing out that recall of events is unreliable, the mummified material of the unconscious is vulnerable to revisionism, and self-serving defenses can dramatically alter personal biography. However, such "softening" does not obliterate historical truth altogether though its unearthing can shift from *en-bloc* recall to piecemeal reconstruction.

Clinical vignette: 1

A middle-aged man undergoing analysis, for instance, offered the memory of a tennis match in which his father badly defeated him after he had lost a game to the patient, as a proof of his father's vindictiveness. Further analytic work, spread over months, however, revealed that the patient had actually let his father win because the father had recently had a heart attack. Still later in the course of this patient's treatment, it became evident that the two games (where the father lost and won, respectively) had been played on different days and had little to do with each other. It was this patient's need to see his father as dangerously retaliatory (in order to keep his own powerful competitive impulses in check) that had led to the conflation of the two memories.

[62] The term "construction" was first used by Freud (1937d) for the analyst's formulation of an account of the patient's forgotten early experience. The analyst draws his inference in this regard from the patient's free associations, transference propensities, nonverbal cues, dreams, and, of course the resonance of all these in the countertransference experience. "Construction" is thus a form of narrative truth. North American analysts' preference for the term "reconstruction" highlights this point (Akhtar, 2009).

Unlike the gradual working through of narcissistically tailored conflation of memory, sometimes the access to a "historical truth" is explosively sudden, convincing, and assertively self-evident. This is Bion's (1965, 1970) "O" or the supreme and absolute truth of the moment.[63]

> **Clinical vignette: 2**
>
> Olga Bokor, a child welfare worker in her forties, once reported what she called a "peculiar" phenomenon. She said that whenever she sees a patch of black-eyed Susans (the yellow flower with a black center) she feels a powerful impulse to lie down and put her head on the flowers; she feels convinced that it would bring her great emotional peace. If this happens while she is driving on a highway, she gets tempted to pull the car off to the shoulder and go lie down among the flowers. In describing this, Olga especially emphasized the "putting my head" on the flower patch, demonstrating it with a gentle tilt of her head. She found the whole thing puzzling because she had grown up in a downtown apartment building and had no memories of being in a garden as a child. Just as she was speculating what this impulse might mean, like a bolt from blue a thought occurred to me. In fact, I became instantly convinced that I knew what this was all about and said, "You know what, I think your mother had a silk dress with such flowers on it and you as a little girl, would put your head in her lap when you were tired or afraid of something." The patient was stunned, could immediately recall such a dress, and found my reconstruction to be astonishingly accurate. She then went on to talk more about that dress and her childhood feelings about it and about her mother.

Regardless of how it is arrived at, historical truth does seem to exist in the clinical process as these two clinical vignettes demonstrate, though it can certainly be argued that painstaking or mysterious interpretive processes of the sort described here do not always yield "actual" information about the patient's past. More often, both parties in the dyad have to accept a reconstruction that appears to be palatable, plausible, and, like Glover's (1931) "inexact interpretation," productive as far as the progress of clinical work is concerned.

---

[63] Bion is of course not the only thinker to talk of "absolute truth." Gandhi too spoke frequently of "*the* truth." Writing long before Bion, but in a similar vein, Gandhi (1927) declared that "deference to tradition" (p. 350) must be put aside in order to find the truth. He stated that "a successful search for Truth means complete deliverance from the dual throng such as of love and hate, happiness and misery" (p. 345). The stoic stance of Gandhi and Bion has a striking resemblance. Gandhi's declaration that "there is no other God than the Truth" (p. 503) echoes in Bion's (1965) emphasis that "O" constitutes the absolute and ultimate truth of the moment and that it is immeasurable. In my reading of it (Akhtar, 2009), Bion's "O" is a truncated form of *Om*, the Sanskrit word for the Omnipotent Creator or God. Gandhi imbued his politics with religion and Bion did the same with his psychoanalysis. To what extent the fact that both were born and raised in India contributes to their mystical inclination remains a matter of speculation.

Narrative truth

Spence (1982a, 1982b) who has written most explicitly and forcefully on this topic, cites the scattered early works of Sherwood (1969), Atkinson (1978), and Ricouer (1977a), and concludes that "narrative truth" is characterized by (i) its intrinsic consistency, (ii) its plausibility, (iii) its satisfactory fit with the other pieces of the mental puzzle, (iv) its acceptability to both its originator and its recipient as (v) its tacit awareness of not having replaced the "historical truth" whatever that might be. Both true and false expositions can be smoothly embroidered into a developing story but "the goodness of fit cannot be used to distinguish the first from the second" (Spence, 1982a, p. 48). Narrative truth also contains an aesthetic element—constituted by its form, timing, phraseology, and intonation of delivery. Moreover, the narrative truth of a moment, in contrast with the absolute truth or "O" (Bion, 1962a, 1962b) of that moment, is open to modification; this can happen by a later-emerging historical truth or by the narrative truth of today transforming itself into a historical truth of tomorrow. Volkan's (1988, 2004) concept of large groups' "chosen trauma" and "chosen glory" are illustrations of how bits and pieces of actual events of the past can be accorded exalted status for political purposes and thus create the possibility of blurring boundaries between narrative and historical truths. More often, though, they remain distinct from each other.

The contrast between these two types of truth resembles that between psychic and external reality. But there is an important difference between the two sets of concepts. Narrative truth is a plug of plausibility in the hole of recall while psychic reality can represent historical truth too. Similarly, historical truth and external reality do not always coincide; the fact that one's husband died two years ago and that one felt profoundly sad for many subsequent months are both historical truths, though one refers to external reality and the other to subjective experience. This goes to show that historical truth and narrative truth can coexist.

However, one area where narrative truth often trumps historical truth is the writing of autobiographies and memoirs (Akhtar, 2022; Gusdorf, 1980). These contain literary devices of condensation, added nuance, juxtaposition, artsy speculation, and omissions of ill-fitting pieces of the story. In essence, these preserve and perpetuate what the writer holds as his or her truth. The biographical self-image for authors of such traits is

> particularly firmly knit and embraces all periods of their lives from childhood on. Their personal history is not only, as one might expect, an essential part of their self-representation, but has become a treasured possession to which the [individual] is attached with a particular devotion. This attachment reflects the fact that the autobiographical self-image has become heir to important early fantasies, which it preserves. In this sense, I propose to speak of it as of a personal myth which, as all living myth, extends from the past into the present. (E. Kris, 1956a, p. 654)

Talking of the "personal myth" (Kris, 1956a) and its oft-needed skirting of reality brings us to consider the place of narrative truth in our clinical work.

In contrast to historical truth that is unearthed either by the analysis of defenses and resistances or by uncanny leaps of intuition, narrative truth emerges from the analyst's "conjecture" (C. Brenner, 1976). However, such formulation must have four characteristics for it to be "valid" and useful: (i) it must not be taken literally and must retain a provisional and make-believe quality, (ii) it must arise from a harmonious blend of the material provided by the patient and the empathic resonance experienced by the analyst, (iii) it must be permitted the freedom to refer to past "events" or to the moment-to-moment experiences in the "here and now" or to a mixture of them, (iv) it must satisfy the "epistemophilic instinct" (Freud, 1916–17; Nunberg, 1931) of both the analyst and the patient; it should make sense to them in a way that brings the matter at hand to closure. A caveat needs to be entered here, though. The degree of conviction and mutual satisfaction felt by the clinical dyad remains variable under such circumstances. Take the following example of "agreement" over the "narrative truth" of a particular clinical moment.

Clinical vignette: 3

Marcy Schectman begins the last session of her nearly ten-year-long analysis by saying that on her way to my office, she felt as if she were coming to a funeral. She describes her experience of there being an air of finality, solemnity, and loss to the afternoon. As I remain silent, Marcy goes on to recount her experiences at a couple of funerals she has attended. She sobs. I too feel sad, but do not say anything. Gradually, her associations shift to her getting a doctorate soon and then to graduation dinners, commencement ceremonies, etc. She begins to be animated. Soon, however, she catches herself and observes that this talk of happy endings (graduations) is defensive against her sadness (funerals). Significantly, she adds that while this might be the case, the two sides most likely represent the two sides of her feelings regarding parting from me for good: "happy and sad, sad and happy." I now say, "Yes, it does seem like that," and, after a momentary pause, add "but you know, all well-timed funerals are graduations of a sort and all graduations contain funeral-like elements." Marcy nods in agreement. She remains silent and so do I for the next couple of minutes. The sense of our being together in each other's apartness is evident as the end of the session approaches.

It is the last component of my intervention (funerals are like graduations and graduations like funerals) that constitutes the empathically derived "narrative truth" of the moment. Perhaps it was this phrase's attention to the "here and now" that solidified its credibility to the patient. In contrast, when the cocreation of "narrative truth" extends far backwards in the patient's history it may lack that "aha" quality of flashy conviction. This is even more true when it comes to early, unmentalized states of childhood.

Clinical vignette: 4

Marilyn McDonough, an attractive architect in her fifties, had sought help following an emotional crisis with one of her children. Once the acute matter was settled and the treatment began to deepen, the centrality of her own mother's death when Marilyn was barely five years old came to the surface. A talented and industrious woman, Marilyn had devoted all her energies to raising her kids (after a tumultuous marriage ended in divorce) and to advancing in the profession she loved. She excelled at both these endeavors and, all along, the pain of her early maternal loss remained psychically sequestered—never repressed but not entirely worked through either. Later, she got married again and had since then maintained a reasonably satisfactory marital life.

Her analysis, for a long time, remained focused upon the pervasive effects of her early loss; it colored transference anxieties, sensitivities to separation, and fear of getting retraumatized by losing me. Provision of ample psychic space, empathic validation, gentle uncovering of defenses against the awareness of the deep impact of the childhood tragedy, and interpretive handling of "survivor guilt" (Niederland, 1968) and the resulting inhibition of healthy entitlement, led to great improvement in her capacity to mourn. Energy thus freed up was then directed to deepening ties with her family and newer sublimations. Such progress did not preclude the repeated return to mourning the loss of her mother at a very young age. The resurgence of this material during later phases of analysis was often accompanied by new recollections and new questions.

One day in the fourth year of her analysis, Marilyn came for her session right after visiting her stepmother, Meg, in the nursing home where she had resided for the past few months. Marilyn began the session by talking about how frail Meg had become and how readily she got fatigued. Soon, the thoughts of Meg's death surfaced. Marilyn sobbed. And, she began wondering about Meg's funeral. This led to the memory of the day Marilyn's biological mother, Mary, had died. A question that had never occurred to her now emerged. Marilyn said, "I think I was told by my father that mom would not be coming back from the hospital and that she had gone to heaven or something like that—I am not sure—around three or four p.m. that afternoon. Since I was four and a half, I suppose my bed time then must have been something like eight p.m. The question is what did I do between four and eight p.m.?" Marilyn went on to say, "I really want to know that. I don't know but I want to, in fact, I need to know that. What did I do? I know I used to write on the walls with crayons and carve something on the coffee table but all that came much later, not that afternoon. Maybe I was just wandering around the house, I don't know. But I want to know, though I am not sure why I want to know." As she was speaking, I found my mind wandering. I recalled that long ago, I had seen Wilhelm Stekel's (1924) monograph on wandering in a psychoanalytic library but had not actually read it. I felt a sense of loss and an aching desire to undo that loss. Taking a cue from this "concordant countertransference" (Racker, 1968) and from this bit of free association of my own, I said, "Of course, you would like to link up with that missing fragment of your life. It's natural for all of us to try to fill in the gaps in our memory to help us experience a sense of continuity. It's like if you lose one earring and are holding on to the other of the pair; you would search for the lost one." Marilyn

> responded, "But why can't I remember?" I said, "I do not really know but think there are many possibilities. One, that you were in a state that is best called 'forlorn' and being only four and a half years old, could not think properly about what had happened. Two, perhaps all the grown-ups in the house were themselves preoccupied. So, left to your own meager resources, you could not feel or think clearly. And, since you were not able to clearly register what was going on during those hours, you can not recall it now. It is all a fog." Marilyn nodded in agreement and cried. Composing herself, she said, "It is like there is a piece of a puzzle or something absent, something not to be found." I responded, "Something and someone! For the very person who could have helped you 'think' about your mother's death—to the extent you could—was your mother and she was gone, not to be found, so to speak." Marilyn listened peacefully. The quiet of the office encased our mutuality. Then I added, "And, of course, we also have to consider if the search for the memory of those missing four hours is a version of a search for her and if the reference includes our four 'hours' and the wish that I would be with you all those hours so that you never feel forlorn now."

Reconstructive and interpretive work, both in the transference and extra-transference realms, was a response to this patient's self-directed curiosity. It helped fill the throbbing and unmentalized gap in the narrative of her trauma and linked it up with her experience in the here and now of the analysis.

Together the two clinical vignettes of the workings of narrative truth in clinical work lead us to the logically weaker but affectively meaningful and alluring world of imagination, metaphor, and yes, poetry.

Poetic truth

Allow me to start with a blunt statement. What is true in poetry is not true in prose. The following lines of poetry illustrate this point well, I think.

- "Listen to presences inside poems" (Rumi, cited in Barks, 1995, p. 99)
- "What is sadder than a train stopped in rain" (Neruda, 1991, p. 32)
- "There is a door that I have closed till the end of this world" (Borges, 1964, p. 49)

Try reading these lines as if they were in prose and the difference between "poetic truth" and the "truth of prose" will become evident to you. Bare-bone prose yields no meaning for "presences inside poems" such as a door that has been "closed till the end of this world" and the "sadness of a train stopped in rain." In fact, such statements appear logically absurd. Now hear these words in the voice of a poet with your verse-friendly ear and suddenly they come alive and seem brightly lit with stars of allusion and moons of metaphor. "Presences in poems" introduces us to those for whom the poem was written and to the writer's internal objects who were the lexical transporters of such message. The impasse between the "train" and "rain" unmasks the clash between machine and nature and, behind that, the encounter between man and God. And the door that has been closed "till the end of this world" does not embody an astronomical prophecy: It tells us that the end of a relationship is the end of the poet's world. What seemed flawed in prose turns out to be flawless in poetry. What is a grotesque equivocation in prose becomes a noble truth in poetry.

In fact, the lexical building blocks of poetry (e.g., alliteration, rhyme, metaphor) are known adversities of well-reasoned prose. Prosodic supremacy is often achieved, in poetry, by defiance of logic and reliance upon a sort of restrained audacity. Borges's 1967 Harvard Lectures, recently brought together as a monograph titled *This Craft of Verse* (Borges, 2000), masterfully elucidated the art of creating—or, letting oneself stumble upon—metaphors. This not only requires a certain freedom from the "truth of prose" but even a striking sophistry of salesmanship. Borges stated:

> Sometimes I have attempted a rather bold metaphor, but have seen that no one would accept it if it came from me (I am a mere contemporary), and so I have attributed it to some out-of-the-way Persian or Norseman. Then my friends have said that it was quite fine; and of course I have never told them that I invented it, because I was fond of the metaphor. (p. 73)

Three decades following Borges lectures, the 1997 US poet, Robert Pinsky (1998), spoke of "vocal reality" (p. 25) and "artful coherence" (p. 26) of a line, as well as "fiendishly charming nature" (p. 80) of sound units to convey action; these physical devices also rebel against the sagacity of prose. That the strictures of custom, formality, and hypnoid obedience to logic have to be broken, if not ruthlessly pulverized, in the process of creativity was put into words, over a hundred years before Borges and Pinsky, by none other than Nietzsche (1873).

> Those enormous beams and planks of concepts to which man clings needily his whole life long to save himself are for the liberated intellect merely a scaffolding and playing for its most daring feats; and in smashing it, mixing it up, reassembling it ironically, combining its most alien elements and separating those most commonly connected, it demonstrates that it has no need for such makeshifts of neediness and from now on be led not by concepts but by intuitions. There is no regular path leading from those intuitions into the land of ghostly schemata, of abstractions; there are no words for them; man falls silent when he sees them or speaks in strictly forbidden metaphors and egregious combinations of concepts in order to correspond creatively to the impression of the powerful present intuition. (p. 46)

This raises poetic truth from the ashes of physical truth and historical truth both of which compose what I have called here the "truth of prose."

Such poetic truth has similarities and differences with the narrative truth described above. Their similarities reside in their band-aid function for bridging the gap between the "unrememberable and the unforgettable" (A. Frank, 1969), their internal coherence, and their appearance of plausibility to the speaker and the audience. Their differences reside in the poetic truth's lesser subservience to the logical "secondary process" (Freud, 1895d) thinking and its greater provision of an "aesthetic bribe"[64] to the listener or reader. Narrative truth is the stuff of novels and history. Poetic truth is the stuff of mythology and dreams.

What does such rumination about the poetic truth have to do with the conduct of clinical psychoanalysis? The answer to this question is simple. Or, is it that the first answer that comes to mind is a simple one? Be that as it may, the answer is that one must listen to patients' speech as both prose and poetry. It is only with such dual attention that one would grasp what the patient is trying to convey. Data arising from these two types of attention are different but complementary and corrective for each other. The composite picture thus derived informs one in a manner that using a single listening approach fails to do. Initially puzzled by such a recommendation, my supervisees gradually see its power. One proudly tells that when a patient reported having lived a third of his life alone, he knew that this betrayed a tendency to withdraw from attachments (prose) and a "warning" that parts of him might never enter the clinical chamber (poetry). Another is radiant with discovering that the woman's persistent weeping over her cat's death not only implies her grief (prose) but also displays a broken heart that has long given up on human relationships (poetry).

Clinical vignette: 5

Sarah Green, a fifty-five-year-old librarian, bought a parakeet to keep as a pet as she was coming out of mourning the loss of a significant romantic relationship. The bird, whom she named Dino, diminished her sense of aloneness, gave some order to her life after working hours, and, over time, became her confidant and *raison d'être* (reason to live). She would talk about Dino as if he possessed in-depth subjectivity, moods, and motivations. I avoided the interpretations that doing dot-to-dot psychoanalysis would have readily offered. I let things be. It was all in the spirit of play. Then Dino died, leaving Sarah devastated. Over the subsequent weeks—no, months—she grieved this loss. The earlier loss of the lover also got reactivated. Sessions were filled with wails and tears. Then one day, Sarah reported the following incident. She had returned to her apartment after work and was sitting near the window. She caught a glimpse, from the corner of her eye, of a dark, little spider on the window sill. She was taken by the spider's quiet beauty and kept looking at it intently. A thought occurred to her: "Could it be that Dino has

[64] The phrase "aesthetic bribe" is my condensation of Freud's (1908e) use of the words "aesthetic" and "bribe" separately in his paper "Creative Writers and Day-Dreaming." He stated that "The writer softens the character of his egoistic day-dreams by altering and disguising it, and he bribes us by the purely formal—that is, aesthetic—yield of pleasure which he offers us in the presentation of his phantasies" (p. 153).

> reincarnated as a spider and come to see me?" As Sarah related this, she emphatically said that she knows that there's no such thing as reincarnation and that birds do not transform themselves into spiders. She paused and then murmured "Who knows? They might." After this, she turned, looked intently at me and said, "You don't think I'm crazy, do you?" Guided by an unknown inner prompter, I spontaneously uttered "No, I do not think you are crazy at all. In fact, I think the spider is actually a poem." Sarah broke into a big and knowing grin which, however, lasted but a few seconds. Somber again, even a bit puzzled, she then said, "What do you mean by that?" I responded by saying that I thought she had immediately grasped my meaning but somehow lost that insight and we should be curious about why that happened. But, I added, that if she wanted, I would be glad to explain what I meant (which I was only then beginning to know myself).

Now, I could wax theoretical and explain the nuances of what, in retrospect, emerged as the rationale for my response to Sarah's asking me if I considered her crazy. That would be hardly suitable for this forum. It should suffice to say that my comment equating the spider with a poem was a spontaneous and, dare I say, poetic, way of saying the following. "Don't worry about reality and don't crowd your mind with what I might or might not think. Just let yourself play with the thought that your mind has come up with. It is beautiful, expressive, and helps you in some ineffable manner. There's no urgency to 'reduce' the thought (that a bird might have become a spider) into its supposed psychic constituents. This space where you and I are at this moment is fun and imagination can have a full rein here. Let us go on with it and see where it might lead us." In prosaic terms, I have "made up" the idea that the spider was a poem because it helped us to stay in the soft space of exploratory dialogue.

Manufactured truth

"Manufactured truth" (Volkan, 1988) is the wicked twin of poetic truth. Unlike the throbbing emotionality and prosodic elegance of the latter, manufactured truth is one-sided and craftily intentional. Poetic truth leaves psychic space between its creator and recipient to negotiate the myriad implications of the message while manufactured truth is delivered with smug certainty and with an attitude of foreclosure. What is "manufactured" here is not only the content but its designation as a fact.

Manufactured truth is the tangible commodity of the contemporary "post-truth" (Keyes, 2004) era. In it, Nietzsche's (1873) early trepidation about the existence of objective truth has found a well-packaged reincarnation that jettisons facts in favor of viewpoint. The *Oxford English Dictionary,* which recognized "post-truth" as the Word of the Year of 2016 regards it as denoting "circumstances in which objective facts are less influential in shaping public opinion than appeals to emotions and personal beliefs" (cited in D'Ancona, 2017). Four occurrences in recent times illustrate this dynamic well.

- In 1989, the Serbian leader, Slobodan Milosevic, "celebrated" the 600th year anniversary of the Battle of Kosovo (in which Serbian King Lazar had died fighting Ottoman forces) by exhuming Lazar's remains and taking them on tour in every Serbian village and town. Each night his remains were buried, then dug up the next morning. The ritual was intended to enhance the cohesion of Serbian identity and, by causing a time collapse (Volkan, 1997), making it appear that the defeat at Kosovo had occurred just recently. The result was expectedly inflammatory and paved the ground for the subsequent ethnic cleansing of Muslim Kosovars and Albanians.
- In 1992, a frenzied Indian Hindu mob, with prominent members of the central government aiding and abetting, destroyed a Muslim mosque, Babri Masjid, built in 1527 AD at the presumed site of the Hindu deity Rama's birth. This dark theater of "messianic sadism" (Akhtar, 2007) was plotted by L. K. Advani, a prominent leader of the ruling party in India, who undertook a 10,000 kilometers *rathyatra* (travel by chariot, which in reality was a Toyota pickup adorned with religious motifs) from the town of Somnath in Northwestern India to the Ayodhya where the allegedly sacrilegious mosque stood. The choice of the starting point was intended to stir up vindictive feeling since a Hindu temple, Somnath, had been destroyed by Muslim invaders in 1020 AD. That the two events (the attack on Somnath and the destruction of Babri Masjid) would occur in different cultural contexts, under different political systems of government, for different purposes, and would be separated by nearly 1,000 years did not matter. Nor did it matter, of course, that there was no way to locate precisely where Rama was born, if indeed he was an actual historical figure and not simply a mythological icon, as is more likely the case.
- In 2003, the Bush administration used the "rationale" of Saddam Hussein possessing nuclear weapons for launching a massive and brutal attack on Iraq which resulted in between 112,000 and 123,000 civilian deaths (Steele, 2010; Tirman, 2011). The fact is that the justification was entirely fabricated (Clarke, 2004; Woodward, 2004) since President Bush had been explicitly told by Ambassador Joseph Wilson, who had been assigned to do due diligence on this matter, that no weapons of mass destruction existed in Iraq and that Saddam Hussein was not purchasing uranium from Niger to make such weapons. All this makes the British Prime Minister Tony Blair's declaration that Saddam Hussein possessed the capacity to destroy the United Kingdom in forty-five seconds a "manufactured truth" of a most diabolical kind.
- The "Big Lie" currently playing havoc with political reality in the United States consists of the former President Donald Trump's assertion that the 2020 election was stolen and he was the real winner in that contest. The lie is believed by millions of his followers and for them it is a truth. Needless to add that the "manufactured" nature of this "truth" is not recognized by those who believe in it; they treat it as "physical" and "historical" truth.

The common element in these instances is a unilateral exaltation of cherished fantasy or known falsehood to the level of fact in order to gain power and political advantage. While the examples I have given come from the sociopolitical arena, the poisonous brew of manufactured truth is served in domestic settings as well. This is something we get to see often in our clinical work.

The commonest variety of manufactured truth encountered in clinical practice involves a parent's refusal to believe a child's report of being sexually abused. The "truth" that's concocted under such circumstances has three features: (i) it whitewashes facts, (ii) it regards the child's emotions as fake, and (iii) it questions the child's perception by declaring the perpetrator to be innocent. A boy who is being regularly beaten up by his older brother is not only left to his own meager resources but is told that his brother "has a heart of gold." A girl who is sexually abused by her uncle is scolded for making up things and casting aspersions on a kind old man who would never harm anyone. Ferenczi's (1949) "confusion of tongues" describes such dynamics in detail and Shengold's (1989) work on "soul murder" gives it a heart-wrenching poignancy.

Matters other than physical and sexual abuse can also be covered up by the family by manufactured truths. An uncle's suicide, a grandmother's affair, father's embezzlement of company funds, sundry miscarriages and abortions, history of political incarceration and torture, the disappearance of a child's cat, and the abrupt cancellation of a wedding are the sort of events that are often patched over by manufactured truths; their real nature is glossed over and rationalized explanations are passed on to family members. Characteristically, deluding others by such manufactured truths benefits those who perpetrate them; the bargain is unilateral, self-serving, and, at its core, dishonest. Children who are chronically exposed to such lying on the parents' part can internalize such tendencies and turn into liars and fabricators themselves. The consumer of yesterday becomes the producer of today and the commerce of manufacturing truth goes on.

In the clinical setting, an important therapeutic task therefore is to make the patient aware that he has been "gaslighted" and to help him or her see the pervasive and deep effects of being fed manufactured truths about important matters about the family or about his or her own development. The validation of having been misled and left bereft of support via "mirroring" (Kohut, 1977) and "affirmative" (Killingmo, 1989) interventions can exert considerable healing impact for such patients. Transforming "manufactured truths" into "manufactured untruths," pointing out their confusion-causing effects, and then interpretively working with the patient's ongoing need to buy into such lies are the sequential steps in this sort of clinical work. Issues of masochism, pathological hope, disengagement from early internalizations, and tolerance of separateness enter forcefully into the resulting analytic dialogue.

Judicial truth

All of us are familiar with the requirement during court proceedings to "tell the truth, the whole truth and nothing but the truth." However, what those of us who are not legal experts do not realize is such proceedings actually deal with two varieties of truth: "substantive truth" and "formal legal truth" (Summers, 1999). "Substantive truth," also called "actual truth," refers to what really is the case, what really happened, who really did what, and so on. It is a combination of what I have termed in this chapter as "physical truth" and "historical truth." It reflects actual actions, actual events, actual people, and actual things. "Formal legal truth," in contrast, refers to whatever is found valid by the legal fact-finder, be it a jury, a judge, or a panel of judges. In an ideal legal setting, formal legal truth is in accordance with substantive truth but in day-to-day legal praxis this is often not the case. Translated back into the classification of truths, I have offered (physical, historical, narrative, poetic, manufactured, judicial, and existential), formal legal truth seems to subsume the categories of narrative and manufactured truths. It can be crafted and makes sense to the authority capable of giving a verdict.

In discussing these issues, Summers (1999) offers two explanations of why formal legal truth can be at variance with substantive truth. *First*, trial procedures in a given case might contribute to such divergence. These might include unequal quality of legal representation, difference in time and money available to each party to document its claims on reality, prejudice or incompetence on the part of fact-finders, and unexpected events such as the death of a key witness. A *second* set of reasons leading to substantive truth and formal legal truth parting company is how certain rules of evidence operate within the judicial system. For instance, a true confession obtained by beating the perpetrator or highly incriminating material procured by a search without a proper warrant might be declared inadmissible by the judge and hence preclude the emergence of substantive truth.

A tension also exists between the law finding the truth (or truths) and creating the truth (or truths). This is because once a fact is declared to be a formal legal truth it becomes true, at least in the eyes of the law.[65] Balkin (2003) makes this explicit by noting that there are several different ways in which law can make that true.

> Sometimes law makes things true just by creating categories and distinctions that define certain situations or conduct vis-à-vis other kinds of situations or conduct, or that make things equivalent or different from the standpoint of legal doctrine. Sometimes law makes things true by creating causes of actions or rights, as in sexual harassment law or intellectual property law. And sometimes law makes things true by creating institutions or devices, like a corporation or Roth IRA or a 401(K) plan. When the law does any of these things, it simultaneously creates the possibility of things being true or false in the eyes of the law ... These things are not true or false from the point of view of mathematics or natural science. Rather, they are true or false from the standpoint of law. (p. 9)

As would be immediately clear, such legal relativism is especially hazardous when it comes to rendering judgment on the highly subjective, imaginary, and metaphorical and yet clinical and therapeutic discourse typical of psychoanalysis.

---

[65] Here, the hackneyed but true phrase that "beauty is in the eye of the beholder" finds its judicial counterpart.

Though brought to attention only by malpractice suits, the judicial system casts its shadow each day upon the practice of psychotherapy and psychoanalysis. Mostly this goes unnoticed. However, with the increasing emphasis upon needing to obtain "informed consent"[66] from the patient, filling insurance company forms for the patient to seek reimbursement, and documenting patients' visits for a potential third-party audit, the legal periphery of the clinical frame has become rather sharply etched. Besides such encroachments on the analyst–patient confidentiality and their regrettable consequences (Bollas & Sundelson, 1996), legal feathers can easily be ruffled by exchanges and transactions within the clinical dyad. Analytic interventions that rely upon metaphor and playfulness are especially vulnerable to judicial criticism. Take a look at the following illustration.

> **Clinical vignette: 6**
> Megan O'Rourke, a forty-year-old schizoid woman, spoke haltingly and sparsely in her sessions. Often, she remained totally silent. When she did speak, she hardly included me in her associations. I felt excluded from her inner world by a thick wall of resistance which mostly emanated from her dread of closeness and intimacy. One day, well into the second year of her four times per week treatment, she began the session by saying "Last night I had a dream." I perked up and was keen to hear more when she added, "But I have completely forgotten what it was." Discouraged but not resigned, I responded rather light-heartedly: "OK, then why don't you make up a dream right now?"

This comment was made in a spirit of playfulness, a stance which has its roots in Winnicott's (1967) comment that:

> Psychotherapy has to do with two people playing. The corollary of this is that when playing is not possible, then the work done by the therapist is directed towards bringing the patient from a state of not being able to play into a state of being able to play. (p. 38)

More recent iterations of this come from Ehrenberg (1990) and Coen (2005). Ehrenberg notes that:

> Playfulness can include the use of humor and irony, affectionate kinds of teasing, banter and repartee, joint fantasy, and a host of other possibilities. Because it can be effective as a means to communicate on multiple levels simultaneously, and can allow for transcending communicative barriers, it can work to cut through distance, and to expand the range of communication. (p. 76)

---

[66] In addition to requiring "informed consent," there is now a growing legislative movement toward telling the patient the expected length and cost of treatment in advance. The havoc such a declaration can play with the psychoanalytic process is either unknown or irrelevant to those proposing the measure.

Coen (2005) makes an even more specific point about the need for such playfulness in the treatment of "patients who would rather remain remote" (p. 811). This certainly was true for the patient with whom I made the playful intervention: "Why don't you make up a dream right now?" Such intervention seems fine given the technical rationale explicated above. However, if we take a legal approach to it, my invitation for her to "make up a dream" can readily be seen as a seduction to produce false memories or fabricated clinical material. In an imaginary court scene, she or her attorney could declare that her analyst asked her to make up dreams and this, as you can imagine, would not go well with a judge or a jury.

Such subtle mistranslations of analytic exchanges into legal transactions pale in comparison to the bolder, if less frequent, provisions we clinicians make in order to provide "ego coverage" (Winnicott, 1945, 1960) to a psychically compromised patient; the same may apply to some of our "interpretative actions" (Jacobs, 2011; Ogden, 1994). For instance, a psychoanalyst might agree to keep a patient's handgun if the patient is totally unwilling to give it to someone else and is potentially suicidal. Or, an analyst might visit a dying patient at her home and hold her hand while she keeps lying on her bed. Or, an analyst might agree to keep a certain amount of cash money for a battered woman who is in the process of divorce and is terrified that her paranoid husband will snatch her private savings accumulated over the last decade or so.[67] In all these situations, it is clear that the analyst is making a choice (hopefully after much thought and consultation with a colleague) that does not comply with strict legalities even though it seems moral and compassionate. Ethics and law do not always travel in parallel and an analyst who possesses the courage to put the former over the latter always remains open to adverse legal action.

Existential truth

The literal meaning of the word "existence" is "reality as presented in experience ... [and] ... the state or fact of having been" (*Webster's*, 1998, p. 407). This compels my designation of "existential truth" to meet two conditions. First, it must refer mainly, if not exclusively, to our subjective being, whether it is from moment to moment or stretched over the canvas of a lifetime; felt experience must be its chief reference point. Second, a conceptualization of this sort of truth must refer to the genre of philosophy called "existentialism," represented by Soren Kierkegaard (1813–1855), Martin Heidegger (1889–1976), Jean-Paul Sartre (1905–1980), and Albert Camus (1913–1960). The concern of this perspective is the anxiety consequent upon man's being and living in a world that is essentially meaningless and absurd. Its chief proposal is that since no a priori meaning of life exists, no divine commandments are valid guides, and no logical order is there to balance inequalities and iron out the wrinkles of randomness,

[67] In an edited volume (Akhtar, 2011), I have gathered a vast array of such "unusual interventions" (e.g., touching the patient, giving gifts to the patient, refusing to listen to certain kinds of material) while underscoring their indications and potential risks.

man is left alone and solely responsible for creating the purpose of his life. There is also an implication in existentialism of free will that is unmoored from destiny and yet compelled to use the tattered fabric of life to stitch together a living garment of genuineness.

I fear my concept of existential truth might not meet this tall agenda since, due to my own existential truth, it is anchored in my psychoanalytic and poetic self. That being said, I regard existential truth to be comprised of the following seven realities.

- Each individual is a separate emotional and intellectual unit and the notion or search for any kind of "dual unity" is illusory.
- Each individual is born out of parental sexual intercourse[68] and, at the deepest layers of his or her psyche, must accept this lineage and its lifelong triangular repercussions.
- Each individual must abide by certain prohibitions, even though these might seem arbitrary and vary from era to era and region to region.
- Each individual must accept lack of omnipotence and having to live with impossibilities.
- Each individual must realize he or she is not merely a victim of life's randomness but himself or herself a contributor to life's problems.
- Each individual must know that time travels only in one direction and no one gets a second chance to do life all over again.
- Each individual must encounter the fact of his or her mortality and accept that life has a limited duration.

Together, these biopsychosocial facts constitute what I have opted to call "existential truth" here. To explicate its clinical relevance would end up covering the entire course of an analysis or, perhaps, more than one full analysis and would also need to invoke the entire psychoanalytic theory. This is because the matters subsumed under "existential truths" are spread over the totality of the life span as well as upon the experiential depth of authenticity and connectedness to self and others. However, the prohibitive nature of such an undertaking must not lead to silence about the ways existential truths appear (or do not appear) in the course of our day-to-day clinical work. Attempting to reach a compromise between their contradicting pulls, I choose here—somewhat arbitrarily—to focus upon three interfaces of existential truth and clinical psychoanalysis.

The first of them refers to the here and now aspect of the therapeutic process and what Strachey (1934) has called the "immediacy" of the interpretations we make. As the focus of clinical work moves from unearthing past traumatic events to discerning their recreations in the transference-countertransference axis, the importance of the present moment became paramount. Kleinians extended the definition of countertransference to include the totality

---

[68] The new and emerging reproductive techniques (e.g., in vitro fertilization, surrogate mothering) account for a miniscule proportion of the world's population and even the individuals thus born might harbor the fantasy of parental sexual intercourse.

of the analyst's subjective experience (Heimann, 1950; Little, 1951), and Bion (1967) sternly declared that psychoanalytic work is not about past or future; it is only about the present. And, this present needs to be viewed with a vision that is devoid of "memory and desire." What is the patient saying, feeling, doing, why, and with what hope or dread is right now the analyst's concern, not what happened in his childhood or what he might or might not do tomorrow or afterwards. Stated differently, is the patient in a state of "going on being" (Winnicott, 1956)? Does he speak and act right now from his "true self" (Winnicott, 1960)? If not, why not? It is this sort of contact with the authentic here and now coupled with openness to the stark and undeniable reality of how things are at this very moment—Bion's (1965, 1970) "O"—that pulls existential truth into the clinical chamber of dialogue.

Second, a patient undergoing analysis must be helped to confront the necessity—in fact inevitability—of living with impossibilities and prohibitions. Thus working through infantile omnipotence and civilization-induced oedipal barriers becomes important clinical talk. At the same time, this must not erase the capacity to play nor should it obliterate any and all traces of intergenerational erotic attraction.

Third, attention must be paid to the existential truth that sooner or later we all end up dead. The temptation to think that only orphaned adults, terminally ill patients, and the elderly talk of death during their analyses must be put aside. All human beings think about their death: young or old, consciously or unconsciously. Having such a perspective would permit the analyst to see that patients make all sorts of efforts to bring this topic up for consideration. When a patient in the termination phase, for instance, talks about death, the reference might not be metaphorical. The patient may be saying to the analyst: "Look, I am leaving the treatment for good and we have not talked about an extremely important topic yet. Can we please do it now?" This is not to say that the usual skepticism about the manifest content of the patient's material should be dispensed with. It is only a plea to sometimes take the patient's talk of death on its surface level. This is also not a recommendation for the analyst to introduce the topic of the patient's mortality, only to discern its ubiquitous, though derivative, presence in the patient's associations. In fact, the analyst needs to explore the patient's feeling about the future death of *both* partners in the clinical dyad. This is existential truth at its best.

Concluding remarks

I began this contribution with the definition and etymology of the word "truth" and then touched upon the various theories that have been deployed to explicate it. Acknowledging my lack of philosophical expertise, I then moved on to seven varieties of truth and their relevance to clinical psychoanalysis. To reiterate, these seven varieties were: (i) physical truth, (ii) historical truth, (iii) narrative truth, (iv) poetic truth, (v) manufactured truth, (vi) judicial truth, and (vii) existential truth. Although I cast my net wide, it is clear that the topic of truth is vast and deep and my discourse has failed to cover it in a genuinely comprehensive manner. Many,

many questions remain unanswered. Here is a list, though it too may not exhaust what there is to learn about this realm of human experience.

- Is there any truth in religion? And, if so, is there more truth in one religion than another?
- Are there differences in the truths of children and adults?
- Does gender affect the perception and grasp of truth? Are women less capable of knowing and handling truth as Freud (1925j, 1933a) implied or do they arrive at truth from different pathways as Bernstein (1983) and Gilligan (1982) have demonstrated?
- In a related vein, is there any truth to the concept of gender itself?
- What is the relationship between truth and honesty?
- Does truth change over time?
- Are all truths or only some truths affected by poverty, disenfranchisement, and oppression?
- Does knowing the truth free one of existential constraints or bind one even more tightly to them?
- Is truth inextricably linked to human goodness or can "bad" people also be truthful?

Clearly the study of truth is labyrinthine and unending. To answer or even attempt to answer these questions is beyond my capacity and skill. While true today, this statement may not be true tomorrow. Who knows?

Epilogue

CHAPTER TWELVE

Truly, what does all this mean?

Louis Rothschild

The popular vernacular contains the idea that "The truth will set you free." One could even say that this is a zeitgeist. If so, the spirit of these times has been with us for quite a long time. In popular thought, the sort of freedom expected through an encounter with the truth is idealized and unlimited: I imagine, something akin to a pot of gold at the end of a rainbow. The aforementioned quote itself is attributed to Jesus speaking to a group of Jews who believed in him (John 8:32, *New Revised Standard Version* of the *Bible*). Yet, I am not certain if Jesus intended such an ecstatic interpretation in regard to an encounter with a singular truth. As the preceding chapters have shown, taken from many divergent perspectives, including varied signifiers pointing to any number of signifieds, truths can implicate the past, future, or present. Further complicating matters, Greek mythology points to some notable exceptions to Jesus's comment that upon being granted the truth, one will be free. For example, in seeing the truth of his future, the Cyclops became rather cranky because he was now able to see his own death (Hamilton, 1942). Perhaps a course of talk therapy would have helped the one-eyed creature in working through his agitated depression regarding that truth. There, in keeping with the severity of his presentation, one can assume a formidable expenditure of time and money. Also within the domain of Greek mythology is Ulysses's restraint found in ordering his men to plug their ears and to be bound to their rowing benches as he also bound himself to the mast in order to maintain a mediated relation to pain and desire so as to escape the tantalizing intoxicant of his lone hearing of a seductive song of Cartesian promise of a total and complete truth offered anew by the Sirens (Homer, 8th–7th century BCE). Ulysses's decision to continue home is wise. There, in line with the dedication of this volume, in being recognized by his dog, working with truth is a different and altogether easier matter, suiters be damned.

I imagine if the Cyclops had the good fortune to find himself in Freud's consulting room, that his depressive certainty would have been met with the idea that quite possibly his misery could be transformed into an ordinary unhappiness (Freud, 1895d). That thought in itself often feels like significant freedom. If such thinking should be considered a psychoanalytic truth or simply a faith in psychoanalysis is a matter of some concern. For example, in a letter to Gandhi, we find developmentally oriented Erik Erikson (1969) considering psychoanalysis a truth-finding method well suited to illuminate the subjective ambivalence found in the conviction of Gandhi's nonviolent truth in action. From Erikson and Freud to the present, faith in psychoanalytically assisted transformation has persisted across a century, as contemporary writers consider clinical work to aim toward developing a capacity to sing "in the center of our gnarled selves" (Eigen, 2007, p. 92) while coming to terms with the truth that we are partial beings who ache for total states (Eigen, 2009). That abundant passion and beauty may be found in partiality, implicating an enigmatic awareness that appreciates limit. Also, a sense that enigmatic abundance exists within partiality necessitates a capacity to tolerate and possibly enjoy paradox. So, in pursuit of truth, a conception of a mature subjectivity is as quickly exposed as is language reified in regard to narrative, historicity, and epistemology. As Avshalom and Ofer show in Chapter Ten (this volume), working with the paucity of partial awareness can facilitate rich transformations.

In addition to granting respect to partiality, plurality matters. There, another quote comes to mind: "We hold these truths to be self evident." This quote found in the Declaration of Independence (1776) (U.S. National Archives and Records Administration, 2020) refers to the existence of unalienable civil rights that need be secured through the creation of a shared government (cf., Nussbaum, 1994). As a concluding act, my chapter rotates around qualities of thinking and listening that curtail truth through an epistemological appreciation of sublime aesthetics found in partiality and plurality with an attendant appreciation of a fallibilism that compassionately makes way for a stupidity that embraces play and creativity as traumatically alienable qualities that warrant protection and care (cf., Voela & Rothschild, 2019). To that end, in consideration of what *this* or *it* means, I find myself considering several apes that will be addressed below. For the sensitive reader, the following trigger warning applies: Comparison to primates illustrates a cognitive difference that is not meant to diminish the value of, or respect I have for, mentation in primates or humans. My aim is simply to illustrate a truth in differences in thinking between species with respect to the profundity of variations in life on this fragile planet where I am humbled to be writing. The first group of primates addresses thinking and relationality through representation of cognitive science and evolutionary theory. Following them are cultural apes who carry a particular perspective or view from somewhere, and in this regard share much with the representatives of evolution and cognition. Lastly, a playful misreading of a psychoanalytic gorilla serves as an awestruck honor guard to a binocular vision of a holistic partiality.

Many is a word that only leaves you guessing[69]

As evolutionary cousins of humans, what might apes be able to contribute in regard to truth and psychoanalysis? This question rotates around the insight that thinking does not begin and end with human language, and also an appreciation of the problem that thought is the very thing necessary to develop concepts and criteria utilized to assess truth. To put matters somewhat convolutedly, our thinking about apes' thinking can help us to think about the truth of our own thinking. For example, Wolfgang Köhler (1917) demonstrated that chimpanzees could solve problems or perceive the validity of a proof by applying insight. Given their willingness to demonstrate novel behaviors such as an ability to join segments of a stick to reach a banana through a cage, it is not surprising that subsequent research has also shown that chimpanzees are able to use symbols such as American Sign Language (ASL) to replicate sentences (Hess, 2008). However, a distinction exists between discovery through banana-grasping insight and mimicry in replication of signs. Simply, there is no conclusive evidence that syntactic knowledge of ASL can be used semantically by chimpanzees in order to facilitate verbally mediated insight (cf., Sebeok, 1991). In addition to demonstrating challenges to understanding the boundary between semantic understanding and replication of syntactic structure, the data provided by these chimps matters in regard to theories of human subjectivity because, it appears that conscious, semantic thinking is not always necessary for insight. To that end, data from cognitive science has relevance for psychoanalysis regarding language, unconscious processing, and truth.

That many human mental functions occur unconsciously is considered a shared truth within cognitive science and psychoanalysis. The enormity of unconscious calculations that we take for granted is expressed in a myriad of examples revealing a distinction between sensation and perception. For example, the lack of photoreceptive cells at the center of the retina constitutes a hole created by the junction of retina and the optic nerve. This sensational hole of transmission creates a perceptual problem that the visual system in most cases solves by filling in a manner that allows humans to consciously perceive a continuous environment. If perception were based only on sensation, we would perceive a hole in the center of our visual field. Although visual perception is not the same thing as a habit, such as my tying my shoe, conscious mental life is aided in both cases by processing that allows much to take place outside of awareness. Here, the popular phrase of being able to "walk and chew gum at the same time" is relevant, as is the truth that in habit formation, conscious experience such as learning implicates unconscious processing. In most cases, unconscious processing makes life easier by freeing up consciousness to focus on other matters. In regard to the ease unconscious mentation affords, the unconscious processing studied by cognitive science has been called the *adaptive unconscious* (Wilson, 2004). Like most unconscious processing in humans, the banana grasping insight utilized by Köhler's apes may not be accessible to conscious reflection on the

[69] Subject headings throughout are from Page and Plant (1971, 1973).

part of a chimpanzee. However, if I attend to and reflect on my shoe-tying, some semblance of procedural memory is accessible to my conscious awareness. Still, no matter how I (as an adult self) try, despite some fleeting images of childhood shoes, I do not have reliably veridical memories of frustration or pleasure felt while learning to tie my shoes. Although some procedural memory of shoe-tying may be found in my conscious mental life, most of the adaptive unconscious, such as the processing required to perceive a stable visual field does not yield to introspection.

Psychoanalytic theory has no difficulty with the idea that much of the unconscious is not admissible to consciousness. Freud (1915e) clearly argued that the unconscious refers to psychic life that lacks consciousness. Still, there are important distinctions in regard to theory building. For example, does one consider childhood amnesia to be a function of language acquisition, oedipal repression, or some combination of each of these factors (cf., Arbuthnott et al., 2006). While many make a sharp distinction between an adaptive unconscious and the psychoanalytic unconscious, others (e.g., Arbuthnott et al., 2006; Bucci, 1997; Westen, 1998) suggest that the unconscious, conflictual, and often traumatic memories that cause suffering may be processed by the same mental mechanisms that aid adaptive functioning. Fortunately, consideration of the adaptive unconscious in relation to maladaptive cognition has been part of psychoanalytic meta-theory prior to the adaptive unconscious finding a home in the cognitive turn of experimental psychology. Within psychoanalysis, Wilfred Bion's conception of an alpha function considers conscious and unconscious adaptive thinking a searching for durable and familiar sense impressions (Bion, 1962b; Eigen, 2011; Williams, 2010). Bion (2015) notes, in a manner consistent with a banana-seeking gorilla, that mental processes are filled with moments of false certainty and uncertainty that may be greater than what is apprehended. Unlike the gorilla, Bion's clinical perspective moves beyond ordinary problems to consider that experiences of bizarre objects are related to a reversal of the alpha function that does violence to its structure. Experimental surprise is interesting. However, the surprise leading to structural breakdown to be labored over clinically is traumatic. The trauma of breakdown facilitates the processing of future experience but only through the violence to mental structures that has occurred (cf., Boulanger, 2007; Eigen, 2004a, 2004b), leading one to live with "a *sense* of catastrophe" (Eigen, 2011, p. 65, italics in original). Participation in a study should not cause such harm. Still, if one is in fact concerned about truth, parsimony has a role in supporting a theory that the same unconscious mental mechanisms are studied within cognitive science and psychoanalysis.

Integrative potential for unconscious processing is found in another ape, the gorilla of selective attention. Glitches in selective attention are often felt when conversing at a cocktail party or in listening to a Global Positioning System suggesting that one "Turn left," while standing at a red light. In one oft cited experiment (Chabris & Simons, 2010), subjects are instructed to count how many times some basketball players pass a ball in a video where midway a person in a gorilla costume walks through the game before leaving the court. Participants have a fifty percent chance of perceiving this novel interruption. As the failure to perceive is considered to be due to engagement in the counting task, this is considered an example of "inattentional blindness." Like the subjects who perceive the gorilla, the subjects who miss the gorilla have the sensation of the image of the gorilla landing on the photoreceptors in their retinas. The remarkable difference is that for half of the subjects, this stimulus remains unconscious. Furthermore, it will remain out of the grasp of introspective reflection. The phrase, "seeing is believing," while phenomenologically true, reveals a fallibility exploited in nature by camouflage. Another difference among approximately fifty percent of subjects is also found in a study measuring an effect in the repetition of implausible statements (Lacassagne et al., 2022). Although half of participants respond to the repetition of implausible statements such as, "Elephants are faster than cheetahs," in a manner that increasingly shows agreement, the other half of the subjects show no changes or an increase in resistance to such statements. In each of these studies, data reveals robust individual differences regarding subjective experience. I find this relevant in thinking about a patient who reports shame and confusion in couple therapy regarding felt deficits experienced in early childhood. Regarding his anxious reflecting on his experiences of childhood boundary violations, all he can report is absence and alexithymia. If in fact this is comparable, a couple's therapist insisting that this patient "find a way to get in touch" with repressed material in order to discuss something other than his felt experience becomes a problem. Simply working with his conscious experiences related to noticing absence may be deep and substantial in its own right. The architects of the gorilla-suit experiment maintain that inattentional blindness accounts for glitches ranging from editing mistakes in popular movies to a police officer running past a criminal. In these cases, one can look back and see via external evidence what has been missed. As Spence (Chapter Eight, this volume) argues, such a luxury is typically absent in psychoanalysis. The demand to attend to one stimulus and not another necessitates an inhibitory function that has been compared to repression (Arbuthnott et al., 2006). Through such a comparison, the demand to only look for one thing is related to a demand to look away from another. Katherine Arbuthnott and her coauthors suggest that when the demand to look away is chronically activated, oftentimes psychiatric symptoms result.

In regard to an explanation of repression, the experimental data does not go quite far enough in accounting for affective motivation and chronic activation. Consider a voice pushing one to tabulate basketball passes, players on a court, a gorilla that terrifies you, and that the scary gorilla is somehow related to the idea that you need to be counting. Furthermore, all of this is taking place not in a lab, but in your mind. That thought experiment only approaches what is often found and felt clinically. For example, an initial hypothesis of repetition with difference (Volkan, Chapter Seven, this volume) suggests that historical awareness does not spare an adult self from experiencing oedipal transgressions felt as a young person in conflicts driving conscious marital choices and emotional outbursts. If the formulation Volkan suggests has some validity, then we have an example of partial awareness mediated by defenses such as identifying with an aggressor that facilitates the relegation of traumatic pain to unconsciousness. Although this is substantially more complicated than missing a gorilla walking across a basketball court, it appears odd to reason that such dynamic processing occurs via a different mechanism. Outside of the laboratory, inhibition is messy because violence does trauma to thinking structures. Feeling what is known is not simple, and individual differences ranging from life histories to neurological and hormonal variation implicate processing. Such a truth is also shown in the loneliness of compulsive sexual activity leading a patient to treatment where through alliance-building and dreaming, he begins to see that his compulsive behavior is an attempt to deny previous sexual abuse. The therapeutic effect of a file providing testament of his abuse, compared here to seeing the gorilla suit after the fact, is a complex factor common to uncertainties held in practice (Avshalom & Ofer, Chapter Ten, this volume). From traumatic confusion regarding a child's identification with an adult (Ferenczi, 1933) to repetitive enactments of unconscious material within a treatment (Black, 2003; McLaughlin, 1991), suffering reveals that as with the visual system, unconscious mental life influences conscious mental life. When unconscious processing is constructively adaptive there is no press to seek treatment or question truth. If unconscious contents reactively motivate one into precarious relationships and lies, analysis can help. Unlike the experimental examples from cognitive science, the pain involved in clinical material motivates one to look away from (Shalvi, 2018) or disavow (Bass, 2007) the very material that in working through resistance, can set one free, or at least, set one freer.

In addition to the idea that the unconscious processes of interest to cognitive science and psychoanalysis are not discrete, is a truth that mental life is uneven. In line with present-day cognitive science, Freud (1926d) asserts that mental life is often divided. As shown in Ulysses and the story of the Cyclops, respecting partiality appears central to the human condition. In contrast, Jean-Paul Sartre (1943) favors a unity of mind whereby he considers the concept of an unconscious to be in bad faith. Sartre's preference for a mind that is unified and transparent has been compared to Descartes's conception of cognition (Neu, 1988). For their respective conceptions of a unified consciousness facilitating objective potentiality, such a view has been linked to that of a machine or computer that can process information without conflicts arising from a motivational bias as opposed to the intentional and biased capacity of a particular organic constitution such as that found in a human or chimp (cf., Flanagan, 1991). The particular or perspectivist view of experiential feeling from somewhere has been considered to contrast with the idea of an objective or detached view in a manner that places arid theories of objectivity as promoting a view from nowhere (cf., Fairfield, 2002; Nagel, 1979). In concert with a perspectivist view, psychoanalytic treatment typically aims at encouraging taking responsibility for awareness and communicating in an increasingly straightforward manner in which one is able to be interested in one's autonomy while working with limited and fluctuating capacities. Furthermore, a mechanized detachment has been linked not with maturity, but to obedience found in traumatized children (Ferenczi, 1933). As humans, we know perspectivism from joy and suffering in waking life and also in our dreaming. Such an awareness leads Brett H. Clarke (Chapter One, this volume) to boldly and simply state that it is a myopic use of philosophy to deny the sort of psychoanalytically friendly experiential perspectivism most every human finds to be true. What also appears true is that humans seek psychoanalysis because consciousness matters. The idea that conscious insight, with its conflicts and attendant sense of privacy, is a gift that often requires care, need not be a philosophical problem (Humphrey, 2002a).

A Darwinian friendliness is found in perspectivism, and Clarke (Chapter One, this volume) suggests that human subjective experience is unique in nature. Indeed, while gorillas and chimpanzees do communicate with sounds, they do not appear to seek talk therapy to help mediate reflexive consciousness. Still, an evolutionary gorilla provides a helpful perspective in regard to linguistics and mentation. While working in Dian Fossey's camp in 1971, Nicholas Humphrey (2002b), perplexed by gorillas who appeared to do little with very large, specialized brains, concluded that the primary function of large brains is the mediation of social problems. What else brings one to treatment? In considering human mental life and culture more complicated than that of a gorilla, Humphrey (2002a, 2002b) further argues that human language evolved from this earlier social intelligence as a sort of abstract grooming. Humphrey's preverbal perspective regarding a theory of mind has been considered an argument in favor of a readiness for cultural and contextual sensitivity that implicates both conscious and unconscious processing (cf., Bruner, 1990). Such an evolutionary leap to consciousness and language acquisition also implicates an awareness of partiality in language or awareness of an enigmatic excess (Laplanche, 1992b) that does not appear to trouble a gorilla. Within a field where semantic use of language is overdetermined (cf., Amati-Mehler et al., 1993) is a challenge to integrate unspoken gorilla-like capacities such as an appreciation of body language to work with conscious awareness such as a sense of empathy in the facilitation of relational communication (cf., S. Stern, 1994). In the spirit of linking to an evolutionary gorilla is an idea that what is not represented can and does return through other routes that a person may be able to utilize (cf., Ogden, Chapter Nine, this volume).

The data from evolutionary and cognitive gorillas favor the truth that experience affords a partial view from somewhere, and that language is accordingly limited and simultaneously overdetermined in its semiotic polysemy. Observed differences or fluctuations in perspectivist and overdetermined cognition support the difficulty of maintaining an epistemological shyness as soft impressions tend to become reified through a tendency to ignore what is complicated (Spence, Chapter Eight, this volume). A press toward humility is supported by philosopher Gadamer's assertion that a method is a method, not a truth (cf., D. B. Stern, 2002). Yet, we are not detached in adherence to successful methodologies, but tend to pledge allegiance through being affected by what we find. Therein is a very human tendency for belief to become tradition (Volkan, Chapter Seven, this volume). Given the ease in which common sense appears ahistorical and natural as opposed to constructed (cf., Moscovici, 2001), cultivating humility regarding attachment to a held truth appears to be a significant achievement. Within psychoanalysis, epistemological analysis of influences such as Gadamer's hermeneutic philosophy that provided a held truth powerful enough to reinvigorate psychoanalysis for Spence and others in the 1970s (cf., D. B. Stern, 2002) is itself an example of the challenge to differentiate method and truth or truth as a method. From a perspective that respects variation, ideas including psychoanalytic ideas are found ready-made like a banana waiting to be picked up (cf., Ogden, Chapter Nine, this volume). There to answer Clarke (Chapter One, this volume), meaning can indeed enter into a relationship with causation in a manner that is able to appreciate that human beings are more than emergent properties of language. In that, however, enigmatic meaning turns on pragmatic meaning in search of truth. In awareness of the enigmatic, a deep humility remains that can, as Clarke finds, resonate with Ricœur's ontological density of subjective experience.

A bustle in your hedgerow

In addition to a perceptual amplification of contextual stimuli, the evolutionary leap illustrated by the complexity of human language acquisition implicates a readiness for human culture that calls to mind the moment in the film *2001: A Space Odyssey* (1968) in which a chimp throws a weapon made of bone into the air that becomes a spaceship in the following scene. Such a radically compressed illustration of human history conjures Martin Heidegger's (1927) *Lichtung* or lighting that points to a clearing where any idea can manifest. Regarding the lighting-like power of conscious mentation is folk psychology, and Volkan (Chapter Seven, this volume) considers the cultural import of shared historical truths or a "chosen trauma" as being intertwined with personal identity in a manner that implicates individual behavior to include health and pathology. Aware of the challenges of working with reflexive consciousness, Bion writes of a clever monkey that can produce an atomic bomb, and asks if we can discriminate from quackery to find truth (Bion, 1991, p. 60).

In a somewhat different key, Spence writes (Chapter Eight, this volume) that psychic reality may, at any one time, contain elements of both historical and narrative truth. The delineation between narrative and history that Spence finds is not easily demarcated, lest we forget that the term *intertwined* that Volkan favors is itself a concept attempting to situate phenomenology through language. In regard to the subjectively intertwined confluence of narrative and history, we may consider that research on collaborative remembering finds that social effects such as a speaker's motive to form a shared reality with listeners can moderate conversational effects on memory (Hirst & Echterhoff, 2012). Additionally, a ten-year study of the attack of September 11, 2001 (Hirst et al., 2015) reveals that flashbulb memories of circumstances such as learning of the attack reveal a rapid forgetting leading to inconsistencies that can persist as a truth unless corrected by an external influence. Determining to what extent an external influence is narrative or history is in many cases a matter of being stuck in a false dichotomy that fails to appreciate the manner in which statements are subjected to transference and modifications that alter a statement very identity (cf., Foucault, 1972). In regard to truth, external and internal influences are powerful, as individuals seeking authenticity fall into or internalize otherness (Shoshani et al., Chapter Six, this volume). Shoshani and coauthors turn to Heidegger to suggest that in such falling one is in effect distancing himself from himself.

Yet, buying into method as truth appears to be the price of a transitional development (Winnicott, 1971) in which one builds object relations and becomes aware of reflexive consciousness.

Although believing occurs across life span development, as evidenced by adult idealizations found in moments such as joining a group like a profession, transitional development is most studied in children. It is fascinating to see that children develop intrapsychic capacities for transitional objects, and for differentiation between truth-telling and telling lies. As Mann (Chapter Two, this volume) considers motivation, we may wonder not only about a child's capacity to lie, but why one child may find concealment through lying to be important in consideration of feeling at home while another finds pleasure through pointing to what is hidden. From a Heideggerian and clinical perspective, a press toward integration of relational states such as dependability and responsibility finds a truth in hoping that like lying, rebellion is a stage related to reworking an earlier distancing from oneself or a distancing for oneself that paradoxically becomes a part of oneself (cf., Smolen, Chapter Three, this volume). Obfuscation, like lying, is a way of working with a press toward differentiation. Waugaman (Chapter Five, this volume) considers the pragmatic value of obfuscating speech for the ability to escape censorship, and that such care may have aided communication with the Queen of England and future generations. If development and the future environment are kind enough, one may be able to dispense with decoding what is cumbersome, and find that being is a bit easier as a result (Wolman, Chapter Four, this volume). Such work appears to implicate an *ontic* density found within (Clarke, Chapter One and Shoshani et al., Chapter Six, this volume).

The tune will come to you

With concern related not to distancing from one's self through child development, but to the adult development and functioning of mental health professionals, Spence (Chapter Eight, this volume) focuses on the implications of the ease in which one apprehends an idiosyncratic method as a categorical truth. Spence considers that in every case one believes a personal system to be a true-enough version of a fuzzy idealization, and that there remains a paucity of opportunities from which to influence such thinking in a manner that makes a significant difference. He puts matters simply through stating that one believes a private theory to be the same as what is held by other, apparently imagined colleagues, and that even through publication, vague logic or the omission of some details can maintain this form of alienation. Indeed, a *confirmation bias* (Nickerson, 1998) or a tendency to interpret data in a matter favorable to a hypothesis is a factor that in my experience is situated by time with trusted mentors, supervisors, and peers who are willing to risk being open and honest in a *truly* vulnerable fashion. Of course, variance in regard to human interaction with hallucinated certainty will persist, and a need to substitute static, objective answers for the challenge of sitting with uncertainty (cf., Bass, 2007) does I think place a limit on the assessment of narrative coherence as a methodology in its own right (cf., Ricœur, 1977b). Concern about such danger or hubris is not new as the Greek poet Archilochus wrote of the fox who utilizes many viewpoints while the hedgehog uses only one. Some have noted (e.g., Gould, 2003; Moscovici, 1993) that researchers often wear the face of either animal, and Moscovici adds that when a researcher is engaged in the task of explaining results, that like the hedgehog, what contradicts and clashes is often rejected. Spence's concern about a misguided hedgehog tendency finds some good company in the underreporting oft referred to as the file-drawer effect (Rosenthal, 1979). Existing across the sciences, the file-drawer effect is considered a problem in which a positive results bias has an effect of leading what is published to be an unbalanced sample of studies undertaken that delays discovery, thinking, and in clinical work, negatively impacts patient care (Dickersin & Chalmers, 2011).

While the hedgehog runs the risk of being rigidly simpleminded, a fox-like practitioner could well become muddleheaded if not frozen in an apprehension of complexity. Consideration of such a possibility leads Mary Gergen (1997) to propose that a fear of chaos upon recognizing a lack in or limit to foundational principles may be considered a syndrome of Cartesian anxiety. There, a remedy in pragmatics often finds good and creative tension with the enigmatic in order for praxis to be behavior relevant (cf., James, 1890; Meehl, 1973; Rothschild & Haslam, 2003). I have argued (Rothschild & Haslam, 2003) that always situated, human desire (or pragmatic need) adds valence to construct a point of view, and that although desire itself may occlude the legitimacy of other points of view, a temporal shift in motivation can reveal other points of view as helpful. For example, paper may be used for writing, or depending on need, to start a fire. Within a psychoanalytic purview, an idea that multiple perspectives are part and parcel of participation in an intersubjective field appears as ordinary as an appreciation of transference. There, muddleheaded stasis may persist, and as such is indicative of a diagnostic and prognostic import emblematic of states such as obsessionality. Concern regarding muddleheaded and simpleminded states within fellow practitioners, is then concern about the effect of rigidity on praxis (cf., D. Shapiro, 1981).

Sharing concern with Spence regarding efficacy among practitioners is Barnaby Barrett (2019) who maintains that many clinicians fail in their use of free association and in understanding libidinal psychic energy, and also suffer from too little interest in cross-fertilization. While the methodology used to make such an assessment is of some concern, Barrett is waging a nonviolent war on structuralist epistemology within psychoanalysis in which thinking fails to include what is incomprehensible while advocating that there can be no final synthesis as desire is never fully represented. Barrett avows a psychoanalytic gorilla, who as a peaceful warrior can find needed supplies through the availability of an openness to pluralism. I must confess that in reading of Barrett's gorilla, I first pictured a silverback known to Fossey. It took several moments before I realized that Barrett was not referring to another species, but to a human member of an irregular and small-scale military force. So, now my psychoanalytic gorilla appears as a confabulated exemplar that is a silverback that speaks English, wears a suit, still has fine glasses, and sometimes enjoys a cigar. Although considered bad form from perspectives of pulmonary health that suggest one forego cigars and from a post-colonial theory that stands against anthropomorphizing animals in a Eurocentric fashion (e.g., Dorfman, 2010), he is a helpful mental representation of engagement in and through multiple perspectives that functions like a security blanket. Consistent with Barrett's intent, the focus of my imaginary gorilla friend of transitional experience differs from Spence. However, each agrees that resting on a laurel of considered truth is a way for a practitioner to become less than effective if not outright dangerous.

A fear of structural consistency can become extreme. In other fields, bakers for example know that methods and recipes vary, and have no trouble agreeing that within such variation exist valid varieties of bread. Clinically, I have overheard surgeons discuss a preferred thickness of thread used for stitching in a fashion that respects a similar variance as personal comfort without concern of outcome. It is notable that truth in questions such as, are instincts primary and therefore mediated by relational experiences, or are instincts secondary and fabricated in relationships, can keep psychoanalysts debating truth in a manner approaching a serious attempt to discern if in fact a chicken did precede the first egg. The truth of the matter being that situating such problems may be best settled by appreciation of multiple methods and theories as opposed to claiming objective truths while efforts to integrate the instinctual into relational phenomena persist (cf., Bass, 2007; A. O. Kris, 2018; Loewald, 1980). The bakers and surgeons I have in mind would have no difficulty considering variation within an epistemology that respects mutual influence in an effort to ground psychoanalysis outside of the mind of an analyst (Bion, 1963, 1970; Ogden, Chapter Nine, this volume). As psychoanalysts have no bread or thread, it may be an envy of the concrete that leads to structuralist enactments be they in the form of concern about what every other practitioner is up to or that of appreciating that each patient brings a world that requires a particular formulation. Still, within such particularity, there appears some evidence that clinical complexity may be studied, and that some agreement of common factors in formulation such as considering a symptom a failing effort to defend against an emotional response (Avshalom & Ofer, Chapter Ten, this volume) may be distilled in addition to the existence of some common ground in technique (Hauser, 2005; Katzenstein et al., 2010; Luborsky et al., 2002). On the technical side, Spence advocates a focus on the *here and now* as opposed to the *there and then* that resonates with Akhtar's (Chapter Eleven, this volume) reminder that Bion declared that psychoanalytic work is only about the present. There remains much to consider in regard to interpreting such thinking. For example, in Spence's reference to Theodore Shapiro's (1981) sense of working in the moment, I began to wonder how that Shapiro might overlap and differ from the here and now focus of David Shapiro (1989). There I think, a security in continued exploration while engaging in practice is a reasonable developmental path.

And it makes me wonder

Difficulty in movement beyond a structuralist epistemology is evidenced in the consideration that "bedrock envy" is a state known to many therapists who are engaged in work to take leave of adherence to a singular truth (Fairfield, 2002). There, metaphysical envy may be soothed by a poetic attitude for clinical work, and as a way to read psychoanalytic meta-theory (cf., Eigen, 2009). Considered a sense of being unencumbered in a pristine moment, poetry (Sarton, 1997) or conscious presence (e.g., Bion, 1970; Symington, 2012) may be the robust common factor of phenomenological encounters across psychoanalysis. In consideration of the poetic, Humphrey (2002a) theorizes that due to the absence of human likeness in the 20,000-year-old cave paintings in Chauvet, those cave-dwellers represent a moment in evolution prior to the mental integration that we enjoy and are challenged by today. Humphrey adds that the loss of the naturalism found in that cave art may well be the price paid for poetry. Hunger for the poetic may then be a need to soothe a mind challenged by evolutionary change. To repeat Ogden (Chapter Nine, this volume): The relative truths arrived at in poetry (and in psychoanalysis) represent "a clarification of life—not necessarily a great clarification, such as sects or cults are founded on, but a momentary stay against confusion." These relative or small truths afford a wisdom that can appreciate Bion's cautionary viewing of Oedipus as a quest to uncover the truth at all cost (Avshalom & Ofer, Chapter Ten, this volume) lest one sink like a dinosaur under an exoskeleton of facts (cf., Bion, 1991). In an introduction to an unpublished collection of poetry, Bion writes that it is easy to lose a capacity for awe. I think Ulysses and the Cyclops knew this to be true, as I suspect did Jesus. A good clinician may benefit from the restraint found in being tethered to the mast.

The seventeenth-century German mystic Angelus Silesius writes that, "The rose is without 'why'," and continues to say that as long as humans need to know and to have, that we have not been delivered (in Campbell, 1991). A popular phrase in Zen Buddhism harmonizes: "The raft is not the shore." In this regard, a poetic attitude is one that holds "metaphorical-ness" as a key to psychoanalytic understanding as metaphor appreciates a polyvalent essence in meaning (Brett H. Clarke, Chapter One, this volume; Rothschild & Haslam, 2003). The humility found in appreciation of a small and poetic truth is one that appreciates an ultimate truth as immeasurable (Ogden, Chapter Nine, this volume), and also that understanding is itself open to modification that can occur in a future transformation of what happens to be true today (Akhtar, Chapter Eleven, this volume). Akhtar's sense (Chapter Eleven, this volume) that a poetic truth or method leaves space for pluralistic negotiation as opposed to a truth that aims toward foreclosure is a distinction found in poet Rainer Maria Rilke's (1996, p. 119) statement that, "No feeling is final." In that, there is a truth that being able to appreciate and savor awe and wonder is a developmental and interminable achievement.

References

Aarons, Z. A. (1970). Normality and abnormality in adolescence—with a digression on "Prince Hal". *Psychoanalytic Study of the Child, 25*: 309–339.

Abraham, K. (1913). On neurotic exogamy: A contribution to the similarities in the psychic of neurotics and of primitive man. In: *Clinical Papers and Essays on Psycho-Analysis* (pp. 312–317). New York: Brunner/Mazel.

Ahbel-Rappe, K. (2006). "I no longer believe": Did Freud abandon the seduction theory? *Journal of the American Psychoanalytic Association, 54*: 171–199.

Ahumada, J. L. (1997). Toward an epistemology of clinical psychoanalysis. *Journal of the American Psychoanalytic Association, 45*: 507–530.

Ahumada, J. L. (2001). The rebirth of the idols: The Freudian unconscious and the Nietzschean unconscious. *International Journal of Psychoanalysis, 82*: 219–234.

Akhtar, S. (1992). *Broken Structures: Severe Personality Disorders and Their Treatment.* Northvale, NJ: Jason Aronson.

Akhtar, S. (1999). *Immigration and Identity: Turmoil, Treatment, Transformation.* Northvale, NJ: Jason Aronson.

Akhtar, S. (2005). Hindu–Muslim relations in India: past, present, and future. In: S. Akhtar (Ed.), *Freud along the Ganges: Psychoanalytic Reflections on the People and Culture of India* (pp. 91–138). New York: Other Press.

Akhtar, S. (2007). From unmentalized xenophobia to messianic sadism: some reflections on the phenomenology of prejudice. In: H. Parens, A. Mahfouz, S. W. Twemlow, & D. E. Scharff (Eds.), *The Future of Prejudice: Psychoanalysis and the Prevention of Prejudice* (pp. 7–19). Lanham, MD: Jason Aronson.

Akhtar, S. (2009). *Comprehensive Dictionary of Psychoanalysis.* London: Karnac.

Akhtar, S. (Ed.) (2011). *Unusual Interventions: Alterations of the Frame, Method, and Relationship in Psychotherapy and Psychoanalysis*. London: Karnac.

Akhtar, S. (2012). Generosity. *Psychoanalytic Review, 99*: 645–767.

Akhtar, S. (2014). *Immigration and Acculturation: Mourning, Adaptation, and the Next Generation*. New York: Rowman & Littlefield.

Akhtar, S. (2022). Review of Patrick Casement's "Credo?: Religion and Psychoanalysis". *Journal of the American Psychoanalytic Association, 69*: 423–428.

Allison, E., & Fonagy, P. (2016). When is truth relevant? *Psychoanalytic Quarterly, 85*: 275–303.

Altman, N. (2007). The children of the children of the Sixties. *Journal of Infant, Child and Adolescent Psychotherapy* 6: 5–23.

Amati-Mehler, J., Argentieri, S., & Canestri, J. (1993). *The Babel of the Unconscious: Mother Tongue and Foreign Languages in the Psychoanalytic Dimension*. J. Whitelaw-Cucco (Trans.). New York: International Universities Press.

Anderson, M. (2005). *Shakespeare by Another Name: The Life of Edward de Vere, Earl of Oxford, the Man who was Shakespeare*. New York: Gotham.

Angels in America (2014). T. Kushner (Dir.). Motion picture produced by Theater Communications Group, USA.

Arbuthnott, K. D., Arbuthnott, D. W., & Thompson, V. A. (2006). *The Mind in Therapy: Cognitive Science for Practice*. Mahwah, NJ: Lawrence Erlbaum.

Arendt, H. (1973). *The Origins of Totalitarianism*. New York: Houghton Mifflin Harcourt.

Aristotle (*c.*335 BCE). *Poetics*. Mineola, NY: Dover Thrift Editions, 2012.

Aristotle (*c.*340 BCE). *The Nicomachean Ethics*. J. L. Ackrill, J. O. Urmson, & D. Ross (Eds.). Oxford: Oxford University Press, 1998.

Arlow, J. A. (1969). Unconscious fantasy and disturbances of conscious experiences. *Psychoanalytic Quarterly, 38*: 1–27.

Arlow, J. A. (1990). The analytic attitude in the service of denial. In: H. J. Schwartz & A.-L. Silver (Eds.), *Illness in the Analyst: Implications for the Treatment Relationship* (pp. 9–25). New York: International Universities Press.

Askay, R., & Farquhar, J. (2006). *Apprehending the Inaccessible: Freudian Psychoanalysis and Existential Phenomenology*. Evanston, IL: Northwestern University Press.

Askay, R., & Farquhar, J. (2011). *Of Philosophers and Madmen: A Disclosure of Martin Heidegger, Medard Boss, and Sigmund Freud*. New York: Rodopi.

Atkinson, R. F. (1978). *Knowledge and Explanation in History*. Ithaca, NY: Cornell University Press.

Bacon, D. (1857). *The Philosophy of the Plays of Shakspere Unfolded*. Boston, MA: Ticknor and Fields.

Baker, R. (1993). The patient's discovery of the analyst as a new object. *International Journal of Psychoanalysis, 74*: 1223–1233.

Bakewell, S. (2016). *At the Existentialist Café: Freedom, Being, and Apricot Cocktails with Jean-Paul Sartre, Simone de Beauvoir, Albert Camus, Martin Heidegger, Karl Jaspers, Edmund Husserl, Maurice Merleau-Ponty and Others*. New York: Other Press.

Balint, M. (1932). *Primary Love and Psychoanalytic Technique*. London: Tavistock.

Balkin, J. M. (2003). The proliferation of legal truth. *Harvard Journal of Law and Public Policy, 26*(1): 5–16.

Barks, C. (1995). *The Essential Rumi*. Edison, NJ: Castle.

Barrett, B. (2019). *Beyond Psychotherapy: On Becoming a (Radical) Psychoanalyst*. London: Routledge.

Barton, R., & Whitehead, J. (1969). The gaslight phenomenon. *Lancet, 1*: 1258–1260.

Bass, A. (2007). When the frame doesn't fit the picture. *Psychoanalytic Dialogues, 17*: 1–27.

Becker, E. (2007). *The Denial of Death*. New York: Simon & Schuster.

Benjamin, J. (2004). Beyond doer and done to: An intersubjective view of thirdness. *Psychoanalytic Quarterly, 73*: 5–46.

Bergstein, A. (2018). The psychotic part of the personality: Bion's expeditions into unmapped mental life. *Journal of the American Psychoanalytic Association, 66*(2): 193–220.

Bergstein, A. (2019). *Bion and Meltzer's Expedition into Unmapped Mental Life*. London: Routledge.

Bernstein, D. (1983). The female superego: a different perspective. *International Journal of Psychoanalysis, 64*: 187–200.

Bialik, H. N. (1915). Language closing and disclosing. In: D. Joseph (Ed.), *The Heart and the Fountain* (pp. 255–261). Oxford: Oxford University Press, 2002.

Bion, W. R. (1958). On arrogance. *International Journal of Psychoanalysis, 39*: 144–146.

Bion, W. R. (1962a). *Learning from Experience*. London: Karnac, 1991.

Bion, W. R. (1962b). A theory of thinking. *International Journal of Psychoanalysis, 43*: 306–310.

Bion, W. R. (1963). *Elements of Psychoanalysis*. In: *Seven Servants*. New York: Jason Aronson, 1997.

Bion, W. R. (1965). *Transformations*. London: Karnac, 1984.

Bion, W. R. (1967). *Second Thoughts*. London: Maresfield.

Bion, W. R. (1970). *Attention and Interpretation*. London: Karnac, 1984.

Bion, W. R. (1975). Brasilia clinical seminars. In: *Clinical Seminars and Four Papers* (pp. 1–130). Oxford: Fleetwood, 1987.

Bion, W. R. (1976). On a quotation from Freud. In: *Clinical Seminars and Four Papers* (pp. 234–238). Oxford: Fleetwood, 1987.

Bion, W. R. (1977). *Seven Servants*. New York: Jason Aronson.

Bion, W. R. (1978). Sao Paulo clinical seminars. In: *Clinical Seminars and Four Papers* (pp. 131–222). Oxford: Fleetwood, 1987.

Bion, W. R. (1982). *The Long Weekend, 1897–1919*. Oxford: Fleetwood.

Bion, W. R. (1991). *A Memoir of the Future*. London: Karnac.

Bion, W. R. (1992). *Cogitations*. F. Bion (Ed.). London: Karnac.

Bion, W. R. (2015). *War Memoirs: 1917–1919*. F. Bion (Ed.). London: Karnac.

Bishop, E. (1979). One art. Poetryfoundation.org/poems.

Black, M. J. (2003). Enactment: Musings on energy, language and personal growth. *Psychoanalytic Dialogues, 13*: 633–655.

Blank, P. (2006). *Shakespeare and the Mismeasure of Renaissance Man*. Ithaca, NY: Cornell University Press.

Blass, R. B. (2016). The quest for truth as the foundation of psychoanalytic practice: A traditional Freudian-Kleinian perspective. *Psychoanalytic Quarterly, 85*(2): 305–337.

Blass, R. B., & Carmeli, Z. (2007). The case against neuropsychoanalysis: On fallacies underlying psychoanalysis' latest scientific trend and its negative impact on psychoanalytic discourse. *International Journal of Psychoanalysis, 88*: 19–40.

Blass, R. B., & Carmeli, Z. (2015). Further evidence for the case against neuropsychoanalysis: How Yovell, Solms, and Fotopoulou's response to our critique confirms the irrelevance and harmfulness to psychoanalysis of the contemporary neuroscientific trend. *International Journal of Psychoanalysis, 96*: 1555–1573.

Bloom, P. (2010). *How Pleasure Works: The New Science of Why We Like What We Like.* New York: W. W. Norton.

Blos, P. (1962). *On Adolescence: A Psychoanalytic Interpretation* New York: Free Press.

Blos, P. (1979). *The Adolescent Passage: Developmental Issues.* New York: International Universities Press.

Blum, H. P. (1976). Acting out, the psychoanalytic process, and interpretation. *Annual of Psychoanalysis, 4*: 163–184.

Boccaccio, G. (1966). *Selections from Boccaccio: The Decameron; Kant: Foundations of the Metaphysics of Morals.* London: The Great Books Foundation.

Böhm, T. (2002). Reflections on psychoanalytic listening. *Scandinavian Psychoanalytic Review, 25*: 20–26.

Bollas, C. J., & Sundelson, D. (1996). *The New Informants: The Betrayal of Confidentiality in Psychoanalysis and Psychotherapy.* Northvale, NJ: Jason Aronson.

Borges, J. L. (1923). Preface. Fervor de Buenos Aires. In: *Jorge Luis Borges: Selected Poems, 1923–1967* (pp. 268–269). N. T. di Giovanni (Ed.). New York: De II, 1973.

Borges, J. L. (1941). Pierre Menard: author of the Quixote. In: J. Irby & D. Yates (Eds.), Labyrinths: Selected Stories and Other Writings. (pp. 36–44). J. Irby (Trans.), New York: New Directions, 1962.

Borges, J. L. (1949). Everything and nothing. In: J. Irby & D. Yates (Eds.), *Labyrinths: Selected Stories and Other Writings* (pp. 248–249). J. Irby (Trans.). New York: New Directions, 1962.

Borges, J. L. (1960). Borges and I. In: A. Hurley (Trans.), *Collected Fictions* (p. 324). London: Penguin, 1998.

Borges, J. L. (1964). Limites (Limits). In: *Obra Poética 1923–1964.* Buenos Aires: Emecé.

Borges, J. L. (2000). *This Craft of Verse.* C.-A. Mihailes (Ed.). Cambridge, MA: Harvard University Press, 2000.

Boss, M. (1949). *Meaning and Content of Sexual Perversions.* L. L. Abell (Trans.). New York: Grune & Stratton.

Boss, M. (1963). *Psychoanalysis and Daseinsanalysis.* New York: Basic Books.

Boulanger, G. (2007). *Wounded by Reality: Understanding and Treating Adult Onset Trauma.* Berkeley, CA: Analytic Press.

Bowlby, J. (1977). *The Making and Breaking of Affectional Bonds.* London: Tavistock.

Boyer, L. B. (1986). One man's need to have enemies: A psychoanalytic perspective. *Journal of Psychoanalytic Anthropology, 9*: 101–120.

Brenner, C. (1976). *Psychoanalytic Technique and Psychic Conflict.* New York: International Universities Press.

Brenner, I. (2002). Foreword. In: V. D. Volkan, G. Ast, & W. Greer, *The Third Reich in the Unconscious: Transgenerational Transmission and Its Consequences* (pp. xi–xvii). New York: Brunner-Routledge.

Bromberg, P. M. (2000). Reply to reviews by Cavell, Sorenson, and Smith. *Psychoanalytic Dialogues, 10*(3): 551–568.

Bromberg, P. M. (2006). *Awakening the Dreamer: Clinical Journeys*. London: Analytic Press.

Bromberg, P. M. (2009). Truth, human relatedness, and the analytic process: An interpersonal/relational perspective. *International Journal of Psychoanalysis, 90*(2): 347–361.

Brothers, L. (2002). The trouble with neurobiological explanations of the mind. *Psychoanalytic Inquiry, 22*: 857–870.

Bruner, J. (1990). *Acts of Meaning*. Cambridge, MA: Harvard University Press.

Bucci, W. (1997). *Psychoanalysis and Cognitive Science: A Multiple Code Theory*. New York: Guilford.

Calderwood, J. L. (1963). The mingled yarn of All's Well. *Journal of English and Germanic Philology, 62*: 61–76.

Cambor, C. G. (1969). Preoedipal factors in superego development: The influence of multiple mothers. *Psychoanalytic Quarterly, 38*: 81–96.

Cameron, N. (1961). Introjection, reprojection, and hallucination in the interaction between schizophrenic patient and therapist. *International Journal of Psychoanalysis, 42*: 86–96.

Campbell, K. J. (1991). *German Mystical Writings: Hildegard of Bingen, Meister Eckhart, Jacob Boehme, and Others*. London: Bloomsbury.

Cavell, M. (1993). *The Psychoanalytic Mind: From Freud to Philosophy*. Cambridge, MA: Harvard University Press.

Caws, P. (2003). Psychoanalysis as the idiosyncratic science of the individual subject. *Psychoanalytic Psycholology, 20*: 618–634.

Chabris, C., & Simons, D. (2010). *The Invisible Gorilla*. New York: Crown/Random House.

Chandler, M. J., Greenspan, S., & Barenboim, C. (1973). Judgments of intentionality in response to videotaped and verbally presented moral dilemmas: The medium is the message. *Child Development, 44*: 315–320.

Changeux, J.-P., & Ricœur, P. (2003). *What Makes Us Think: A Neuroscientist and a Philosopher Argue about Ethics, Human Nature, and the Brain*. M. B. DeBevoise (Trans.). Princeton, NJ: Princeton University Press.

Chekov, A. (1901). *The Three Sisters*. Mineola, NY: Dover Thrift Editions, 2012.

Chused, J. (1982). The role of analytic neutrality in the use of the child analyst as a new object. *Journal of the American Psychoanalytic Association, 30*: 3–28.

Civitarese, G. (2019). The concept of time in Bion's "A Theory of Thinking". *International Journal of Psychoanalysis, 100*(2): 182–205.

Clarke, B. H. (2017). The epistemology behind the curtain: Thoughts on the science of psychoanalysis. *Psychoanalytic Quarterly, 86*(3): 575–608.

Clarke, B. H. (2018). A cat is not a battleship: Thoughts on the meaning of neuropsychoanalysis. *International Journal of Psychoanalysis, 99*(2): 425–449.

Clarke, B. H. (2022). "It was and it was not": Metaphoric tension in psychoanalysis. *Psychoanalytic Review, 109*(2): 121–150.

Clarke, R. A. (2004). *Against All Enemies: Inside America's War on Terrorism.* New York: Free Press.

Coen, S. J. (2005). How to play with patients who would rather remain remote. *Journal of the American Psychoanalytic Association, 53*: 811–834.

Colarusso, C. A. (2005). The evolution of paternal identity in late adulthood. *Journal of the American Psychoanalytic Association, 53*: 51–81.

Cooper, A. M. (1993). Discussion: On empirical research. *Journal of the American Psychoanalytic Association, 41*: 381–392.

Cooper, A. M. (Ed.) (2006). *Contemporary Psychoanalysis in America: Leading Analysts Present Their Work.* Washington, DC: American Psychiatric Publishing.

D'Ancona, M. (2017). *Post-Truth: The New War and How to Fight Back.* London: Ebury.

De Masi, F. (2019). Essential elements of the work of a supervisor. *American Journal of Psychoanalysis, 79*: 388–407.

Dickersin, K., & Chalmers, I. (2011). Recognizing, investigating and dealing with incomplete and biased reporting of clinical research: from Francis Bacon to the WHO. *Journal of the Royal Society of Medicine, 104*(12): 532–538.

Dickinson, E. (1872). Poem 1129. In: M. L. Todd (Ed.), *Collected Poems of Emily Dickinson* (p. 202). New York: Gramercy, 1988.

Dorfman, A. (2010). *The Empire's Old Clothes: What the Lone Ranger, Babar, and Other Innocent Heroes Do to Our Minds.* Durham, NC: Duke University Press.

Durban, J. (2016). From The Scream to The Pieta: Murderous mourning and evil. In: *Talking about Evil* (pp. 115–133). New York: Routledge.

Durban, J. (2019). "Making a person"—Clinical considerations regarding the interpretation of anxieties in the analyses of children on the autisto-psychotic spectrum. *International Journal of Psychoanalysis, 100*(5): 57.

Dutton, R. (2016). *Shakespeare, Court Dramatist.* Oxford: Oxford University Press.

Dreyfus, H. L., & Wakefield, J. (1988). From depth psychology to breadth psychology: A phenomenological approach to psychopathology. In: S. B. Messer, L. A. Sass, & R. L. Woolfolk (Eds.), *Hermeneutics and Psychological Theory: Interpretive Perspectives on Personality, Psychotherapy, and Psychopathology* (pp. 272–288). New Brunswick, NJ: Rutgers University Press.

Eagle, M. N. (1980a). Psychoanalytic interpretation: veridicality and therapeutic effectiveness. *Nous, 14*: 405–425.

Eagle, M. N. (1980b). A critical examination of motivational explanation in psychoanalysis. *Psychoanalysis and Contemporary Thought, 3*: 329–380.

Eagle, M. N., Wolitzky, D. L., & Wakefield, J. C. (2001). The analyst's knowledge and authority: A critique of the "new view" in psychoanalysis. *Journal of the American Psychoanalytic Association, 49*: 457–489.

Earle, J. (1881). The history of the word "mind". *Mind, 6*: 301–320.

Edelson, M. (1988). *Psychoanalysis: A Theory in Crisis.* Chicago, IL: University of Chicago Press.

Ehrenberg, D. (1990). Playfulness in the psychoanalytic relationship. *Contemporary Psychoanalysis, 26*: 74–95.

Eigen, M. (2004a). *The Sensitive Self.* Middletown, CT: Wesleyan University Press.

Eigen, M. (2004b). *Psychic Deadness.* London: Karnac.

Eigen, M. (2007). *Feeling Matters.* London: Karnac.

Eigen, M. (2009). *Flames from the Unconscious: Trauma, Madness, and Faith.* London: Karnac.

Eigen, M. (2011). *Contact with the Depths.* London: Karnac.

Enckell, H. (2001). Psychic reality and psychoanalysis: A look through the theory of metaphor. *Psychoanalysis and Contemporary Thought, 24*(3): 231–252.

Erikson, E. H. (1950). *Childhood and Society.* New York: W. W. Norton.

Erikson, E. H. (1956). The problem of ego identity. *Journal of the American Psychoanalytic Association, 4*: 56–121.

Erikson, E. H. (1959). *Identity and the Life Cycle.* New York: International Universities Press.

Erikson, E. H. (1963). *Childhood and Society.* New York: W. W. Norton.

Erikson, E. H. (1968). *Identity, Youth and Crisis.* New York: W. W. Norton.

Erikson, E. H. (1969). *Gandhi's Truth: On the Origins of Militant Nonviolence.* New York: W. W. Norton, 1993.

Esman, A. (1979). On evidence and inference, or the Babel of tongues. *Psychoanalytic Quarterly, 48*: 628–630.

Fairbairn, W. R. D. (1952). *Psychoanalytic Studies of the Personality.* London: Routledge & Regan Paul, 1981.

Fairfield, S. (2002). Analyzing multiplicity: A postmodern perspective on some current psychoanalytic theories of subjectivity. In: S. Fairfield, L. Layton, & C. Stack (Eds.), *Bringing the Plague: Toward a Postmodern Psychoanalysis* (pp. 69–101). New York: Other Press.

Ferenczi, S. (1933). Confusion of tongues between adults and the child. In: M. Balint (Ed.), E. Mosbacher (Trans.), *Final Contributions to the Problems and Methods of Psycho-analysis* (pp. 156–174). Levittown, PA: Brunner/Mazel.

Ferenczi, S. (1949). Confusion of the tongues between the adults and the child. *International Journal of Psychoanalysis, 30*: 225–230.

Ferro, A. (2019). *Psychoanalysis and Dreams.* New York: Routledge.

Fink, B. (2010). Against understanding: why understanding should not be viewed as an essential aim of psychoanalytic treatment. *Journal of the American Psychoanalytic Association, 58*: 259–285.

Finnerty, P. (2006). *Emily Dickinson's Shakespeare.* Amherst, MA: University of Massachusetts Press.

Fischer, R. M. (2009). What it takes to tell a lie. In: S. Akhtar & S. Parens (Eds.), *Lying, Cheating, and Carrying-On* (pp. 17–31). Lanham, MD: Jason Aronson.

Flanagan, O. (1991). *The Science of the Mind.* Cambridge, MA: MIT Press.

Fonagy, P. (2001). *Attachment Theory and Psychoanalysis.* New York: Other Press.

Fotopoulou, A. (2012a). The history and progress of neuropsychoanalysis. In: A. Fotopoulou, D. Pfaff, & M. A. Conway (Eds.), *From the Couch to the Lab: Trends in Psychodynamic Neuroscience.* Oxford: Oxford University Press.

Fotopoulou, A. (2012b). Towards a psychodynamic neuroscience. In: A. Fotopoulou, D. Pfaff, & M. A. Conway (Eds.), *From the Couch to the Lab: Trends in Psychodynamic Neuroscience*. Oxford: Oxford University Press.

Foucault, M. (1972). *The Archaeology of Knowledge and the Discourse on Language*. A. M. Sheridan Smith (Trans.). New York: Pantheon.

Frank, A. (1969). The unrememberable and the unforgettable: passive primal repression. *Psychoanalytic Study of the Child, 24*: 48–77.

Frank, J. (2018). *Trump on the Couch*. New York: Avery.

Frankfurt, H. (2006). *On Truth*. New York: Alfred A. Knopf.

Frege, G. (1918). *Logical Investigations*. Oxford: Blackwell, 1977.

Freud, A. (1958). Adolescence. *Psychoanalytic Study of the Child, 13*: 255–278.

Freud, S. (1893). Miss Lucy R. Case histories from *Studies on Hysteria*. *S. E., 2*: 106–124. London: Hogarth.

Freud, S. (1895d). *Studies on Hysteria* (with J. Breuer). *S. E., 2*: 19–312. London: Hogarth.

Freud, S. (1899a). Screen memories. *S. E., 3*: 301–323. London: Hogarth.

Freud, S. (1905d). *Three Essays on the Theory of Sexuality*. *S. E., 7*. London: Hogarth.

Freud, S. (1905e). Fragment of an analysis of a case of hysteria. *S. E., 7*: 1–122. London: Hogarth.

Freud, S. (1907a). *Delusions and Dreams in Jensen's "Gradiva"*. *S. E., 9*: 9–196. London: Hogarth.

Freud, S. (1908e). Creative writers and day-dreaming. *S. E., 9*: 141–154. London: Hogarth.

Freud, S. (1909b). Analysis of a phobia in a five-year-old boy. *S. E., 10*: 1–150. London: Hogarth.

Freud, S. (1911b). Formulations on the two principles of mental functioning. *S. E., 12*: 213–226. London: Hogarth.

Freud, S. (1912e). Recommendations to physicians practising psycho-analysis. *S. E., 12*. London: Hogarth.

Freud, S. (1913c). On beginning the treatment (further recommendations on the technique of psycho-analysis, I). *S. E., 12*. London: Hogarth.

Freud, S. (1914c). On narcissism: an introduction. *S. E., 14*: 67–102. London: Hogarth.

Freud, S. (1914d). On the history of the psycho-analytic movement. *S. E., 14*: 7–66. London: Hogarth.

Freud, S. (1914g). Remembering, repeating and working-through (further recommendations on the technique of psychoanalysis, II). *S. E., 12*: 145–156. London: Hogarth.

Freud, S. (1915b). Thoughts for the times on war and death. *S. E., 14*: 273–300. London: Hogarth.

Freud, S. (1915e). The unconscious. *S. E., 14*: 159–215. London: Hogarth.

Freud, S. (1916a). On transience. *S. E., 14*: 303–307. London: Hogarth.

Freud, S. (1916d). Some character-types met with in psycho-analytic work. *S. E., 14*: 310–333. London: Hogarth.

Freud, S. (1916–17). *Introductory Lectures on Psycho-Analysis*. *S. E., 15–16*: 3–463. London: Hogarth.

Freud, S. (1917e). Mourning and melancholia. *S. E., 14*: 237–258. London: Hogarth.

Freud, S. (1921c). *Group Psychology and the Analysis of the Ego*. *S. E., 18*: 63–143. London: Hogarth.

Freud, S. (1923c). Remarks on the theory and practice of dream-interpretation. *S. E., 19*: 109–124. London: Hogarth.

Freud, S. (1925j). Some psychical consequences of the anatomical distinction between the sexes. *S. E., 19*: 241–258. London: Hogarth.

Freud, S. (1926d). *Inhibitions, Symptoms and Anxiety. S. E., 20*: 75–176. London: Hogarth.

Freud, S. (1930a). *Civilization and Its Discontents*. London: W. W. Norton, 1989.

Freud, S. (1933a). *New Introductory Lectures on Psycho-Analysis. S. E., 22*: 7–182. London: Hogarth.

Freud, S. (1933b). Why war? *S. E., 22*: 197–215. London: Hogarth.

Freud, S. (1937d). Constructions in analysis. *S. E., 23*: 255–269. London: Hogarth.

Freud, S. (1940a). *An Outline of Psycho-Analysis. S. E., 23*: 211–253. London: Hogarth.

Freud, S. (1957). *The Standard Edition of the Complete Psychological Works of Sigmund Freud. Vol. 24*. J. Strachey (Ed. & Trans.). London: Hogarth.

Friedman, L. (2000). Modern hermeneutics and psychoanalysis. *Psychoanalytic Quarterly, 69*: 225–264.

Frosch, J. (1964). The psychotic character. *Psychiatric Quarterly, 38*: 81–96.

Frost, R. (1939). The figure a poem makes. In: R. Poirier & M. Richardson (Eds.), *Robert Frost: Collected Poems, Prose and Plays* (pp. 776–778). New York: Library of America, 1995.

Gadamer, H.-G. (1960). *Truth and Method*, 2nd rev. edn. J. Weinsheimer & D. G. Marshall (Trans.). New York: Crossroad, 1989.

Gandhi, M. K. (1927). *An Autobiography: The Story of My Experiments with Truth*. Boston, MA: Beacon, 1957.

Garber, M. (2004). *Shakespeare After All*. New York: Anchor.

Gerald, M. (2021). *In the Shadow of Freud's Couch: Portraits of Psychoanalysts in Their Offices*. London: Routledge.

Gergen, M. (1997). Skipping stone: Circles in the pond. In: M. Gergen & S. N. Davis (Eds.), *Toward a New Psychology of Gender: A Reader* (pp. 605–611). London: Routledge.

Gilbert, S. (2020). *Shakespeare Beyond Science: When Poetry Was the World*. Toronto, Canada: Guernica Editions.

Gilligan, C. (1982). *In a Different Voice: Psychological Theory and Women's Development*. Cambridge, MA: Harvard University Press.

Glover, E. (1931). The therapeutic effect of inexact interpretation. *International Journal of Psychoanalysis, 12*: 397–418.

Goldfarb, W. (1963). Self-awareness in schizophrenic children. *Archives of General Psychiatry, 8*: 47–60.

Gould, S. J. (2003). *The Hedgehog, the Fox, and the Magister's Pox: Mending the Gap between Science and the Humanities*. Nevada City, CA: Harmony.

Green, A. (2001). *Life Narcissism, Death Narcissism*. London: Free Association.

Green, H. (1964). *I Never Promised You a Rose Garden*. New York: Holt, Rinehart & Winston.

Greenberg, J. (2016). Editor's introduction: Is truth relevant? *Psychoanalytic Quarterly, 85*(2): 269–274.

Grondin, J. (1994). *Introduction to Philosophical Hermeneutics*. J. Weinsheimer (Trans.). New Haven, CT: Harvard University Press.

Grotstein, J. S. (2007). *A Beam of Intense Darkness: Wilfred Bion's Legacy to Psychoanalysis*. London: Karnac.

Gusdorf, G. (1980). Conditions and limits of autobiography. In: J. Olney (Ed.), *Autobiography* (pp. 32–46). Princeton, NJ: Princeton University Press.

Hamilton, E. (1942). *Mythology: Timeless Tales of Gods and Heroes*. Dublin: Mentor, 1969.

Hanly, C. (1990). The concept of truth in psychoanalysis. *International Journal of Psychoanalysis, 71*: 375–383.

Hanly, C. (1992). *The Problem of Truth in Applied Psychoanalysis*. New York: Guilford.

Hanly, C. (1999). On subjectivity and objectivity in psychoanalysis. *Journal of the American Psychoanalytic Association, 47*: 427–444.

Hanly, C. (2006). Pragmatism, tradition, and truth in psychoanalysis. *American* Imago, *63*: 261–282.

Hanly, C. (2014a). The interplay of deductive and inductive reasoning in psychoanalytic theorizing. *Psychoanalytic Quarterly, 83*: 897–915.

Hanly, C. (2014b). Skeptical reflection on subjectivist epistemologies. *Psychoanalytic Quarterly, 83*: 949–968.

Hanly, C., & Fitzpatrick Hanly, M. A. (2001). Critical realism: Distinguishing the psychological subjectivity of the analyst from epistemological subjectivism. *Journal of the American Psychoanalytic Association, 49*: 515–532.

Harari, Y. N. (2014). *Sapiens: A Brief History of Humankind*. London: Vintage.

Hartmann, H. (1939). *Ego Psychology and the Problem of Adaptation*. D. Rapaport (Trans.). New York: International Universities Press, 1958.

Hartmann, H. (1964). *Essays on Ego Psychology. Selected Problems in Psychoanalytic Theory*. New York: International Universities Press.

Hass, L. (2008). *Merleau-Ponty's Philosophy*. Bloomington, IN: Indiana University Press.

Hauser, S. T. (2005). The legacy of Enrico Jones. *Journal of the American Psychoanalytic Association, 53*(2): 535–540.

Heaney, S. (1979). Song. In: *Opened Ground: Selected Poems, 1966–1996* (p. 178). New York: Farrar, Straus & Giroux, 1998.

Heidegger, M. (1927). *Being and Time*. J. Stambaugh (Trans.). Albany, NY: State University of New York Press, 1996.

Heidegger, M. (1947). Letter on "humanism". F. A. Capuzzi (Trans.). In: W. McNeill (Ed.), *Heidegger, Pathmarks* (p. 272). Cambridge: Cambridge University Press, 1998.

Heidegger, M. (1963). What is metaphysics? In: D. Krell (Trans.), *Basic Writings* (pp. 89–110). New York: Harper & Row, 1977.

Heidegger, M. (1987). *Zollikon Seminars: Protocols–Conversations–Letters*. Evanston, IL: Northwestern University Press, 2011.

Heimann, P. (1950). On countertransference. *International Journal of Psychoanalysis, 31*: 81–84.

Herzog, B. (2015). Compliance, defiance, and the development of relational technique: what a ballerina taught me about myself and the supervisory process. *Psychoanalytic Inquiry, 35*: 298–311.

Hess, E. (2008). *Nim Chimpsky: The Chimp Who Would Be Human*. New York: Bantam.

Hirst, W., & Echterhoff, G. (2012). Remembering in conversations: the social sharing and reshaping of memories. *Annual Review of Psychology, 63*(1): 55–79.

Hirst, W., Phelps, E. A., Meksin, R., Vaidya, C. J., Johnson, M. K., Mitchell, K. J., Buckner, R. L., Budson, A. E., Gabrieli, J. D. E., Lustig, C., Mather, M., Ochsner, K. N., Schacter, D., Simons, J. S., Lyle, K. B., Cuc, A. F., & Olsson, A. (2015). A ten-year follow-up of a study of memory for the attack of September 11, 2001: Flashbulb memories and memories for flashbulb events. *Journal of Experimental Psychology: General, 144*(3): 604–623.

Homer (8th–7th century BCE). *The Odyssey.* R. Fagles (Trans.). London: Penguin Classics, 1997.

Humphrey, N. (2002a). *The Mind Made Flesh: Frontiers of Psychology and Evolution.* Oxford: Oxford University Press.

Humphrey, N. (2002b). *The Inner Eye: Social Intelligence in Evolution.* Oxford: Oxford University Press.

Ikiru (1952). A. Kurosawa (Dir.). Motion picture distributed by Toho, Japan.

Incendies (2010). D. Villeneuve (Dir.). Motion picture produced by micro_scope, Canada.

Jacobs, M. (2011). Interpreting in the form of action. In: S. Akhtar (Ed.), *Unusual Interventions: Alterations of the Frame, Method, and Relationship in Psychotherapy and Psychoanalysis*, (pp. 113–137). London: Karnac.

James, W. (1890). *The Principles of Psychology.* New York: Dover, 1950.

Jeffery, E. H. (2001). The mortality of psychoanalysts. *Journal of the American Psychoanalytic Association 49*(1): 103–111. https://doi.org/10.1177/000306510104900110

Jiménez, R. (2018). *Vero Nihil Verius*—Nothing truer than *what*? *Shakespeare Oxford Newsletter, 54*: 16–17.

Kandel, E. R. (2005). Biology and the future of psychoanalysis: A new intellectual framework for psychiatry revisited. In: *Psychiatry, Psychoanalysis, and the New Biology of Mind.* Washington, DC: American Psychiatric Publishing. Reprinted from *American Journal of Psychiatry, 156*: 505–524, 1999.

Kaplan-Solms, K., & Solms, M. (2000). *Clinical Studies in Neuro-psychoanalysis: Introduction to a Depth Neuropsychology.* London: Karnac.

Karlsson, G. (2010). *Psychoanalysis in a New Light.* Cambridge: Cambridge University Press.

Katz, M. S. (2011). Unconscious metaphoric processes as the basis for an inclusive model of psychoanalytic perspectives. *Psychoanalytic Inquiry, 31*(2): 134–146.

Katz, M. S. (Ed.) (2013). *Metaphor and Fields: Common Ground, Common Language, and the Future of Psychoanalysis.* New York: Routledge.

Katzenstein, T., Fonagy, P., & Ablon, J. S. (2010). Enrico Jones: Appreciating complexity. In: L. G. Castonguay, J. C. Muran, L. Angus, J. A. Hayes, N. Ladany, & T. Anderson (Eds.), *Bringing Psychotherapy Research to Life: Understanding Change through the Work of Leading Clinical Researchers* (pp. 259–269). Washington, DC: American Psychological Association.

Kernberg, O. F. (1975a). *Borderline Conditions and Pathological Narcissism.* New York: Jason Aronson.

Keyes, R. (2004). *The Post-Truth Era: Dishonesty and Deception in Contemporary Life.* New York: St. Martin's.

Killingmo, B. (1989). Conflict and deficit: implications for technique. *International Journal of Psychoanalysis, 70*: 65–79.

Köhler, W. (1917). *The Mentality of Apes.* London: Routledge, 2019.

Kohut, H. (1959). Introspection, empathy, and psychoanalysis: An examination of the relationship between mode of observation and theory. In: P. H. Ornstein (Ed.), *The Search for the Self: Selected Writings of Heinz Kohut, Volume 1, 1950–1978* (pp. 205–232). New York: International Universities Press, 1978.

Kohut, H. (1977). *The Restoration of the Self.* New York: International Universities Press.

Kris, A. O. (2018). "Love's not times's fool": Some continuities, discontinuities, and alterations in psychoanalysis during my lifetime. *Psychoanalytic Study of the Child, 71*: 123–129.

Kris, E. (1956a). The personal myth: a problem in psychoanalytic technique. *Journal of the American Psychoanalytic Association, 4*: 653–681.

Kris, E. (1956b). The recovery of childhood memories in psychoanalysis. *Psychoanalytic Study of the Child, 11*: 54

Lacassagne, D., Jérémy Béna, J., & Corneille, O. (2022). Is Earth a perfect square? Repetition increases the perceived truth of highly implausible statements. *Cognition, 223.*

Laing, R. D. (1960). *The Divided Self: An Existential Study in Sanity and Madness.* London: Penguin, 2010.

Lakatos, I. (1976). *Proofs and Refutations: The Logic of Mathematical Discovery.* Cambridge: Cambridge University Press.

Lake, P. (2016). *How Shakespeare Put Politics on the Stage: Power and Succession in the History Plays.* New Haven, CT: Yale University Press.

Lakoff, G., & Johnson, M. (1980). *Metaphors We Live By.* Chicago, IL: University of Chicago Press.

Lampl-de Groot, J. (1960). On adolescence. *Psychoanalytic Study of the Child, 15*: 95–103.

Langs, R. (1981). Modes of "cure" in psychoanalysis and psychoanalytic psychotherapy. *International Journal of Psychoanalysis, 62*(2): 199–214.

Laplanche, J. (1970). *Life and Death in Psychoanalysis.* J. Mehlman (Trans.). Baltimore, MD: Johns Hopkins University Press, 1976.

Laplanche, J. (1992a). Interpretation between determinism and hermeneutics: A restatement of the problem. P. Slotkin (Trans.). In: *Essays on Otherness.* New York: Routledge, 1999.

Laplanche, J. (1992b). *Essays on Otherness.* New York: Routledge, 1999.

Laplanche, J. (1995). Seduction, persecution, revelation. *International Journal of Psychoanalysis, 76*: 663–682.

Laplanche, J. (2006). *Après-coup.* J. House (Trans.). New York: The Unconscious in Translation, 2017.

Lear, J. (2003). *Therapeutic Action: An Earnest Plea for Irony.* New York: Other Press.

Levin, H. (1999). Those who walk in darkness. In: *Those Who Walk in Darkness and Other Plays* (pp. 7–70). Tel Aviv, Israel: Am Oved. [In Hebrew.]

Little, M. I. (1951). Countertransference and the patient's response to it. *International Journal of Psychoanalysis, 32*: 32–40.

Loewald, H. W. (1951). Ego and reality. *International Journal of Psychoanalysis, 32*: 10–18.

Loewald, H. W. (1960). On the therapeutic action of psychoanalysis. *International Journal of Psychoanalysis, 41*: 16–33.

Loewald, H. W. (1971). Some considerations on repetition and repetition compulsion. *International Journal of Psychoanalysis, 52*: 59–66.

Loewald, H. W. (1980). *Papers on Psychoanalysis.* New Haven, CT: Yale University Press.

Loewenberg, P. (1995). *Fantasy and Reality in History.* London: Oxford University Press.

Loftus, E. R. (1979). *Eyewitness Testimony.* Cambridge, MA: Harvard University Press.

Loftus, E. R., & Palmer, J. (1974). Reconstruction of automobile destruction: example of the interaction within language and memory. *Journal of Verbal Learning and Verbal Behavior, 13*: 585–589.

Luborsky, L., Rosenthal, R., Diguer, L., Andrusyna, T. P., Berman, J. S., Levitt, J. T., Seligman, D. A., & Krause, E. D. (2002). The dodo bird verdict is alive and well—mostly. *Clinical Psychology: Science and Practice, 9*(1): 2–12.

Lyotard, J.-F. (1990). *Heidegger and the Jews.* A. Michel & M. S. Roberts (Trans.). Minneapolis, MN: University of Minnesota Press.

Mahler, M. S., & Furer, M. (1968). *On Human Symbiosis and the Vicissitudes of Individualization.* New York: International Universities Press.

Mahler, M. S., Pine, F., & Bergman, A. (1975). *The Psychological Birth of the Human Infant.* New York: Basic Books.

Markides, K. C. (1977.) *The Rise and Fall of the Cyprus Republic.* New Haven, CT: Yale University Press.

Masson, J. M. (1984). *The Assault on Truth: Freud's Suppression of the Seduction Theory.* New York: Farrar, Straus, and Giroux.

Masson, J. M. (Ed.) (1985). *The Complete Letters of Sigmund Freud to Wilhelm Fliess.* Cambridge, MA: Harvard University Press.

McDougall, J. (1978). Primitive communication and the use of countertransference: Reflections on early psychic trauma and its transference effects. *Contemporary Psychoanalysis, 14*: 173–209.

McGuire, J. (Ed.) (1974). *Freud-Jung Letters: The Correspondence Between Sigmund Freud and Carl Jung.* Princeton, NJ: Princeton University Press.

McLaughlin, J. T. (1991). Clinical and theoretical aspects of enactment. *Journal of the American Psychoanalytic Association, 39*: 595–614.

Meehl, P. (1973). *Psychodiagnosis: Selected Papers.* New York: W. W. Norton.

Meltzer, D. (1984). *Dream Life: A Re-examination of the Psychoanalytic Theory and Technique.* Strathtay, UK: Clunie.

Melzer, A. M. (2014). *Philosophy Between the Lines: The Lost History of Esoteric Writing.* Chicago, IL: University of Chicago Press.

Messer, S. B., Sass, L. A., & Woolfolk, R. L. (Eds.) (1988). *Hermeneutics and Psychological Theory: Interpretive Perspectives on Personality, Psychotherapy, and Psychopathology.* New Brunswick, NJ: Rutgers University Press.

Miller, S. A., Custer, W. L., & Nassau, G. (2000). Children's understanding of the necessity of logically necessary truths. *Cognitive Development, 15*: 383–403.

Mills, J. (1997). The false Dasein: From Heidegger to Sartre and psychoanalysis. *Journal of Phenomenological Psychology, 28*(1): 42–65.

Mills, J. (2014). Truth. *Journal of the American Psychoanalytic Association, 62*(2): 267–293.

Mitchell, S. (1988). *Relational Concepts in Psychoanalysis: An Integration.* Cambridge, MA: Harvard University Press.

Mitchell, S. (1999). Personal communication.

Modell, A. H. (1993). *The Private Self.* Cambridge, MA: Harvard University Press.

Modell, A. H. (2003). *Imagination and the Meaningful Brain*. Cambridge, MA: MIT Press.

Modell, A. H. (2005). Emotional memory, metaphor, and meaning. *Psychoanalytic Inquiry, 25*(4): 555–568.

Modell, A. H. (2011). Not even wrong. *Psychoanalytic Inquiry, 31*(2): 126–133.

Money-Kyrle, R. E. (1952). Psycho-analysis and ethics. *International Journal of Psychoanalysis, 33*: 225–234.

Money-Kyrle, R. E. (1968). Cognitive development. *International Journal of Psychoanalysis, 49*: 691–698.

Morag, T. (2016). *Emotion, Imagination, and the Limits of Reason*. New York: Routledge.

Moscovici, S. (1993). *The Invention of Society*. W. D. Halls (Trans.). Cambridge: Polity.

Moscovici, S. (2001). Why a theory of social representation? In: K. Deaux & G. Philogène (Eds.), *Representations of the Social: Bridging Theoretical Traditions* (pp. 8–35). London: Blackwell.

Murphy, R. F. (1957). Ingroup hostility and social cohesion. *American Anthropologist, 59*: 1018–1035.

Nagel, T. (1979). *Mortal Questions*. Cambridge: Cambridge University Press.

Nagel, T. (1995). Searle: Why we are not computers. In: *Other Minds: Critical Essays 1969–1994*. New York: Oxford University Press.

Neruda, P. (1991). *The Book of Questions*. W. O'Daly (Trans.). Washington, DC: Townsend.

Neu, J. (1988). Divided minds: Sartre's "bad faith" critique of Freud. *Review of Metaphysics, 42*(1): 79–101.

Nickerson, R. S. (1998). Confirmation bias: A ubiquitous phenomenon in many guises. *Review of General Psychology, 2*(2): 175–220.

Niederland, W. (1968). Clinical observations on the "survivor syndrome". *International Journal of Psychoanalysis, 49*: 313–315.

Nietzsche, F. (1873). On truth and lie in a nonmoral sense. In: *On Truth and Untruth*. T. Carmen (Trans.). New York: HarperCollins, 2010.

Nunberg, H. (1931). The synthetic function of the ego. *International Journal of Psychoanalysis, 12*: 123–140.

Nussbaum, M. (1994, October 1). Patriotism and cosmopolitanism. *Boston Review*, pp. 3–6.

Ofer, G., & Durban, Y. (1999). Curiosity: Reflections on its nature and functions. *American Journal of Psychotherapy, 53*(1): 35–51.

Ofer, G., Shoshani, B., & Shoshani, M. (2021). When one plus one equals one: Truth and blindness in the Oedipal myth and Denis Villeneuve's film *Incendies*. *Free Associations*, 81–82.

Ogden, T. H. (1994). The analytic third: Working with intersubjective clinical facts. *International Journal Psychoanalysis, 75*: 3–20.

Ogden, T. H. (1997). Some thoughts on the use of language in psychoanalysis. *Psychoanalytic Dialogues, 7*: 1–21.

Ogden, T. H. (2001). *Conversations at the Frontier of Dreaming*. Northvale, NJ: Jason Aronson.

Ogden, T. H. (2002). A new reading of the origins of object-relations theory. *International Journal Psychoanalysis, 83*: 767–782.

Ogden, T. H. (2003). On not being able to dream. *International Journal of Psychoanalysis, 84*(1): 17–30.

Ogden, T. H. (2005). *This Art of Psychoanalysis: Dreaming Undreamt Dreams and Interrupted Cries.* London: Routledge.

Ogden, T. H. (2009). *Rediscovering Psychoanalysis: Thinking and Dreaming, Learning and Forgetting.* London: Routledge.

Ogden, T. H. (2016). On language and truth in psychoanalysis. *Psychoanalytic Quarterly, 85*: 411–426.

Opatow, B. (1999). Affect and the integration problem of mind and brain. *Neuropsychoanalysis, 1*: 97–110.

Ostrowski, D. (2020). *Who Wrote That? Authorship Controversies from Moses to Sholokhov.* Dekalb, IL: Northern Illinois University Press.

Page, J., & Plant, R. (1971). Stairway to heaven. [Song.] *Led Zeppelin IV* [Album]. Atlantic.

Page, J., & Plant, R. (1973). Over the hills and far away. [Song.] *Houses of the Holy* [Album]. Atlantic.

Pearl, J. (2011). *A Question of Time: Between Philosophy and Psychoanalysis.* Tel Aviv, Israel: Bar-Ilan University Press.

Person, E. S. (2001). Knowledge and authority: The godfather fantasy. *Journal of the American Psychoanalytic Association, 49*: 1133–1155.

Piaget, J. (1948). *The Moral Judgement of the Child.* Glencoe, IL: Free Press.

Pickhardt, C. E. (2009). Rebel with a cause: Rebellion in adolescence. Retrieved from: https://psychologytoday.com/blog/surviving-your-childs-adolescence/200912/ (last accessed May 12, 2022).

Pierce, C. S. (1901). Truth and falsity and error. In: J. M. Baldwin (Ed.), *Dictionary of Philosophy and Psychology, vol. 2* (pp. 716–720). New York: Atheneum.

Pimentel, D. (2018). Afterword in *Brief über den "Humanismus"* by Heidegger, M. (1947). [In Hebrew] Tel Aviv, Israel, Bar-Ilan University Press.

Pinsky, R. (1998). *The Sounds of Poetry.* New York: Farrar, Straus, and Giroux.

Plato (*c.*381 BCE). Allegory of the cave. In: *The Republic.* Oxford: Rowman & Littlefield, 1997.

Quine, W. V. (1960). *Word and Object.* Cambridge, MA: Harvard University Press.

Quine, W. V., & Ullian, J. S. (1978). *The Web of Belief.* New York: Random House.

Quirk, M. J. (2016). *Martin Heidegger: Being, Beings, and Truth.* Online: Sophia Project, Philosophy Archives.

Racker, H. (1968). *Transference and Countertransference.* London: Hogarth.

Rangell, L. (2002). The theory of psychoanalysis: Vicissitudes of its evolution. *Journal of the American Psychoanalytic Association, 50*(4): 1109–1137.

Rank, O. (1945). *Will Therapy.* New York: Alfred A. Knopf.

Razinsky, L. (2013). *Freud, Psychoanalysis and Death.* Cambridge: Cambridge University Press.

Reichenbach, H. (1951). *The Rise of Scientific Philosophy.* Berkeley, CA: University of California Press.

Ricœur, P. (1970). *Freud and Philosophy: An Essay on Interpretation.* D. Savage (Trans.). New Haven, CT: Yale University Press.

Ricœur, P. (1971). The model of the text: Meaningful action considered as a text. In: K. Blamey K. & J. B. Thompson (Trans.), *From Text to Action: Essays in Hermeneutics, II* (pp. 144–167). Evanston, IL: Northwestern University Press, 1991.

Ricœur, P. (1973). The hermeneutical function of distanciation. In: K. Blamey K. & J. B. Thompson (Trans.), *From Text to Action: Essays in Hermeneutics, II* (pp. 75–88). Evanston, IL: Northwestern University Press, 1991.

Ricœur, P. (1977a). The question of proof in Freud's psychoanalytic writings. *Journal of the American Psychoanalytic Association, 25*: 835–871.

Ricœur, P. (1977b). *The Rule of Metaphor: Multi-disciplinary Studies of the Creation of Meaning in Language.* R. Czerny (Trans.). Toronto, Canada: University of Toronto Press.

Ricœur, P. (1978). The metaphorical process as cognition, imagination, and feeling. *Critical Inquiry, 5*(1): 143–160.

Rilke, R. M. (1996). *Rilke's Book of Hours: Love Poems to God.* A. Barrows & J. Macy (Trans.). New York: Riverhead, 2005.

Rorty, R. (1999). Endorsement. In: R. Safranski, *Martin Heidegger: Between Good and Evil.* E. Osers (Trans.). Cambridge, MA: Harvard University Press.

Rose, G. (1969). Transference birth fantasies and narcissism. *Journal of the American Psychoanalytic Association, 17*: 1015–1029.

Rosenthal, R. (1979). The file drawer problem and tolerance for null results. *Psychological Bulletin, 86*(3): 638–641.

Rothschild, L., & Haslam, N. (2003). Thirsty for H_2O? Multiple essences and psychological essentialism. *New Ideas in Psychology, 21*: 31–41.

Rudnytsky, P. (2022). *Mutual Analysis: Ferenczi, Severn, and the Origins of Trauma Theory.* London: Routledge.

Russell, B. (1912). *The Problems of Philosophy.* New York: Holt.

Sarton, M. (1997). *Coming into Eighty.* New York: W. W. Norton.

Sartre, J.-P. (1915). *No Exit and Three Other Plays.* New York: Vintage.

Sartre, J.-P. (1943). *Being and Nothingness.* H. E. Barnes (Trans.). New York: Philosophical Library, 1956.

Sartre, J.-P. (1946). *Existentialism Is Humanism.* Paris: Les Editions Nagel.

Scenes from a Marriage (1973). I. Bergman (Dir.). Motion picture produced by Svensk Filmindustri, Sweden.

Schafer, R. (1973). Concepts of self and identity and the experience of separation-individuation in adolescence. *Psychoanalytic Quarterly, 42*: 42–59.

Searle, J. (1992). *The Rediscovery of the Mind.* Boston, MA: MIT Press.

Sebeok, T. A. (1991). *A Sign Is Just a Sign (Advances in Semiotics).* Bloomington, IN: Indiana University Press.

Shalvi, H. M. (2018). *From Ultrasound to Army: the Trajectory of Masculinity in Israel.* London: Routledge.

Shapiro, D. (1981). *Autonomy and Rigid Character.* New York: Basic Books.

Shapiro, D. (1989). *Psychotherapy and Neurotic Character.* New York: Basic Books.

Shapiro, T. (1981). On the quest for the origins of conflict. *Psychoanalytic Quarterly, 50*(1): 1–21.

Shengold, L. (1989). *Soul Murder: The Effects of Childhood Abuse and Deprivation.* New Haven, CT: Yale University Press.

Sherwood, M. (1969). *The Logic of Explanation in Psychoanalysis*. New York: Academic Press.

Shoshani, B., Ofer, G., & Shoshani, M. (2021). When one plus one equals one: truth and blindness in the oedipal myth and the film *Incendies*. In: *Timeless Grandiosity and Eroticised Contempt: Technical Challenges Posed by Cases of Narcissism and Perversion* (pp. 169–187). Bicester, UK: Phoenix.

Shoshani, M., & Shoshani, B. (2013). Borges in my office: The analysis of a man dwelling outside of time. *Psychoanalytic Quarterly*, *82*(3): 635–669.

Shoshani, M., & Shoshani, B. (2021). Fear and shame in an Israeli psychoanalyst and his patient: lessons learned in times of war. In: *Timeless Grandiosity and Eroticised Contempt: Technical Challenges Posed by Cases of Narcissism and Perversion* (pp. 95–124). Bicester, UK: Phoenix.

Sigad, R. (1975). *Studies in Existentialism*. Jerusalem: Bialik Institute. [In Hebrew.]

Smith, L. (1949). *Killers of the Dream*. New York: W. W. Norton.

Solms, M. (1998). Before and after Freud's *Project*. In: R. M. Bilder & F. F. LeFever (Eds.), *Neuroscience of the Mind on the Centennial of Freud's* Project for a Scientific Psychology. New York: The New York Academy of Sciences.

Solms, M. (2000). Foreword. In: Pally, R., *The Mind-Brain Relationship*. International Journal of Psychoanalysis Key Papers Series. London: Karnac.

Solms, M., & Turnbull, O. (2002). *The Brain and the Inner World:An Introduction to the Neuroscience of Subjective Experience*. New York: Other Press.

Spence, D. P. (1981). Psychoanalytic competence. *International Journal of Psychoanalysis*, *62*: 113–124.

Spence, D. P. (1982a). Narrative truth and theoretical truth. *Psychoanalytic Quarterly*, *51*: 43–61.

Spence, D. P. (1982b). *Narrative Truth and Historical Truth*. New York: W. W. Norton.

Spinoza, B. (*c*.1660). *Ethics*. New York: Prometheus, 1989.

Spitz, R. A. (1957). *On the Genesis of Human Communication*. New York: International Universities Press.

Steele, J. (2010, August 27). Chilcot Inquiry accused of fixating on West and ignoring real victims. *Guardian*.

Steiner, J. (1985). Turning a blind eye: The cover up for Oedipus. *International Journal of Psychoanalysis*, *12*: 161–172.

Steiner, J. (1993). *Psychic Retreats: Pathological Organizations of the Personality in Psychotic Neurotic, and Borderline Patients*. London: Routledge.

Stekel, W. (1924). The impulse to wander. In: *Peculiarities of Behavior: Wandering Mania, Dipsomania, Cleptomania, Pyromania and Allied Impulsive Acts, Volume I* (pp. 18–91). New York: Liveright, 1943

Stern, D. B. (1994). Empathy is interpretation (And who ever said it wasn't?): Commentary on papers by Hayes, Kiersky and Beebe, Feiner and Kiersky. *Psychoanalytic Dialogues*, *4*: 441–471.

Stern, D. B. (2002). What you know first: Construction and deconstruction in relational psychoanalysis. In: S. Fairfield, L. Layton, & C. Stack (Eds.), *Bringing the Plague: Toward a Postmodern Psychoanalysis* (pp. 167–194). New York: Other Press.

Stern, S. (1994). Needed relationships and repeated relationships. *Psychoanalytic Dialogues*, *4*: 317–345.

Still Alice (2014). R. Glatzer & W. Westmoreland (Dirs.). Motion picture produced by Sony Picture Classics, USA.

Stogner, J., Miller, B. L., & Marcum, C. (2013). Learning to e-cheat: A criminological test of internet facilitated academic cheating. *Journal of Criminal Justice Education, 24*: 175–199.

Strachey, J. (1934). The nature of the therapeutic action of psychoanalysis. *International Journal of Psycho-Analysis, 50*: 275–292.

Strenger, C. (2013). Why psychoanalysis must not discard science and human nature. *Psychoanal Dialogues, 23*: 197–210.

Suistola, J., & Volkan, V. D. (2017). *Religious Knives: Historical and Psychological Dimensions of International Terrorism.* Durham, NC: Pitchstone.

Sullivan, H. S. (1953). *Conceptions of Modern Psychiatry.* New York: W. W. Norton.

Summers, R. S. (1999). Formal legal truth and substantive truth in judicial fact-finding. *Law and Philosophy, 18*: 497–511.

Symington, N. (2006). Sanity and madness. *International Journal of Psychoanalysis, 87*: 1059–1068.

Symington, N. (2012). The essence of psycho-analysis as opposed to what is secondary. *Psychoanalytic Dialogues, 22*: 395–409.

Tähkä, V. (1993). *Mind and Its Treatment: A Psychoanalytic Approach.* Madison, CT: International Universities Press.

Target, M., & Fonagy, P. (1996). Playing with reality: II. The development of psychic reality from a theoretical perspective. *International Journal of Psychoanalysis, 77*: 459–479.

Tarski, A. (1944). The semantic conception of truth and the foundations of semantics. In: *Collected Papers, Vol. II* (pp. 665–699). Basel, Switzerland: Birkhäuser.

Taylor, G. H. (2011). Understanding as metaphoric, not a fusion of horizons. In: F. J. Mootz III & G. H. Taylor (Eds.), *Gadamer and Ricœur: Critical Horizons for Contemporary Hermeneutics* (pp. 104–118). London: Bloomsbury.

The Father (2020). F. Zeller (Dir.). Motion picture produced by Lionsgate, USA.

The Holy Bible: Containing the Old and New Testaments: New revised standard version. New York: Zondervan, 1989.

The Messenger (2009). O. Moverman (Dir.) Motion picture produced by Oscilloscope Laboratories, USA.

Tirman, J. (2011). *The Deaths of Others: the Fate of Civilians in America's Wars.* New York: Oxford University Press.

Tolstoy, L. N. (1886). *The Death of Ivan Ilyich and Other Stories.* Ware, UK: Wordsworth, 2004.

Turkle, S. (2004). Whither psychoanalysis in computer culture? *Psychoanalytic Psychology, 21*(1): 16–30.

Tustin, F. (1987). *Autistic Barriers in Neurotic Patients.* New Haven, CT: Yale University Press.

2001: A Space Odyssey (1968). S. Kubrick (Dir.). Motion picture produced by Metro-Goldwyn-Mayer, USA.

Tyminski, R. (2015). Lost in (cyber) space: finding two adolescent boys hiding from their own humanity. *Journal of Analytical Psychology, 60*: 220–244.

Tyson, P. (1996). Object relations, affect management and psychic structure formation: the concept of object constancy. *Psychoanalytic Study of the Child, 51*: 172–189.

U.S. National Archives and Records Administration (2020, July 24). *Declaration of Independence: A Transcription*. Original work, 1776. https://archives.gov/founding-docs/declaration-transcript (last accessed November 15, 2021).

Valvo, M. (2007). Discussion of Neil Altman's paper, "The children of the children of the sixties". *Journal of Infant, Child and Adolescent Psychotherapy*, 6: 30–33.

Vendler, H. (1999). *The Art of Shakespeare's Sonnets*. Cambridge, MA: Harvard University Press.

Viderman, S. (1979). The analytic space: meaning and problems. *Psychoanalytic Quarterly*, *48*: 257–291.

Vision, G. (1989). *Modern Anti-Realism and Manufactured Truth*. New York: Routledge.

Voela, A., & Rothschild, L. (2019). Creative failure: Stiegler, psychoanalysis and the promise of a life worth living. *New Formations: A Journal of Culture/theory/politics*, 95: 54–69.

Volkan, V. D. (1976). *Primitive Internalized Object Relations: A Clinical Study of Schizophrenic, Borderline and Narcissistic Patients*. New York: International Universities Press.

Volkan, V. D. (1987). *Six Steps in the Treatment of Borderline Personality Organization*. Northvale, NJ: Jason Aronson.

Volkan, V. D. (1988). *The Need to Have Enemies and Allies: From Clinical Practice to International Relationships*. Northvale, NJ: Jason Aronson.

Volkan, V. D. (1997). *Bloodlines: From Ethnic Pride to Ethnic Terrorism*. New York: Farrar, Straus, and Giroux.

Volkan, V. D. (2004). *Blind Trust: Large Groups and Their Leaders in Times of Crisis and Terror*. Charlottesville, VA: Pitchstone.

Volkan, V. D. (2006). *Killing in the Name of Identity: A Study of Bloody Conflicts*. Charlottesville, VA: Pitchstone.

Volkan, V. D. (2010). *Psychoanalytic Technique Expanded: A Textbook on Psychoanalytic Treatment*. Istanbul: Oa Press.

Volkan, V. D. (2013). *Enemies on the Couch: A Psychopolitical Journey through War and Peace*. Durham, NC: Pitchstone.

Volkan, V. D. (2014). *Animal Killer: Transmission of War Trauma from One Generation to the Next*. London: Karnac.

Volkan, V. D. (2015a). *A Nazi Legacy: A Study of Depositing, Transgenerational Transmission, Dissociation and Remembering Through Action*. London: Karnac.

Volkan, V. D. (2015b). *Would-be Wife Killer: A Clinical Study of Primitive Mental Functions, Actualized Unconscious Fantasies, Satellite States, and Developmental Steps*. London: Karnac.

Volkan, V. D. (2017). *Immigrants and Refugees: Trauma, Perennial Mourning, and Border Psychology*. London: Karnac.

Volkan, V. D. (2019). *A Study of Ghosts in the Human Psyche: Story of a Muslim Armenian*. London: Phoenix.

Volkan, V. D. (2020). *Large-Group Psychology: Racism, Social Divisions, Narcissistic Leaders and Who We Are Now*. London: Phoenix.

Volkan, V. D. (2021). *Sexual Addiction and Hunger for Maternal Care*. London: Phoenix.

Volkan, V. D., & Fowler, C. (2009). *Searching for a Perfect Woman: The Story of a Complete Psychoanalysis.* New York: Jason Aronson.

Volkan, V. D., & Itzkowitz, N. (1994). *Turks and Greeks: Neighbours in Conflict.* Huntingdon, UK: Eothen.

Volkan, V. D., Ast, G., & Greer, W. (2002). *The Third Reich in the Unconscious: Transgenerational Transmission and Its Consequences.* New York: Brunner-Routledge.

Waelder, R. (1936). The principle of multiple function: Observations on over-determination. *Psychoanalytic Quarterly, 5*: 45–62.

Waugaman, R. (1973). The intellectual relationship between Nietzsche and Freud. *Psychiatry, 36*: 458–467.

Waugaman, R. M. (2007). A wanderlust poem, newly attributed to Edward de Vere. *Shakespeare Matters, 7*: 21–23.

Waugaman, R. M. (2008). A snail poem, newly attributed to Edward de Vere. *Shakespeare Matters, 7*: 6–11.

Waugaman, R. M. (2010). *The Arte of English Poesie:* the case for Edward de Vere's authorship. *Brief Chronicles: The Interdisciplinary Journal of the Shakespeare Fellowship, 2*: 121–141.

Waugaman, R. M. (2013). A new 1569 poem by Arthur Golding, re-attributed to Edward de Vere. *Shakespeare Oxford Society Newsletter, 49*: 9–10.

Waugaman, R. M. (2014). The 1574 "Mirror for Magistrates" is a possible "source for 'Feath'red King" in Shakespeare's "The Phoenix and the Turtle". *Cahiers Élisabéthains, 85*: 67–72.

Waugaman, R. M. (2015). A 1578 poem about de Vere's trip to Italy. *Shakespeare Oxford Society Newsletter, 51*: 27–32.

Waugaman, R. M. (2016). Edward de Vere translated the 1570 *A Ritch Storehouse or Treasurie for Nobilitie and Gentlemen* by Johann Sturm. *Brief Chronicles: The Interdisciplinary Journal of the Shakespeare Fellowship, 7*: 131–146.

Waugaman, R. (2017). An unpublished letter by Sigmund Freud on the Shakespeare authorship question. *Scandinavian Review of Psychoanalysis, 39*: 148–151.

Waugaman, R. M. (2018). Did Edward de Vere translate Ovid's "Metamorphoses?" *The Oxfordian, 20*: 1–20.

Waugaman, R. M. (in press). Did Edward de Vere translate Boccaccio's "Decameron" into English, published in 1620? *The Oxfordian.*

Webster's Ninth Collegiate Dictionary (1998). Springfield, MA: Merriam-Webster.

Westen, D. (1998). The scientific legacy of Sigmund Freud: Toward a psychodynamically informed psychological science. *Psychological Bulletin, 124*: 333–371.

Westphal, M. (2011). The dialectic of belonging and distanciation in Gadamer and Ricœur. In: F. J. Mootz III & G. H. Taylor (Eds.), *Gadamer and Ricœur: Critical Horizons for Contemporary Hermeneutics* (pp. 43–62). London: Bloomsbury.

Wilde, O. (1897). *De Profundis.* New York: Modern Library, 2000.

Williams, M. H. (2010). *Bion's Dream: A Reading of the Autobiographies.* London: Karnac.

Wilson, T. D. (2004). *Strangers to Ourselves: Discovering the Adaptive Unconscious*. Cambridge, MA: Harvard University Press.

Winnicott, D. W. (1940). Discussion at a Scientific Meeting of the British Psychoanalytic Society. In: *The Maturational Processes and the Facilitating Environment* (p. 39). New York: International Universities Press, 1965.

Winnicott, D. W. (1945). Primitive emotional development. *International Journal of Psychoanalysis, 26*: 137–143.

Winnicott, D. W. (1951). Transitional objects and transitional phenomena. In: *Playing and Reality* (pp. 1–25). London: Tavistock, 1971.

Winnicott, D. W. (1952). Anxiety associated with insecurity. In: *Collected Papers: Through Paediatrics to Psychoanalysis* (pp. 97–100). London: Karnac, 1984.

Winnicott, D. W. (1956). Primary maternal preoccupation. In: *Collected Papers: Through Paediatrics to Psychoanalysis* (pp. 300–305). New York, Basic Books, 1958.

Winnicott, D. W. (1960). Ego distortion in terms of true and false self. In: *The Maturational Processes and the Facilitating Environment* (pp. 140–152). New York: International Universities Press, 1965.

Winnicott, D. W. (1966). The ordinary devoted mother. In: C. Winnicott, R. Shepherd, & M. Davis (Eds.), *Babies and Their Mothers* (pp. 3–14). Reading, MA: Addison-Wiley, 1987.

Winnicott, D. W. (1967). D.W.W. on D.W.W. In: J. Abram (Ed.), *Donald Winnicott Today* (pp. 29–45). London: Routledge.

Winnicott, D. W. (1971). *Playing and Reality*. London: Tavistock.

Winnicott, D. W. (1974). Fear of breakdown. *International Review of Psycho-Analysis, 1*: 101–107.

Wolman, T. (1990). The death of the analyst in the post-termination phase of analysis: impact and resolution. In: H. Schwartz & A.-L. Silver (Eds.), *Illness in the Analyst: Implications for the Treatment Relationship* (pp. 267–298). New York: International Universities Press.

Woods, M. (1994). *The Magician's Doubts: Nabokov and the Risks of Fiction*. Princeton, NJ: Princeton University Press.

Woodward, R. (2004). *Plan of Attack*. New York: Simon & Schuster.

Yadlin-Gadot, S. (2016). *Truth Matters: Theory and Practice in Psychoanalysis*. Leiden, the Netherlands: Brill.

Yadlin-Gadot, S. (2017). Truth axes and the transformation of self. *Psychoanalytic Review, 104*(2): 163–201.

Zaltz, T. (2018). *Madness or Knowing the Unbearable Truth: A Psychoanalytic Journey in Search of Sanity*. London: Routledge.

Index